FE 19

P9-CMW-053

Russia

Kazakhstan

Kyrgyzstan
Tajikistan

China

Dem. Rep.
Korea

Korea

Japan

Belarus

Turkey

Lebanon
Israel
Jordan

Syria
Iraq

Iran

Afghani-
stan

Pakistan

Taiwan

Libya

Egypt

Kuwait

Saudi
Arabia

UAE

Oman

India

Bangla-
desh

Vietnam

Philippines

Chad

Sudan

Eritrea

Yemen

Djibouti
Somaliland

Sri
Lanka

Malaysia
Singa-
pore

Brunei

C.A.E.

South
Sudan

Ethiopia

Somalia

Maldives

ongo

Uganda
Kenya

Papua
New Guinea

Dem. Rep.
Congo

Tanzania

Seychelles

ngola

Zambia

Malawi

Zimb.

Mozambique

Madagascar

Mauritius

Botswana

Indonesia

Timor-Leste

Australia

South
Africa

New Zealand

Arabic	Hindi-Urdu	Mandarin	Spanish
Bengali	Japanese	Persian	Swahili
English	Javanese	Portuguese	Tamil
French	Korean	Punjabi	Turkish
German	Malay	Russian	Vietnamese

Babel

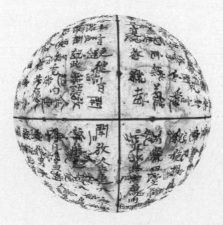

Babel

Around the world
in twenty languages

Gaston Dorren

Atlantic Monthly Press
New York

First published in Great Britain in 2018 by
Profile Books

Published simultaneously in Canada
Printed in Canada

First Grove Atlantic hardcover edition: December 2018

ISBN 978-0-8021-2879-9
eISBN 978-0-8021-4672-4

Library of Congress Cataloging-in-Publication data is available for this title.

Atlantic Monthly Press
an imprint of Grove Atlantic
154 West 14th Street
New York, NY 10011

Distributed by Publishers Group West

groveatlantic.com

18 19 20 21 10 9 8 7 6 5 4 3 2 1

*Language is such an intimate possession,
something that one possesses in the same
measure that one is possessed by it. Language
is bound up with the foundations of one's being,
with memories and emotions, with the subtle
structures of the worlds in which one lives.*

Alok Rai, *Hindi Nationalism*

Contents

Babel

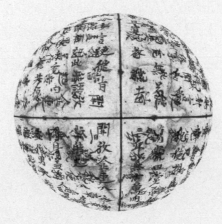

Introduction

Twenty languages: half the world

COUNTING THE WORLD'S LANGUAGES is as difficult as counting colours. There are scores of standardised languages, such as English, French, Russian and Thai; making a tally of them is as easy as counting the colours in a Mondrian painting. But most languages have never been standardised. In many areas, there is only a multitude of local varieties, and deciding where one language ends and the next one begins is as hard as distinguishing individual colours in a Turner painting. So there can be no definitive total. That said, 6,000 is a common estimate for the number of languages spoken and signed in today's world – an average of one for every 1.25 million people. Such amazing diversity – what a Babel we live in!

Or do we? Here's another statistic: with proficiency in just four languages – English, Mandarin, Spanish and Hindi-Urdu – you could smoothly navigate most of the world, without any need for an interpreter. Hindi-Urdu and Mandarin are widely understood in the two most populous countries on earth, Spanish will serve you well in much of the Americas and English is the nearest thing we have to a global linguistic currency. So much for Babel, one might think.

The world's biggest languages, which are the subject of this book, are causing the decline of hundreds, even thousands of smaller ones. This is a tragedy, as smaller languages fall out of use across every continent, wiping out valuable knowledge codified in words, stories and names – Alok Rai's 'subtle structures of the worlds in which one lives'. At the same time, the dominant languages in themselves represent more linguistic, cultural and historical variety than is commonly realised. The contrast makes *Babel* a bittersweet book: the twenty tongues portrayed herein are delicious and dangerous in equal measure.

Between them, these languages are the mother tongues of no less than half the population of the world. Take second-language speakers into account, and the numbers are much larger still. Again, the figures are debatable, but it's safe to claim that at least 75 per cent of people on this planet are able to communicate in one of the Babel Twenty. A less pertinent but more exact figure would be this: over 90 per cent of humankind live in countries where one or more of the twenty are routinely used by central government.

How have these big languages risen to their current station? Individual stories differ, but most have this in common: they are lingua francas – languages that bridge the gap between people with different mother tongues.

Two of *Babel*'s lingua francas – Swahili and Malay – first thrived as trade languages. Later on, several governments embraced them as languages of administration, but even today they're spoken more as second languages – useful gap-bridgers – than as mother tongues. But the primary creator and carrier of lingua francas has always been imperialism – Persian, Portuguese and English all outgrew their cradles in this way. Other Asian languages went through similar episodes: Arabic was spread by the caliphate, Mandarin by successive Chinese dynasties, Turkish by the Ottomans and Vietnamese by the kings and armies of the Việt people. Like Portuguese and English, other European languages also piggybacked on colonial empires. Spanish and French were spread by sea, and Russian overland. Nor has history changed its ways – or so the people of South India feel, as they vehemently resist the advancement of Hindi as the all-Indian language.

I have mentioned thirteen languages so far. The remaining seven are German, Japanese, Javanese, Korean and three languages of South Asia: Bengali, Punjabi and Tamil. To categorise these as lingua francas would be a stretch. What they have in common is that they happen to occupy compact but densely populated regions.

If the Babel Twenty have triumphed in different ways, that's only the beginning of their diversity. Unsurprisingly, all languages are different in the words they offer, the grammar they employ and the sounds they travel on. Their writing systems are not just alluringly varied in appearance, but also profoundly dissimilar in their functioning. People have different collective feelings about their languages: we find veneration, pride, protectiveness and sometimes indifference, but also, especially among second-language speakers, resignation and even loathing. Languages are put to different uses: most, but not all, are popular with governments and businesses; some have long and rich literary traditions, others less so; some will be maintained by migrants for several generations, while others are soon given up. All languages display internal diversity, but the patterns differ: usually, there are regional varieties; sometimes, there's one for speech, another for writing; or one for formal conversations, the other for informal chats; or different varieties for speaking to one's social superiors, inferiors or peers, et cetera. In other words, apart from being a unique system of communication, each of the Babel Twenty also has its own language history and its own linguistic culture. They are worlds unto themselves.

In the following twenty chapters (plus one bonus semi-chapter) I will peer into one of these worlds, starting with the smallest of the bunch and working towards the biggest, the world's 'linguistic superpower'. But while each story will focus on a language, it will also focus on an issue, on one particular feature of that particular language. For instance, what does it actually mean for Russian to be 'related' to English? How do non-alphabetic scripts, such as those of India and China, do the same job as our twenty-six letters? If Belgium and Canada have trouble keeping the linguistic peace, how do multilingual countries such as Indonesia manage? How did tiny but colonial Portugal spawn a major world language – and why didn't the Netherlands? Why do Japanese women talk differently from men? And how did this book gain the author two Vietnamese nieces?

About Babel – some (im)practicalities

Each chapter begins with a short profile of the language under discussion: its various names, its linguistic pedigree, the numbers of speakers, some basics about grammar, sounds and the writing system as well as information about loanwords (which are the main sources of borrowing and which words English has adopted from this language?). The numbers, of course, are questionable, as language statistics are highly erratic; I've consulted many sources, ignored the implausible outliers, averaged the others and rounded the outcome to the nearest catchy figure.

It's hard to represent the unfamiliar sounds of foreign languages without making use of the International Phonetic Alphabet, which can be opaque for non-specialists. I've tackled the problem in two ways. In most cases, I've tried to approximate the pronunciation of the foreign words by referring to either English spelling conventions (e.g. by using /ee/, as in *bee*) or some 'continental' spelling (where the same sound would be represented as /i/ or even, in passages where vowel length matters, /ī/). In a few cases, where this wouldn't work, I've included references to my website (*languagewriter.com*), where under the menu item 'BABEL', there's a page with sound files.

When citing words, phrases or sentences as examples, I've tried to be typographically consistent in the following way:

BABELI Small caps: words in foreign languages. But for legibility, whole sentences are quoted in italics.

Babel Italics: English words, but also sentences in other languages. Italics for emphasis are used too.

/baybl/ Slashes: phonetic approximations.

'Babel' Inverted commas: English translations of words.

(Babel) When English translations are placed in parentheses, no inverted commas have been added.

Precisely half of the Babel languages are written in a script other than our Roman alphabet. Words in Russian, Mandarin and so on have been transliterated or transcribed. More than one system is in circulation for each of several languages, so if you feel that Korean, Japanese or Arabic words in *Babel* look somewhat different from what you were taught, this may be the explanation.

I've taken great pains over the many foreign words cited in this book, but it is nonetheless likely to contain spelling errors, especially in the non-European languages. I would be grateful for any corrections that readers might send me (through the contact page on my website – *languagewriter.com*); they will inform later editions and translations. Meanwhile, let's appreciate such errors for what they are: evidence that we live in Babel still.

Gaston Dorren, 2018

20

Vietnamese

TIẾNG VIỆT

85 million speakers

Around 75 million native Vietnamese speakers live in Vietnam, where it is the only official language; half a million in Cambodia. Some 2 million Vietnamese live in the US and substantial numbers in France, Australia, Canada, Germany, the Czech Republic and the UK. There are 5 to 10 million second-language speakers, mostly ethnic minorities, in Vietnam.

Vietnamese

SELF-DESIGNATION TIẾNG VIỆT, sometimes TIẾNG VIỆT NAM or VIỆT NGỮ

FAMILY Vietnamese is far and away the most widely spoken member of the Austroasiatic family, which also includes Khmer, the national language of Cambodia. More than 100 smaller Austroasiatic languages are spoken by minorities throughout Southeast Asia and eastern India.

SCRIPT Roman alphabet, with a remarkable number of diacritics (accents). Until the early twentieth century, a character script based on Chinese was in use.

GRAMMAR See main text.

SOUNDS See main text.

LOANWORDS In prehistory, agricultural terminology was adopted from the neighbouring Tai languages. A huge number of words from Chinese languages were borrowed over a period of some two thousand years, up until the mid-twentieth century; according to estimates, 30 to 60 per cent of Vietnamese vocabulary is of Chinese origin. During French colonial rule, scores of French words were adopted and adapted to the Vietnamese sound system and spelling. Today, English words trickle in. For examples, see main text.

EXPORTS English mainly uses Vietnamese words to refer to elements of Vietnamese culture. The best known may be *pho* (PHỞ), a popular broth-based dish. During the Vietnam war, some Vietnamese words temporarily trickled into American military jargon, such as *di di* (ĐI ĐI) for 'go away', *Quan Canh* (QUÂN CẢNH) for 'Military Police' and *so mot* (SỐ MỘT) for 'the best', literally 'the number one'.

ACCENT OBSTACLES Vietnamese has strong regional variety in terms of pronunciation and vocabulary, though not in grammar. For the language student, this is a major obstacle: it's easy to tell the major accents apart, but more difficult to understand them, especially the ones spoken in the south. Indeed, even northern native speakers have trouble dealing with some of the less familiar southern dialects. The recommended standard pronunciation is a mixed bag of some southern and rather more northern characteristics.

20: **Vietnamese**

Linguistic mountaineering

I'M HALFWAY THROUGH my three-week stay in Hanoi when I hear myself say: '*Bác học tiếng Việt một năm và ruỗi* - no, wait: *rưỡi - rồi nhưng chưa có thể nói không được!*'

The words come out haltingly, but I see Loan, my teacher, nod, so I may indeed be saying what I'm trying to say: that I've been studying Vietnamese for a year and a half now and I still can't speak it. Have I really managed to get that across? If so, I've just produced my longest – and most paradoxical – Vietnamese utterance so far.

Loan (pronounced 'lwahn') is silent for a second or two. Then she shakes her head. 'Let's correct that.'

I ignore the sinking feeling in my stomach and try to make my answer sound light-hearted: 'Why? You feel I'm wrong in saying that I can't speak the language?'

'The sentence has several errors,' and she starts listing them. 'Now say it again.'

'*Bác học tiếng Việt một năm rưỡi rồi nhưng chưa thể nói được.*'

I like studying with Loan. Not only does she speak good English (though that may be a double-edged sword), but she's also lively, fun and full of enthusiasm for language study, both her students' and her own. We've been to a museum, a bookshop and an eatery together, and she's even introduced me to a few of her friends. But while she's a dedicated teacher, there's no denying that she can be a little stern. Rather than praise what progress I may make, she firmly believes in the motivational force of her disappointment, saying things like, 'Why don't you know that word, *bác* (uncle)? We read it only yesterday!'

'Undoubtedly, but I can't possibly memorise every single word we come across, *cháu* (niece), or even half of them! Learning Vietnamese vocab is *khó khăn* – it's difficult!'

'You should, though. You're such a good student!'

I sit up.

'But it's true that your conversational skills haven't improved much.'

I slouch.

'Yet they have somewhat. And your pronunciation certainly has.'

But not right now, it hasn't, because the rare compliment leaves me speechless. That's how we roll, my twenty-year-young Vietnamese teacher and I.

But why am I here in the first place, 6,000 miles away from my friends and family, struggling with a language that, except for the odd expat, only the oddest foreigner ever ventures into? What made me do it? The answer is: this book did.

The Temple of the Jade Mountain in central Hanoi. For centuries, most writing was done in Classical Chinese. An adapted version of its script was also used for Vietnamese.

As I mentioned in the introduction, one would need to learn twenty languages to be able to speak to half the world population in their mother tongues. Some people have actually pulled that off. I once shook hands with the American polyglot Alexander Argüelles, who speaks sixteen or seventeen of the Babel languages and many more that aren't in the top twenty. Personally, I've studied seven of the twenty at some point in my life (English, German, Spanish, French, Portuguese, Russian and Turkish), resulting in levels of familiarity ranging from fluency to (more often) mere acquaintance. The idea of having a go at the full set of twenty did briefly tickle me. But I soon realised that I would never even cover the basics of them all within a time frame that my publisher, my bank account or, indeed, my life expectancy would allow. So I decided to try just one – but a challenging one.

Vietnamese seemed a good choice. Unlike most other options, such as Arabic, Hindi and Korean, it wouldn't require learning a whole new alphabet, nor, heaven forbid, thousands of Chinese characters. And since Vietnamese was going to be the protagonist of the opening chapter, it would allow me to dip into many features of foreign languages early on in the book. An additional, private motive was that I hoped I might address Tuyet, our Vietnamese cleaning lady, in her mother tongue, preferably by surprise. So I made my choice, picked a self-study book that appealed to me* and set out on my journey. This chapter is an account of that journey.

Early acquaintance

Written Vietnamese makes a striking first impression: no other language that I know of has so many diacritics. As a young boy, I found my father's *Paris Match* exotic because of the numerous é's, à's and î's and endless apostrophes, yet French looks stark and unadorned compared to Vietnamese. With no fewer than nine different diacritics (á, à, ả, ã, ạ, â, ă, đ and ơ – I love the informal term 'whiskered o' for this last one), it's a language for people with keen eyes. Words and even letters with several diacritics are by

---

* I'm grateful to Assimil for providing me with their Vietnamese course. In the 'Sources and further reading' section at the end of this book, I list the learning resources I've used.

no means rare: I soon discover that Tuyet's name is actually spelt Tuyết (and that it means 'snow').

These accents are necessary to ensure correct pronunciation, but they add considerably to the burden of memorisation. Fortunately, written Vietnamese also seems to have a plus side: nearly all words are monosyllabic. Words of up to six letters must be easier to memorise than those centipede-shaped things that German, Russian and Turkish are so fond of.

More good news: unlike English, Vietnamese spelling reflects pronunciation pretty accurately. Not that all spelling rules make intuitive sense. Why have three different ways of writing a /z/ sound – and why should the letter z not be one of them? Also, why have three different ways of writing a /k/ sound? (Though of course, in English, we write *can*, *keen* and *queen* rather than *kan, keen* and *kween*.) Another intricacy of Vietnamese is the distinction between *t* and *th*, the former a /t/ sound, the latter a /tʰ/ sound – that is to say, a /t/ with a little puff of air. In English we write both as *t*, so we can hardly complain if Vietnamese prefers to be more precise.

On the whole, I would call Vietnamese pronunciation easy if it weren't for the elephant in the room, the big fat singing elephant that bedevils most East Asian languages: *tone*. Each word must be vocalised according to one 'tune' from a total repertoire of six. I knew this beforehand, but I hoped that as a native speaker of a tonal regional language (Limburgish) I would take it in my stride. No such luck: six tones is very different from the paltry two I'm used to. Use the wrong tone, and 'here' becomes 'there' (ĐÂY, ĐẤY) and the meaning of ĐI changes from 'go' to 'prostitute' (ĐĨ), 'scrotum' or 'ill-treat' (both Đì). Fortunately, Vietnamese spelling is helpful: five of the nine diacritics are there to indicate the correct tone; the sixth tone is marked by the absence of these five. The result of this is that Vietnamese writing is equal parts text and score.

There's something insidious about the grammar of Vietnamese. On the one hand, it's easy in all the places where experience has taught me to expect hard work. Verbal conjugation, the ordeal of most European languages? None to speak of: you just add a handful of simple particles that never change, and even those can often be omitted. Cases, as in Latin and Greek, the Slavic group and German? Entirely non-existent. Irregular plurals, as in the Slavic group,* Danish and German? Vietnam doesn't even have plurals as we know them. All of which can be summarised as: no endings! Vietnamese words stay as they are. They never change. Hard to believe, but true.

But just when I'm beginning to hope that Vietnamese might turn out to be rather easier than I thought, several gremlins emerge.

Gremlin 1: the personal pronouns, which are ... hell, where do we even start? The trouble with Vietnamese pronouns is that there are so many. You do not simply say 'I' and 'you' – there is a multitude of Is and yous to choose from, partly depending on gender, but also on respect and age. The pronoun you choose creates a specific type of relationship. Even if you use the most neutral word for 'I', TÔI, it's not *really* neutral, because it makes you sound terribly aloof, which is no way to win friends.

Much more common than the neutral or distant pronouns are pronouns that, in literal translation, designate all sorts of family relationships. If you are somewhat older than me, I will address you as ANH (older brother) or CHỊ (older sister), while referring to myself as EM (younger sibling). However, if you're younger, I will call you EM and refer to myself (being male) as ANH. Note that all three words may mean either 'I' or 'you', depending on who is saying them to whom. If the characters in a Vietnamese dialogue use these pronouns, the first thing to do is figure out, from context, who's junior and who's senior, so you can tell which pronoun refers to whom. Entirely different words again come into play if the age difference is wider. The reason why Loan and I in the above dialogue called each other BÁC and CHÁU (literally: 'uncle/aunt' and 'niece/nephew') is that I'm about the same age as her parents. Incidentally, I didn't insert these words into the dialogue for local colour: Vietnamese people commonly use them even in English.

The second gremlin is what I will call 'labyrinthine sentences'. Of course, when you're starting on a new language, it's normal to feel

---

* Note that the Slavic languages are in several ways the diametrical opposites of Vietnamese. For decades, the Soviet Union was Vietnam's main ally, which drove two suffering generations to studying Russian – which is Slavic.

clueless. But with other languages, even if the meaning of words is unclear, I can usually tell what *sorts* of words they are. Numerous signals – endings, neighbouring articles and pronouns, et cetera – help me recognise if I am being baffled by a verb, puzzled by a noun or beaten by an adjective. That is comforting and useful, like being able to make out vague shapes in the darkness. Since Vietnamese has no endings and no articles but too many pronouns, it's all too easy to get utterly and completely lost in a sentence.

I soon discover another complication. Many common Vietnamese words can be verbs, nouns, prepositions or yet another part of speech, with meanings that may or may not be related. CHỈ can be 'to point' or 'only'. Ở often means 'at' but can also mean 'to be, to stay'. LÀ can mean 'to be' ('is', 'are', 'was', et cetera) but also 'that', as in 'she said that...' And ĐƯỢC has so many meanings and grammatical purposes, I'm warned, that one can only ever hope to develop a feel for it through lots and lots of practice.

There is yet another gremlin: word order. The *basic* word order is child's play: subject, verb, object, same as in English. Adjectives follow their nouns, which is different from English, but familiar from French or Spanish. Unfortunately, other types of Vietnamese words and phrases are both fussy and fickle in their placement preferences. One word for 'very' precedes the adjective (RẤT LỚN, 'very big'), the other insists on following it (LỚN LẮM, 'big very'). KHI NÀO (when) at the end of a sentence tends to refer back to the past, whereas it eyes the future when employed at the beginning. One particle for past tense comes before the verb (ĐÃ), the other after it (RỒI). Et cetera, et maddening cetera.

Pronunciation and grammar have hard bits, but also quite a few easy ones. In vocabulary, the easy bits are few and far between. Given the European influences that Vietnam has undergone since the late nineteenth century, I expected to find numerous loanwords. If only! Barring foreign names and some rare words of foreign extraction, Vietnamese text consists of deeply alien, impenetrable gatherings of one to six letters which have to be learnt by rote. I can't say the prospect does much to strengthen my motivation.

Nor do my first real-life encounters with the language. I've just given a TED talk about the individual and collective blessings of multilingualism, in which I've briefly mentioned my romp with Vietnamese, when I'm addressed by a friendly young man of East Asian appearance. I don't understand a word he says. He helpfully shifts to German, explaining that he has just said hello to me in the language of his parents – a phrase from my very first lesson, actually, which I have failed to recognise. And when some time later I greet our cleaning lady, Tuyết, in Vietnamese, her reaction is one of irritation rather than pleasant surprise. I guess that the pronoun I chose suggested that she was younger than her sixty years, which in Vietnamese culture is not a compliment.

In early April, after a six-month struggle, I call a halt.

Estrangement and renewed acquaintance

Throughout the summer, while I'm working on this book, Vietnamese leaves me cold. But these months also take me to several places on the margins of Europe where relatively small languages are spoken (Bulgarian, Norwegian, Irish), and I feel my linguistic hunger returning. As the writing of this Vietnamese chapter draws nearer, I begin to hate the idea that I've thrown in the towel so soon. And one chilly October evening, while huffing and puffing at the gym, I make up my mind: I'm going to pick up the thread, but under more inspiring conditions. I will find myself an online teacher and plan a trip to Vietnam. That same week, I book a flight and apartment for March. And through italki.com, I contact Huyền, who describes herself as 'an accidental polyglot'. She met her boyfriend when she was looking for a Spanish teacher, and since he's a native speaker of Catalan, she went on to master that as well. When talking to his parents, she likes to throw in elements of their insular dialect, Menorquí. She seems right up my street.

The plan works out. Our one-on-one classes are fun and since I don't want to make a fool of myself, I diligently revise the grammar and refresh my vocabulary. The good news is that Huyền understands what I say. I can't say much by myself, mind you, but when I read sentences aloud, they are intelligible. The bad news is that when she speaks, it almost sounds like white noise to me. To a tiny degree, that is due to her very slight regional accent, but the real problem is me – as well as Vietnamese, I think it's fair to say. Me, because understanding speech is my poorest skill in any language. And Vietnamese, because the obstacles to reading – all the non-existent endings and articles and the overdose of pronouns – are even more cumbersome at the moment of listening. Moreover, several groups of vowels (ơ and â, e and ê, a, o and ă) sound quite similar to me, and many word-final consonants are barely audible: pairs like BÁT and BÁC are best distinguished by lip-reading, while for BẠT versus BẠN, even that won't do the trick.

When I'm not studying, I read about the language. I discover why so few Vietnamese words sound familiar to Westerners. In spite of eight decades of French colonialism and four decades of Soviet alliance, Chinese* remained the main source of borrowing until well into the twentieth century. This was a matter partly of 2,000-year habit, partly of phonetic affinity, which made borrowing Chinese relatively easy. Of course, Chinese words are as alien to me as Vietnamese words. With at least one exception, Huyền points out: the Vietnamese word HIỆN ĐẠI derives from the same Chinese word as the Korean brand name Hyundai. Their common meaning is 'modern'.

But wait a sec: weren't all Vietnamese words supposed to be short and monosyllabic? It turns out that they only *look* that way. Thousands of them really consist of two syllables, sometimes more. It's just that every syllable gets written separately – a legacy of the time when the language was written in Chinese-style characters, one character per syllable. The same group of letters with spaces on either side may be a word or a syllable, depending on context. It's as if English were to write *context* as 'con text', or *protocol* as 'pro to col'.

Russian loanwords in Vietnamese are surprisingly scarce: I've only found internationalisms such as 'kulak', 'soviet', 'ruble' and 'tsar' (CU-LẮC, XÔ VIẾT, RÚP, SA HOÀNG – literally 'tsar emperor'). My favourite is 'Marxism-Leninism': CHỦ NGHĨA MÁC-LÊNIN. MacLenin! The Vietnamese flag shows one golden star against the typical red background of most MacLeninist states – but whenever I see it now, the golden arches of McJunkfood superimpose themselves.

---

* I use the word 'Chinese' because Mandarin has not been the primary source from which Vietnamese has borrowed. Southern Chinese languages have played a more important role.

Since Vietnam has opened up to a global economy dominated by English, some words from that language have entered Vietnamese, e.g. *internet*, *photocopy*, *data*, *blog* and *golf*. But it's a trickle, not a deluge. For English words like *website*, *cyberspace* and *app*, which are widespread elsewhere, indigenous terms are in common use. And even borrowings are rewarded with a new spelling, reflecting Vietnamese pronunciation: IN-TƠ-NÉT, ĐA-TA, BỜ LÓC (blog), GÔN (golf).

If these spelling changes make some loanwords from English hard to recognise, this is all the more true for thóse from French, which have had more time to blend in. In the colonial era (late nineteenth century and the first half of the twentieth), dozens, perhaps hundreds of words were adopted, mostly cultural novelties and technical innovations. Can you identify the following? SÔ-CÔ-LA, SÂM BANH, MÙ TẠC, CÔNG-TẮC, GIĂM BÔNG, XI MĂNG, KEM, KI-ỐT, LƠ. *

If Vietnamese dislikes borrowing from the West and loves to naturalise what little it does borrow, it follows that, for a newcomer to the language, building up a decent vocabulary implies starting near zero and working hard to lay just a foundation. We do not always realise what an abundance of vocabulary we are handed on a plate when we study French, Spanish or German, from *organisation* to *hygiene* and from *algebra* to *yogurt*. True, the plate is not quite as laden with gifts when we move to Europe's linguistic margins, but neither is it empty, thanks to centuries of cultural cross-pollination: our *manager* and the French word PAYSAGE for 'landscape' are also present in both Russian and Turkish. Even in languages spoken further afield, such as Swahili, Tamil and Malay, words of European stock are far from rare. And with Arabic, which seems so outlandish to Anglophones, centuries of exchange have produced more commonality than we tend to think (see chapter 5). In Vietnamese, on the other hand, we have to make do with MÙ TẠC and SÂM BANH.

The grammar in particular proves to be more intractable than it had at first appeared to be. A simple sentence like 'Do you live in this beautiful house?' assumes a very different sort of simplicity in Vietnamese, and it takes quite a few steps to get from one to the other. Step 1: choose a form for 'you' that correctly expresses

---

* The French sources of the Vietnamese loanwords are: CHOCOLAT, CHAMPAGNE, MOUTARDE, CONTACT, JAMBON, CIMENT, CRÈME, KIOSQUE and BLEU.

gender, age and respect. Step 2: place this 'you' word at the very start. Step 3: for the sentence to be a question, delete the English 'do' and add a question word at the end. Step 4: reorder 'this beautiful house' to 'house beautiful this'. Hey presto: *Chị sống ở nhà đẹp này không?*

'Almost correct', Huyền says. 'Just one word missing.' Ah, right. Step 5 then: 'house' has to be preceded by a little something to turn the general concept of 'any house' into this specific specimen we're talking about. In English, the determiner *this* will do the job just fine, but Vietnamese usually insists that the noun should be preceded by a so-called classifier, which in this case is CÁI. And so I gradually discover that some grammatical rules *are* complex. The one about classifiers is a prime example, because the correct choice of these pesky little words is governed by dozens of rules with even peskier exceptions. Thankfully, CÁI can be used for most concrete objects, but there are numerous other categories too, each of which requires its own classifier: one for vehicles, another one for books, one for plants. There's also one for round things, such as eggs and balls, and okay, I can see that this should be a fitting class for most fruits – but why do bananas get the same classifier? Also, why do rivers, knives, eyes and other assorted items grammatically behave as if they were animals? And then there are some self-sufficient nouns that resist any classifier. I can't figure out what defines this group.

Some grammatical surprises are fun (to some people anyway). For example, the Vietnamese language would use different words for 'how' in questions meaning 'how long was the snake?' and 'how scary was the snake?' Length can be measured, therefore the first question is rendered as 'the snake is long how much?' Degrees of scariness on the other hand cannot be conveyed very precisely, and therefore the correct wording is more along the lines of 'The snake is scary like how?' It's reminiscent of the difference in English between *many* and *few* versus *much* and *little*. The Vietnamese realise that a snake of *few* centimetres has *little* scariness, whereas *many* result in *much* more of it.

Even after months of trying, I still don't understand Huyền when she speaks Vietnamese. Fortunately, however, my reading skills are benefiting from her teaching. The meanings of some words are now immediately evident to me, without consciously looking them up in my mental lexicon. As a result, the structure of sentences is becoming clearer. Which isn't to say that I understand them. When my eyes flit across a line of Vietnamese text, what registers in my brain might be rendered as follows (each number represents one word, or perhaps syllable, who knows?):

1. young male or female; 2. does something; 3. in; 4. some place; 5. already (must be past tense then); 6. because; 7. s/he; 8. wants to – or rather, wanted to; 9. được (God help me, that's 'được' of the 99 meanings – passive voice here perhaps?); 10. must be a verb, but no idea which; 11. could be anything; 12. house (or family, or expert); 13. no idea; 14. no idea, I'm lost; 15. much/many.

That's what progress looks like.

Poor show, you'll be saying to yourself. Yet in a way, I'm doing better than Google Translate. More often than not, the software spouts pure gobbledygook. It is stumped by the pronouns, flummoxed by the grammar and wrong-footed by the many homonyms. 'I only ever use it when I want to have a laugh,' Huyền says. On the other hand, Google does know thousands of words, so it has that advantage over me.

At some point, I also discover how to input Vietnamese diacritics on my laptop and telephone (two different systems, unfortunately, called VNI and Telex respectively), and within weeks I'm conjuring up ể's, đ's and ự's like a pro.

A few weeks before departure, I'm going to the embassy for a visa. I decide against trying to say anything in Vietnamese, as I'd be bound to embarrass myself. While the embassy official reads my application, I try to decipher the information signs behind him, but I come up empty. The official looks up and says: 'Language study? In three weeks?'

A few days later, a book about Hanoi written by two European expats tells me, 'Expect your efforts in Vietnamese to go unrecognised at first. Your attempts to speak the language may well be rewarded with "Sorry, no English."'

Can it really be as bad as that? I'll soon find out.

Being there

As soon as I've shaken off my jet lag, I take a liking to Hanoi. Granted, it's crowded, cluttered and dirty. It's huge, almost preposterously noisy and not over-endowed with parks and historical buildings. Its streets are mostly taken up by an oozing mass of scooters and small motorbikes. The continuous din of engines, horns, building sites and telephones vibrates in an almost liquid atmospheric soup of dust, exhaust gases and water vapour. Being a pedestrian is hard work, because the pavements too are mostly taken up by motorbikes, always parked at right angles so as to better block the way. What gaps remain are filled with racks of clothes and other merchandise, street-food cooks, repairers, and the collections of child-sized furniture that pass for café terraces here.

If I enjoy Hanoi nonetheless, it's because of its people. For starters, they don't stare at you, not even when they see one's *tây* (Western) features approaching at the rarefied height of 6 feet 1½. In Hanoi, people mind their own business as long as you mind yours. Once you approach them, they nearly always respond politely, and often in a friendly manner. (Even my *least* favourite Hanoi folks, motorcycle taxi drivers, try to remain friendly while working their swindles.) When there's a language barrier, they're patient and inventive. Whenever I say or do something clumsy or culturally insensitive, they're discreet. In a word, people in Hanoi seem to live their public lives in the key of C, for civil, frequently modulating to F (friendly). Like everyone else, of course, they at times express anger (A sharp), blues (B flat) or desperation (D) , but rather than modulating their public behaviour to these keys, they'll just shift from C to C minor or from F to F minor. It's all rather refreshing – I'd almost call it a tonic.

Back to the language. How's my progress?

I'm having mini dialogues with my Airbnb hostess, Huệ, but they're based more on mutual goodwill than any real comprehension. On one occasion, I talk to the housekeeper, thanking her for hanging out my laundry, or so I believe. In fact, some grammatical error makes it sound – so I later understand from my host, Phong, who speaks English – as if I'm *asking* her to help me with the laundry.

'Because we understand you' reads the TPBank slogan – and for once, I understand *them*.

But I *am* learning, slowly. Most weekdays, I spend two hours or more working with Loan. In restaurants, I place orders in Vietnamese – but if I ask a question, no matter in which language, English-speaking co-workers are called upon to save the day. I have rudimentary chats with cabbies, but we sit in silence most of the time. All day long, at home, on the streets and in shops, I see Vietnamese words, and some of them put down roots in my memory: THẺ for '(telephone) card', SIÊU THỊ for 'supermarket', XOÀI for 'mango', RỬA XE 'carwash', HẠT SEN for 'lotus seeds'. It strikes me how rare English words are in public space, while French, the former colonial language, is practically absent. (More about the fate of colonial languages in chapter 9.)

I gradually discover more about the intricacies of respect and politeness. When Loan says 'yes' to me, the word for her to use is VÂNG; for me, on the other hand, the correct word to use in response to her is Ờ or Ừ. At the end of a sentence, she regularly adds Ạ, whose only function is to express respect where respect is due – but it would be silly if I, being older, said that to her. The most common way of forming a question is by attaching KHÔNG to the sentence; I could replace the word with the more casual HẢ when asking her a question, but her doing so when addressing me would be taking a liberty. Learning these things is part of a Vietnamese education, and when children are careless or recalcitrant enough to break the rules, parents will scold them for talking *trống không*, something like 'empty and plain'.

To me, as an egalitarian Western European, such linguistic etiquette is awkward and old-fashioned, and I wonder if it has any chance of surviving in a society that is rapidly modernising. Don't young Vietnamese people hate it? One young woman tells me that, *vâng*, she would much prefer the language to be like English and have just one word for 'you', one for 'I' et cetera, with none of this 'younger sibling', 'uncle' and 'grandma' business. But I speak to other young people who value the practice. One of them is Huyền, whom I get to meet during my stay. 'By calling you "uncle", my friend "sister" and my Dad "father", I feel part of a bigger whole,' she says. 'I have my own place. And it's not as if my father or you can boss me about. Regardless of pronouns, I'm my own person, with my own life' (and her own company). If an urban, well-travelled young person with a European partner feels this way about it, then people with more traditional lifestyles are likely to embrace the custom even more wholeheartedly. And while I am the product of a tradition quite different to hers, I begin to relate to at least one aspect of it. Young people calling me 'uncle' and me reciprocating with 'niece/ nephew' feels weird at first, but I grow to appreciate it. It is neither needlessly remote nor too close for comfort.

The strong Vietnamese sense of respect owed to age shows in more than just grammar. One evening, I sit in a coffee shop with Loan and a friend of hers, chatting and waiting for Mike, who runs the language school that employs her. When he arrives, we shake hands, and while he finds himself a chair and orders a drink, I turn to Loan to wrap up our previous topic of conversation. Her slightly startled words and gestures, however, immediately impress upon me that I am now supposed to focus my undivided attention on Mike, as he is noticeably older than her – and her boss. I'm keenly aware that I've just behaved like a *tây*.

And thus, studying and reading, wandering around and blundering about, I feel my vocabulary grow. Even the tones are becoming inseparable parts of the words I know. Or perhaps I should say: the tonal *signs*, for my speaking feels a lot like reading out loud what my mind's eye sees. Indeed, I notice that while I speak, my hand behaves like something between a prompter and a musical director, gesturing the approximate shapes of the tones.

Words of Chinese origin comprise an increasing proportion of the new words that I'm trying to learn, and many of them are compounds consisting of two syllables. Most of these syllables have a meaning of their own in Chinese, but less often in Vietnamese. Even when their meanings can be figured out, these borrowed syllables are often bothersome. CHỦ, for instance, is derived from a Chinese word for 'owner', 'master', 'lord' or 'principal'. Vietnamese has borrowed quite a few Chinese compounds containing this word, in some of which this meaning is recognisable, while in others, not so much. CHỦ NHÂN for instance, literally 'owner-person', means simply 'owner'. DÂN CHỦ, 'people (being) lord', is 'democracy'. Much less transparent is CHỦ TỊCH for 'president, chair(man)', because the second part, TỊCH, from a Chinese word for 'seat' or 'banquet', does not occur as a separate word in Vietnamese. Even more mysterious is CHỦ NGHĨA: the second half stands for 'sense' or 'morality', but the compound means 'doctrine' – it represented 'ism' in the word for 'Marxism-Leninism' we saw above.

The Vietnamese have also created their own compounds with CHỦ. An old one is CHỦ NHẬT for 'Sunday', literally 'Lord-day'. This compound follows the grammatical pattern of Chinese, which usually functions like English in this respect: *day* comes at the end, while the noun or adjective giving additional information about the day (Sun-, Lord-) goes before it. But more recent compounds have been coined in accordance with Vietnamese grammar, which works the opposite way: main word first, additional information second. Examples of this are CHỦ XE for 'car owner' (literally owner-vehicle) and CHỦ NỢ debtor ('owner-debt'). Compounds-of-compounds may contain *both* orders: a TRƯỜNG CHỦ NHẬT or 'Sunday school', literally a 'school lord day'.

All of this fascinates the linguist in me, but it horrifies the student. For what am I to think when I encounter CHỦ? I have to consider the option that it occurs here as a one-syllable word. However, it's more likely to be part of a compound, either with the preceding word (as in the word for 'democracy') or with the following word (as in 'Sunday', 'car owner' and many others) – or with both. In compounds, the overall meaning may be completely transparent ('owner-car', hence 'car owner'), easy to grasp ('owner of debt', hence 'debtor'; 'people-lord', hence 'democracy') or pretty much unfathomable ('master-seat' for 'president').

Curiously, this whole complex and daunting business is paralleled closely by things that English and other Western European languages also do. Take this habit of plundering a prestigious foreign language. Just as Vietnamese has endlessly drawn from Chinese, so English has drawn from both Latin and Greek. Words like *construction*, *instructor* and *structure* have all come to us from Latin, either directly

Posters are fertile ground for language learners. This one asks us to 'Celebrate the Reformation, Celebrate the Glorious Party, Celebrate the Spring of the Year of the Dog'.

or through French. Few people know or care that they've all been derived from the Latin verb STRUĔRE meaning 'to build', nor do they need to. And just as the Vietnamese have taken CHỦ and run with it, building new words as they saw fit, so English words such as *infrastructure* and *deconstruct* weren't coined until modern times, even though they look as Latin as anything else with *struct* in it. Ditto with Greek: *philosophy* and *democracy* are classical terms, but *anthroposophy* and *kleptocracy* aren't, even though they were formed from Greek elements.

As for disorderly compounds, just compare English *bring up* with *upbringing*, *in-depth* with *lie-in*, *outrun* and *run out* ... And now imagine having to master all this while your first language is Vietnamese. (Yet Huyền has managed somehow. She's a niece-prodigy.)

I have to face it: even when my three weeks are nearly up, I can still say very little and understand less. That's for two reasons. Firstly, I haven't talked enough. I'm interested not primarily in understanding language – utterances – but in understanding *the* language – the structure of Vietnamese. I do want to communicate, to be sure, but there's just enough English around me to meet that need. When I was in Spain as a student, I was mostly surrounded by Spaniards whose English was worse than my Spanish, and I'm still grateful to them for it. But Loan and her friends, Huyền and her boyfriend, my admirable host Phong: while I'm grateful to them for other reasons, they speak English so well that it remains our language of choice. Many cabbies, shopkeepers and waiters don't, but how much time does one spend with them?

The second reason is that Vietnamese *is* difficult. Let me add one last piece of evidence. Vietnamese expresses many things in a fundamentally different way from European languages. Information is presented by means of other formulas, with other types of words. At Hanoi Central Station, a public panel with a timetable and some legal provisions isn't captioned 'Information' but 'Dear travellers ought to know'. If you say 'I was taken to the theatre', the correct word for 'was' can be 'got' or something like 'endured', depending on whether you went gladly or reluctantly. For 'What's the difference?' you use 'Where different?' For 'thing', you have to choose from a whole range of options, such as 'story', 'object' or a classifier – the *correct* classifier, that is. Of course, there's nothing *wrong* with any of these aspects of Vietnamese; they all make as much or as little sense as our own phrases and formulas. But as speakers of European languages, we have to learn them, one by one.

The more I realise how pervasive these differences are, the more I tend to agree with the Chinese polyglot who once remarked that 'European languages are a lot like dialects of each other'. Seen from afar, they really are.

Going home

The last few days before returning home I let my discipline slip as I afford myself the luxury of agonising over whether I should give up or press on. Vietnamese is tough and, let's face it, not enormously useful in practical terms. I would like to visit the country again, but as a tourist you don't really *need* the language. And outside Vietnam, it's not much more than a party trick. Literature? More Vietnamese novels have been translated into English than I'm ever likely to read.

'Can you think of reasons for me to continue?' I ask Huyền. 'Vietnam offers good economic opportunities', she says after some thought. 'And once you know Vietnamese, it's much easier to learn Chinese.' I'm not sure if that is a comforting thought.

19

Korean

한국어

han'gugŏ (South Korea)

조선말

chosŏnmal (North Korea)

85 million speakers

Korean has more than 80 million native speakers and a few million second-language speakers. Significant Korean communities exist in China, Japan, Russia, Uzbekistan, Kazakhstan and the United States.

Korean

SELF-DESIGNATION 한국어 (Han'gugŏ; South Korea); 조선말 (Chosŏnmal; North Korea). The name of South Korea's standard language is 표준어 (P'yojunŏ), that of North Korea's 문화어 (Munhwaŏ).

FAMILY Korean is considered a language isolate, which means it has no living relatives. However, the variety spoken by a few thousand people on Cheju island is so different that it is considered a separate language. Historical family links with Japanese, Mongolian and perhaps other Asian languages have been proposed but rejected.

SCRIPT In the twentieth century, the fifteenth-century Hangeul alphabet finally became widespread. Previously, the Chinese character script was cherished by the intellectual elite.

GRAMMAR Korean has no gender. The case system consists of seven cases, indicated by particles, i.e. small separate words after the noun. Verbs can have several out of forty suffixes, which indicate person, formality, mood and tense.

SOUNDS Somewhat unusually for East Asia, Korean is not a tonal language. Korean used to have ten different vowel sounds, but in modern speech only eight remain. There are twenty-one different consonants. The /p/, /t/, /k/ and /ch/ sounds exist in three different varieties, together making up more than half of the complete set. The vowel (or diphthong) of a syllable cannot be preceded or followed by more than one consonant.

LOANWORDS Historically, Korean has borrowed massively from Chinese. Since the twentieth century, North Korea has adopted Russian words, South Korea English ones.

EXPORTS Two familiar Korean words are *kimchi* (pickled vegetables) and the sport of *taekwondo*. Several well-known brand names are of Korean origin, including Samsung (from SAMSŎNG, 'three stars'), Hyundai (HYŎNDAE, 'modern') and Daewoo (or TAEU, 'great Woo', Woo being the founder).

JARGONS APART The languages of North and South Korea are drifting apart, especially in modern terminology. In the run-up to the 2018 Winter Olympics, players of the joint ice-hockey team found they used completely different jargons: English-derived in the South, home-grown in the North. The same is undoubtedly true in other sectors, such as technology and information sciences.

19: **Korean**

Sound and sensibility

There should be a word for words that sound like things would sound like if they made a noise, he thought. The word 'glisten' does indeed gleam oilily, and if there ever was a word that sounded exactly the way sparks look as they creep across burned paper, or the way the lights of cities would creep across the world if the whole of human civilization was crammed into one night, then you couldn't do better than 'coruscate'.

EQUAL RITES, TERRY PRATCHETT

IF ONE LINGUISTIC NOTION was hammered home by my adventures in Vietnamese, it was this: the sound of a word bears precious little relation to its meaning. Learning the basic vocab of a language is mostly a matter of brute perseverance, of memorising one damn word after another. There's nothing about GIƯỜNG to suggest it means 'bed'. It might just as well be 'awake', 'seven' or a swear word. In Korean, the word is CH'IMDAE, which is no more inherently beddish than GIƯỜNG, LIT, CAMA, KITANDA, YATAK (Vietnamese, French, Spanish/Portuguese, Swahili and Turkish) or indeed the word *bed*.

The randomness of vocabulary is a basic characteristic of human language, or at least this is what highly influential Swiss linguist Ferdinand de Saussure claimed in the early twentieth century. He taught his students that 'the entire linguistic system is founded upon the irrational principle that the sign [i.e. the word] is arbitrary'. Centuries earlier, William Shakespeare had Juliet phrase a similar thought rather more memorably when she mused on the rose, its name and its smell.

Saussure did allow for what he thought of as an inconsequential exception. Onomatopoeias, he realised, resemble the sounds they signify, or the sounds made by the things they signify. Take 'meow', cats' main contribution to the human lexicon. English has turned this into a verb, *meow* (or *mew* or *miaow*); in Vietnamese, MÈO is the noun for 'cat', while MEO and MÉO are verbs, the former referring to the workaday 'meow' of a cat giving orders, the latter a poignant rendering of its cry when scared or in pain.

Not all onomatopoeias are so alike across different languages. Farm animals in particular would seem to be giving their daily concert from different sheet music in different places. The rooster, for instance, cries *cock-a-doodle-doo* in English, COCORICO in French, KIKERIKI in German, GAGGALAGÚ in Icelandic, KKOKKIO KKOKKO in Korean, wōwōwō in Mandarin and ɪ'ííʼʾʌóó in Navajo; in Vietnamese it sings ò ó o. There are two reasons for this wide variety. Animal cries contain sounds that our speech organs can't faithfully reproduce. Moreover, languages are constrained in two ways: they have to choose from their particular sets of sounds and obey their particular word-forming rules (though onomatopoeias cut them more slack than most other words do). The differences between onomatopoeias from one language to the next enabled Saussure and later linguists to maintain that this special category was not much of a problem for their sweeping claim that 'the sign is arbitrary'. If we, as English speakers, can't tell that ò ó o represents the crowing of a rooster in Vietnamese, this suggests that the word can still be regarded as arbitrary.

Not that Saussure knew much about Vietnamese, Korean or other Asian languages. Western linguists have a somewhat shameful tradition of generalising about language on the basis of a smallish sample: English, French, German, Latin, Greek and perhaps a sprinkling of Arabic (mostly clichés) and Chinese (frequently misconceptions). Even though several Asian languages, dead and alive, have been studied in Europe for centuries, this specialist knowledge somehow failed to properly feed into general linguistic theory. As late as the 1960s and 1970s, Noam Chomsky and his followers tried to work out the universal grammar of human language on the basis of just a few specimens. Or rather, one: English.

This parochial perspective has changed. Today, many native speakers of Asian and African languages are questioning the long-held views of Western linguistics, which are also being challenged by scholars who have travelled to places that are as poor in modern conveniences as they are rich in linguistic treasure. One of the things that African and Asian linguists as well as linguistic field-workers have called into question is Saussure's assertion that language is essentially arbitrary. Especially in the languages of sub-Saharan Africa and East and Southeast Asia, they've documented extensive use of what has come to be known as *sound symbolism*. These languages have words, numbering in their hundreds or even thousands, whose sounds map on to certain meanings: *ideophones*. This is a category of which onomatopoeias are merely a subgroup; we'll meet other subgroups shortly.

The joy of ideophones

Two East Asian languages have been found to be particularly rich in this respect: Korean and Vietnamese. If I were more talented a language learner, I might now be able to draw on my first-hand experience with Vietnamese, but alas, no such luck. I did suspect that the words for 'cat', 'cow' and 'goat' (MEO, BÒ and DÊ), might be onomatopoeias, and the colloquial word for 'sneeze' left no room for doubt: HẮT XÌ. But I seem to have missed all the sound symbolism that isn't onomatopoeia.

Korean, the protagonist of this chapter, has literally thousands of ideophones. Indeed, in books about Korean, they are mentioned as one of its defining characteristics. Native-speaking linguists have long been aware of this, and have coined two terms for these ideophones: ŬISŎNGŎ are the ones that imitate sounds (onomatopoeias), while ŬIT'AEŎ convey visual, tactile or mental sensations.

The main point of using ideophones, in Korean as in other languages, is to make stories more lifelike. These are words that stand out, because there is something expressive and pictorial about them. They often display some sort of rhyme or even full repetition of syllables. In speech, the specialness of ideophones is frequently reflected in the performance: they may be set off by minute silences or accompanied by gestures; the volume, speed or pitch may be different from the surrounding words.

Because of these theatrics, it would be reasonable to assume that ideophones are limited to story-telling. But while they are indeed a valued literary resource in many cultures, they serve other purposes too, especially that of making a speaker more

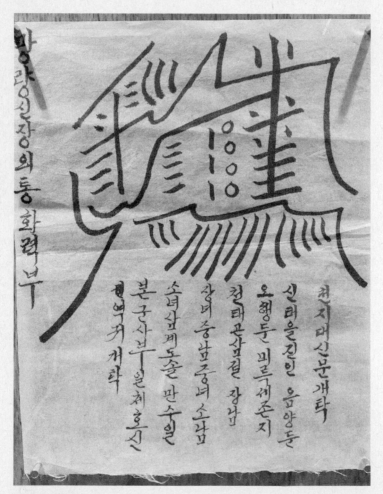

Korean talisman. Today, the Hangeul script runs left to right, but in previous centuries, top-to-bottom in right-to-left columns was preferred, as it was in Chinese and Japanese.

convincing and trustworthy. Ideophones reflect physical sensations and states of mind, and someone who makes a believable job of describing those must have experienced the story in person, or so the reasoning goes. Liars shun such details; when asked for an alibi, they will say they were 'at a party' and not become specific until prompted, whereas actual party-goers are likely to volunteer details (about people, feelings and incidents). Therefore, details bestow trust.

God's wallop

In Western languages and literatures, there is a whiff of childishness about onomatopoeia and what we consider excessively expressive terms. The German-British linguist Max Müller wrote in 1862 that they 'are the playthings, not the tools of language'. And in 1910, French anthropologist Lucien Lévy-Bruhl adduced ideophones as evidence that in 'inferior societies', the natives have an 'irresistible tendency' to 'imitate all one perceives'.

It's important to realise that the use or avoidance of such words is a cultural preference, not a universal. As Westerners, we would be taken aback if instead of 'God smote the Philistines' we were to read that he 'whacked' or 'walloped' them. Western missionaries translating the Bible into non-Western languages avoid such expressive terms, but in many languages this is a stylistic choice that weakens rather than strengthens the impact of the text. In East and Southeast Asia and Africa, very far from being childish, the effective use of ideophones is a mark of eloquence and literary sophistication.

Let's have a look at some real-life specimens from Korean (and a listen, if you like). Overleaf, in the columns headed 'Hangeul' and 'Romanisation', you can see the words in the Korean Hangeul alphabet and in a Romanised version respectively.* The next column

---

* Unfortunately, there are several Romanisation systems in circulation for Korean, and even more unfortunately, the one that is currently official in South Korea lumps together sounds that are relevantly different. Therefore, I've consistently used the previous system, which is still in use in North Korea. However, I've followed the increasingly current practice of spelling the name of the Korean alphabet as Hangeul instead of Han'gŭl, as the old system would have it.

translates them into English. If you want to hear them, there are sound file links on the 'BABEL' page of my website (*languagewriter.com*).

Korean sets of ideophones

	HANGEUL	ROMANISATION	MEANING
1	감감 깜깜 캄캄	kam-gam kkam-kkam k'am-k'am	in the dark in the pitch-dark in a spooky, desolate dark
2	빙빙 삥삥 핑핑	ping-bing pping-pping p'ing-p'ing	round and round round and round, faster round and round, in wider circles
3	반짝 빤짝	pantchak ppantchak	twinkle, glitter sparkle, twinkle brightly
4	빙빙 뱅뱅	ping-bing paeng-baeng	round and round round and round, in small circles
5	끄뚝끄뚝 까딱까딱	kkŭttok-kkŭttok kkattak-kkattak	nodding in a heavy way nodding in a light way
6	벅벅 박박	pŏk-pŏk pak-pak	rubbing hard rubbing or polishing
7	박 팍 죽 쑥 발딱 픽	pak p'ak chuk ssuk palttak p'ik	with a rip with a strong rip briefly, roughly abruptly with a jerk sudden fall

The pronunciation of Romanised Korean words often runs counter to English intuitions. For present purposes, the main thing that needs explaining is the spelling of four groups of consonants. These groups roughly correspond to the English sounds written as *k*, *t*, *ch* and *p*, each of which in Korean has three subtly different pronunciations. Let's take the k-sounds as an example. One version, written as a simple *k* (or sometimes *g*) in Romanised Korean, requires the consonant to be spoken without exhaling, the same as in French and Spanish. This pronunciation is considered basic or neutral in Korean. In English, we hear this when the *k* is preceded by an *s*, e.g. *skin*. The second type of k-sound is called 'aspirated', meaning that it comes with a puff of air. This is the pronunciation that English and German speakers are most used to: the word *kin* is pronounced as /k^{h}in/. It's written as *k'* in Romanised Korean; in other contexts, k^h is a more common notation. The third and final type of *k* is hard to describe, but there's somehow more tension involved; it's written as *kk*.

Thlv-thlv-thlv

Equipped with this knowledge and looking at the table once more, we may wonder: how do the sounds symbolise the meanings of these words? To answer that, we first have to find regular correlations between sounds and meanings.

The easiest regularities to detect are in the rows 1, 2 and 3. The first word in each of these – KAM-GAM, PING-BING, PANTCHAK – begins with a neutral consonant, whereas the second word begins with a tense consonant, and sometimes the second syllable does too: KKAM-KKAM, PPING-PPING and PPANTCHAK. This changes the meaning from neutral to intensive, e.g. from 'dark' to 'pitch-dark'. Apparently the tense initial consonant conveys a more intense sensation. In rows 1 and 2, the third words in the list pull off a similar trick by substituting the aspirated variety of the consonant: K'AM-K'AM, P'ING-P'ING. This too intensifies the meaning, but with some sort of twist, adding the dimension of 'spookiness' in row 1 and 'wideness' in row 2. The fact that row 3 doesn't have a third word is interesting in itself, because it shows that speakers know which of the potential forms are part of the Korean lexicon and which ones aren't. If a Korean speaker were to say P'ANTCHAK, which is the form missing in row 3, it would be considered an inspired coinage: perfectly good Korean, but not conventional. It would be a bit like calling something 'sensmashingsational' in English: the word has a transparent meaning, only a pedantic stick-in-the-mud would call it 'wrong', yet it can't be said to *exist* in any but the most ephemeral sense. In other words, ideophones are expressive, but they are not primarily a tool for *individual* expression.

Ideophones should therefore not be confused with the expressive noises we make when reading a bedtime story to a child. After saying 'And the snake slithered across the lawn' we may go something like 'THLV-THLV-THLV' or 'WZHV-WZHV-WZHV' to paint a sound-picture of the slithering. Great fun of course, but it's not how the typical ideophone works. Speakers of Korean and other languages don't spend their days ad-libbing; for their ideophones, they mostly draw on a large set of vocabulary that can be looked up in dictionaries. For a snake slithering through grass, there's probably a ready-made word.

Returning to the examples, we see that in rows 4, 5 and 6 the vowels play a significant role. The details are somewhat complex, but the long and the short of it is this: in ideophones, vowels known as 'bright' carry connotations such as small, affectionate, happy, flimsy and feminine, whereas 'dark' vowels are associated with concepts like big, heavy, clumsy, gloomy and masculine. (If you're wondering if this has anything to do with yin and yang: yes, absolutely. Rather unusually, though, in Korean ideophones dark is associated with yin, bright with yang. We'll see the consequences further on.) There are four bright vowels, and each one is paired with one or two dark vowels. For instance, since both the dark vowels ŭ (as in *curl*) and o (as in *lot*) have a (as in *ah-ha*) as their bright partner, the 'dark word' KKŬTTOK, with its heavy, gloomy undertones, has a more light-hearted counterpart in KKATTAK.

The two types of regularity discussed so far will sometimes team up. The word ping-bing appears in both row 2 and row 4. An even better example is the word PINGGŬL (similar in meaning to PING-BING), which has all the six forms that are logically possible: PINGGŬL, PPINGGŬL, P'INGGŬL, PAENGGŬL, PPAENGGŬL and P'AENGGŬL.

Finally, row 7 represents a less systematic group of Korean ideophones. Words ending in the same consonant often express similar sensations. Those ending in *k* tend to signify something abrupt, shrill or tight. Words ending in *l* often refer to smooth or flowing things, those in *ng* to round, hollow and open things (PING-

BING!), those in *t* to small, fine things and pointed details, et cetera. Unlike the examples in row 1 to 6, however, the words under 7 do not form duos or other combinations, with different meanings based on their final consonant. They're all loners.

Topsy-turvy symbolism

So yes, ideophones do display regular correlations between sound and meaning. But then, sound and meaning are sometimes correlated in English in a similar way: if you put un- or in- in front of an adjective, you (usually) negate it; if you add -s, you make it a plural. It would be silly to claim that those regularities are sound-symbolic; they aren't. What is it about the Korean sounds then that does make them symbolic? Do they really convey meaning all by themselves?

To settle that question, we need to find out if people who don't speak Korean have a hunch about these words. Of course, no one would be likely to guess the exact meaning of KAM-GAM, KKAM-KKAM and K'AM-K'AM, but it just *might* be possible for non-Koreans to intuit that the second and third words refer to a blacker darkness than the first.

They might – and they actually do, as Korean linguist Nahyun Kwon discovered in her PhD research. She had a number of Australians listen to quasi-Korean nonsense words displaying the sorts of regular patterns discussed above. Without knowing any Korean whatsoever, they correctly guessed (significantly more often than can be accounted for by mere chance) that KKAM-KKAM and K'AM-K'AM type words had a more intensive meaning than the KAM-GAM type, and not the other way round. So did Korean participants in the experiment – and remember these were nonsense words, so it wasn't as if they knew them to begin with. The effect was not very strong in either group, but it was unmistakable.

Kwon also had her English-speaking participants listen to pairs of Korean-style nonsense words, one with a dark vowel, the other with a bright one (as exemplified in rows 4, 5 and 6 of the table). Again, they had statistically significant intuitions, but here's another surprise: this time, they were *wrong* somewhat more often than chance would predict. Weirder still, her Korean-speaking participants simply seemed at a complete loss when trying to interpret these nonsense words. These startling results begin to make sense if we assume that the Korean language somehow has its vowel symbolism the wrong way round. And well we might, because there is a well-documented tendency for humans worldwide to associate low, open vowels such as /ah/ with bigness – words like *vast* and *large* fit the bill, as does *yang* – and high, closed vowels such as /ee/ with smallness – think *mini*, *teeny-weeny* and *wee* as well as *yin*. Other research has shown that Koreans actually share this widespread intuition, but only when hearing words that are evidently not Korean. Words that appear Korean but aren't, as in Kwon's research, put them in a bind: their general intuition clashes with their specific knowledge of Korean, the result being that they can't make up their minds. Just why the Korean language has reversed the widespread correlation is anybody's guess; no explanation has proved satisfactory so far. Let's chalk it up as a linguistic accident.

What *is* understood is why most of us associate /ah/ with big and /ee/ with small: when we say /ah/, our oral cavity (otherwise known as 'mouth') is big, when we say /ee/, it's small. This is sound symbolism at its most basic: size of mouth reflects size of thing referred to. You may object that when you're talking, you're hardly aware of the size of your mouth, which is true. But try thinking of sound symbolism as a special manner of gesturing. Even though you hardly realise what you're doing with your hands during a conversation, your manual gestures are highly meaningful and symbolic. Similarly, 'oral gestures' can be meaningful and symbolic. However, the oral gestures also do something that manual gestures don't: they form the sounds that you utter. Oral gestures therefore, being both unconsciously expressive and the mechanism to produce our speech sounds, could easily be a mechanism that links meanings to sounds. Exactly this is thought to be the case for the sounds of many words in some languages, such as Korean and other Asian as well as African languages, and also for some words in languages elsewhere. More about those later.

Turning from vowels to consonants, we've seen that Korean ideophones beginning with tense consonants rather than neutral ones (*pp* or *kk* instead of *p* or *k*) convey a more emphatic meaning,

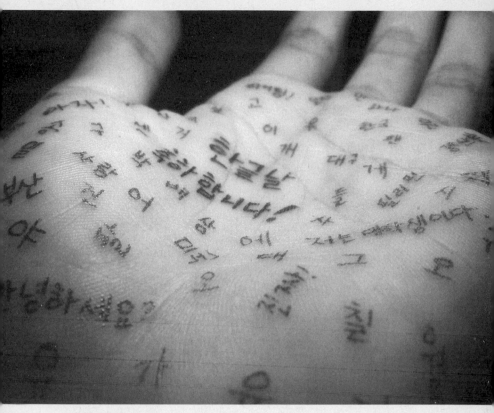

Korean handwriting, as it were.

and so do the aspirated ones (*p'*, *k'*). Those correlations, especially the former, make even more obvious and intuitive sense than a wide-mouthed /ah/ being suggestive of something big.

This leaves us with the third type of Korean sound symbolism seen above, the one that manifests itself in the final consonant. Kwon didn't examine it, but this type seems to reflect another general human intuition: words ending in *k* sound more abrupt, because the consonant itself consists in an abrupt, sharp burst of sound, unlike *g* or *m*. So does the *t*, but here the burst of sound is smaller, produced by only the tip of the tongue – hence the connotation of something small, fine or with pointed details. It's also tempting to see the *t* as another oral gesture, presenting the tip of the tongue: a pointed part or detail that makes small, nimble movements.

There are other real-world phenomena that can help explain symbolic links between sound and meaning, some widely accepted, others more speculative. If a certain movement can be heard and therefore expressed in an onomatopoeia, say sand *sliding* down a slope, the same word can then also be applied to other movements that are similar yet silent: think of a raindrop sliding down a leaf. Another link can form when certain types of sounds often go together with conspicuous features: if time and again we notice that children, short people and small animals such as mice make softer, higher noises than sturdy adults and large beasts such as lions, we will come to associate loudness and pitch with size. This is also an (additional or alternative) explanation for the 'ah-as-in-vast' versus 'ee-as-in-wee' contrast: /ah/ reminds us of a roaring lion, /ee/ of a squeaking mouse. Yet another conceptual link may be found in duration, with longer sounds representing longer and therefore slower things and movements.

Taking it further

Once such links are established in our minds, we can base ever more abstract associations on them. If we think of a certain sound as 'soft', for instance /b/ as compared to /p/, we can easily extend this to a general sense of 'pleasantness' and from there to 'sweetness'. If we feel that /ah/ represents 'big', and thus high on the scale of size, we may also think of it as high on other scales, for instance thickness, danger or bitterness. In this way, ideophones can become abstract to the point of having cognitive rather than sensory meaning.

The Korean word CHIGŬLCHIGŬL can illustrate how ideophones can leap from one sense to another, and I mean 'sense' in both senses of the word: from one meaning to the other and from one sensory organ to the other. The first meaning the dictionary gives for CHIGŬLCHIGŬL is straightforwardly onomatopoetic: 'sizzlingly; used to describe the sounds made when a small amount of water, oil, etc., boils, or such a motion.' Note the addendum, 'or such a motion', which extends the word's domain from sound to movement. Another translation of CHIGŬLCHIGŬL is fully visual: 'glaringly; blazingly; in the manner of sunlight shining intensely.' This makes easy sense from an English-language perspective: a Google search for 'sizzling sunlight' yields – to my surprise, I must admit – a substantial number of hits, albeit far fewer than for 'glaring sunlight' or 'blazing sunlight'. Things get even more interesting with the third translation of CHIGŬLCHIGŬL. The dictionary simply states that there is 'no equivalent expression [in English]' and goes on to explain: 'in the manner of one being sick and one's body getting hot due to fever.' Here the original image of the sizzling liquid, which can of course hurt a cook's hands, has been transferred to the bodily sensation of being hot and uncomfortable. Finally, CHIGŬLCHIGŬL can even describe a state of mind: 'worrisomely; anxiously; in the manner of the speaker being agitated with anger or worry.'

The more abstract meanings ideophones acquire, the harder it becomes for outsiders – non-Koreans – to guess their meaning. In the case of CHIGŬLCHIGŬL, we can easily hop on this train of associations and stay aboard all the way from 'sizzling' through 'glaring' and 'feverish' to 'anxious' – but only as long as we're told that this is how it goes. Linking sound to meaning spontaneously, however, becomes more difficult with each stop on the line. CHIGŬLCHIGŬL does remind me of 'sizzling', but I'd be hard-pressed to say whether it refers to feeling hot or cold – the association with chattering teeth would probably lead my intuition astray. So while ideophones are firmly rooted in sensory perception, they can branch into unpredictable directions. They make sense, but often not in obvious ways.

N as in nose

It was French, English and the other European languages that inspired Ferdinand de Saussure to believe that 'the sign is arbitrary'. Yet even here, some sounds are less arbitrary than others.

English has several groups of words that seem to suggest that something other than randomness is at work. One such group, which includes the likes of *glitter*, *glimmer* and *glow*, all signify a certain kind of light effect; *sprout*, *sprinkle*, *sprawl* and their ilk are *spreading* one thing or another; while *swerve*, *sway*, *swagger* and *swing* describe smooth, wide movements. But why? Try as we might, we're unlikely to find anything intrinsically luminescent in *gl-*, anything dispersive in *spr-* or anything swaggerish in *sw-*. They might be ideophones whose onomatopoetic roots have become untraceable, as described above. Alternatively, each of the groups may have clustered around two words that just happened to have similar sounds and somewhat similar meanings; these might then have influenced the form or the meaning of other words, pulling them into their acoustic or semantic orbit, so to speak. These things have been known to happen: Old Latin DINGUA ('tongue') changed its form into LINGUA under the influence of the verb LINGERE meaning 'lick'. And the English word *glamour* used to mean 'enchantment', but shifted its meaning the better to align with the *gl-* group mentioned above.

Other English words are more directly sound-symbolic. When I mentioned that Korean words ending in *k* suggest abruptness, you may have thought, 'Wait a minute, how about English words like *flick*, *pick* and *smack* – don't they describe abrupt movements too?' They do, and it's unlikely to be a mere coincidence. Words ending in *p* (*pop*, *hop*, *flip*, *thump*) and *t* (*hit*, *punt*, *butt* as a verb) are equally

Sejung the Great, who is said to have personally created the unique Korean alphabet, Hangeul, in the fifteenth century.

suggestive of movements with a sudden beginning or ending, and *roll* is an excellent word to describe just that movement.

Against every one of these examples – a sceptic might argue – can be set a counterexample, revealing the seeming correlation as a mere fluke. But here's the thing: there aren't enough counterexamples to do that. Linguists have compared thousands of English words and established that they are more sound-symbolic than chance would have it. English has much less sound symbolism than Korean, Vietnamese or many African languages,* but it's still a feature of the language. It turns out, moreover, that sound symbolism is more prevalent among the sorts of basic words that young children learn than among those acquired somewhat later in life. That makes sense, because words are more readily understood (and memorised) if their sounds hint at their meaning. After all, beginning learners can use all the help they can get.

Some types of sound symbolism cut across linguistic borders. A comparison of one hundred basic items of vocabulary from over 4,000 languages showed some neat correlations. The ee-as-in-wee effect proved to hold across this huge sample, though somehow the ah-as-in-vast effect didn't. More surprisingly, words for several body parts proved to have clear preferences for certain sounds. 'Nose' in many languages begins with /n/, this being a nasal sound – and unlike /m/ and /ng/, which are also nasal sounds, /n/ has the tongue pointing towards the nose. Words for 'tongue' (and words for 'lick' too, I would expect, but it wasn't part of the sample) like to have an /l/, a sound which puts said organ nicely on display. The word for 'a woman's breast' often begins with *m* (think of Latin MAMA), as does the word for 'mother' – probably the result of babies' making a *ma* sound in between suckling. Other scholars have found that the word for 'lip' often contains a b or p, consonants of a group called bilabial or 'double-lipped'. Both the English *lip* and Romance words such as LABIO and BUZĂ fit the bill. Unfortunately, Korean lets us down with a thump here: its words for 'nose', 'tongue' and 'breast' are nothing like what they should be (K'O, HYŎ, YUBANG); only 'lip' is a decent IPSUL.

---

* It so happens that the only language of sub-Saharan Africa discussed in this book, Swahili, displays less sound symbolism than most other languages in the region.

Senses talking

In spite of all these ideophones, it remains true that the majority of words in all of today's spoken languages have an arbitrary form. This is particularly true for the numerous terms referring to entities, qualities and actions that we refer to in a neutral, matter-of-fact way: cups, plumbers and sitting are sensorially observable, but the words for them are meant to be neutral references, in Korean as in English. In contrast, as soon as we try to convey our sensations more graphically and vividly, the proportion of ideophones rises – manifestly in Korean, hidden in full sight where English is concerned. That's where words like *wobbly*, *swagger* and *twiddle*, *titillate*, *bling* and *snide* as well as Terry Pratchett's *coruscate* come into their own. We hear our senses talking.

For a categorical statement such as 'the sign is arbitrary', to be true in most cases is not good enough. We have to face that the claim has been falsified. Tough luck for Saussure, of course. The great man must be rolling in his grave – *paeng-baeng,* if not *ppaeng-ppaeng.*

18

Tamil

தமிழ்

90 million speakers

80 million Tamil speakers, including some 10 million second-language speakers, live in Tamil Nadu (South India), with around 3 million in Sri Lanka. Tamil-speaking minorities have long existed in Malaysia (over 2 million), Singapore, Myanmar, South Africa and several Indian Ocean islands. More recent migration has created substantial communities in the UK, the US, Australia and Canada.

Tamil

SELF-DESIGNATION தமிழ் (Tamil).

FAMILY Dravidian, which comprises three other large languages (Telugu, Kannada and Malayalam) as well as a few dozen smaller ones that are not usually written. Most of them are spoken in Southern India and in Sri Lanka, a few farther north in India, one in Pakistan and Afghanistan. Tamil, Kannada and Malayalam all belong to the Southern group, but mutual intelligibility is limited.

SCRIPT Tamil has its own writing system. See Bengali (chapter 6) which deals with the writing systems of India.

GRAMMAR Tamil grammar is agglutinative, which means that words can have several suffixes in a row, to indicate their grammatical function. Nouns have two categories: rational (humans and gods) and irrational (everything else). Singular rational nouns can be feminine or masculine; plurals are gender-free.

SOUNDS Tamil has five vowel sounds, each of which can be either long or short. Some Tamil consonants are 'retroflex', which means the tongue is curled in a way that is unusual in English (except some American dialects) and in European languages generally, except Swedish.

LOANWORDS Historically Sanskrit, today English.

EXPORTS *Rice* and *ginger* seem to have a very old Tamil (or rather, Dravidian) origin. More modern loans include *mango, curry, catamaran, cheroot* and *pariah*.

CLASSIC In 2004, Tamil became the first language to be recognised as classical by the Indian government; Sanskrit followed in 2005.

18: **Tamil**

A matter of life and death

CHANCES ARE THAT when you see the word Tamil, 'tigers' is the next word to come to mind. It's a reasonable association, for the Tamil Tigers were the protagonists in a civil war that tore the island of Sri Lanka apart for more than a quarter of a century. And the conflict was triggered by language. After the country's independence, a nationalist government dominated by the majority Sinhalese introduced a disastrous 'Sinhala Only Act' that led to riots and the massacre of Tamils, and to a resistance that turned into terror and bloodshed. It was a war that had roots both in language and religion (Tamils are mainly Hindu with small numbers of Christians; Sinhalese are almost exclusively Buddhist). But it was an attack on the Tamil language that lit the fires.

We will return to Sri Lanka at the end of this chapter, which concerns itself mainly with the Tamil heartland of South India. Even there, however, being a speaker of Tamil has been a matter of life and death. In the 1960s, the Tamil language became a cause to be defended against the perceived imposition of Hindi, and over the following decades led numerous activists to 'sacrifice themselves at the altar of Tamil', often killing themselves publicly. Conversely, the Tamil scholar and nationalist 'Ma.Po.Si' (M.P. Sivagnanam; 1906–1995) claimed that it was his deep devotion to Tamil that stopped him seeking relief in suicide when he was suffering an agonising illness.

Other nations have a long history of extolling the beauty of their own language, its copiousness and its unequalled capacity to express all subtleties of thought. The French are a case in point. So are the Arabs. Even the English. The difference is of course that we've all heard of French and Arabic, whereas Tamil, notwithstanding its 90 million speakers, somehow scarcely registers. Yet their language is considered something sacred, the object of nothing less than *Tamiḻpparru*, or 'devotion to Tamil', as the historian Sumathi Ramaswamy translates the term. Tamil is, in effect, divine – a goddess, or, perhaps more aptly, an equivalent of the Virgin Mary, lauded by her followers with the titles of Queen, Mother and Virgin.

Tamil language personified as a goddess. Note the book and writing tool flourished by the goddess's secondary arms.

Ugly duckling

The adoration of the Tamil language is not quite the age-old tradition that the devotees would have us believe. At the turn of the nineteenth century, its status was as low as could be. The British colonials didn't think much of the Indians and their culture generally, and what appreciation they could muster was reserved for the lighter-skinned Aryans of the North. They had only just discovered that Sanskrit, the ancient and highly literary Indo-Aryan language, was historically related to Europe's classical Greek and Latin. The dark-skinned southerners, thought to be lacking in any appreciable culture and to be speaking abominably bastardised Sanskrit dialects, were disdained by Brits and North Indians alike.

But then a few maverick British scholars in the southern city of Madras began to study the Tamil language and old documents written in it. Helped by native speakers, what they found was spectacular: a rich, refined and almost completely forgotten literature spanning two thousand years. Part secular, part religious, it bore witness to a golden age. It turned out that South India had been ruled in this era by various mighty dynasties called Pandyan, Chola and Chera. Today, these names are as familiar to southern Indians as Alexander, Caesar and Charlemagne are to Europeans.

In 1856, a grammar of Tamil was published. In it, the linguist and bishop Robert Caldwell refuted the idea that it was a dialect of Sanskrit, corrupted out of all recognition. Together with three large neighbouring languages (Telugu, Kannada and Malayalam) and dozens of smaller, unwritten ones, it in fact forms what has since become known as the Dravidian family. Suddenly, what had seemed like an Indo-Aryan ugly duckling was transformed into the 'purest' of the Dravidian swans – and linguistic purity was at a premium in the nationalistic ideology of the day, in India as in Europe.

An unexpected stroke of luck came Tamil's way in the 1930s. Short inscriptions in an unknown language had been found in the Indus Valley since the 1870s, and some European scholars now proposed that they represented a Dravidian language. If true, this would give Dravidian writing an exceptionally long (although interrupted) history of some 5,500 years and a rather grand origin: the Indus Valley or Harappan Civilisation, as old and sophisticated as those of Egypt and Mesopotamia, and covering a much larger area. Today, it is still considered quite possible that the underlying language of the Indus script is an early form of Dravidian. Other contenders vie for the same prize though, including Proto-Aryan – mother of Sanskrit, grandmother of Hindi, and hence arch-enemy of Tamil. It will be hard to settle the question as long as the script is not deciphered, which seems impossible without finding something like a Rosetta Stone. And language chauvinists of all persuasions may ultimately be in for a disappointment: some scholars suspect that the Indus symbols aren't a script at all.

It's hard to believe that millions and millions of Tamilians, most of them poor and illiterate, should have felt deeply about some indecipherable symbols found 2,000 kilometres away. Yet that is exactly what they did. So why was this? Why should this scholarly stuff matter to folks who couldn't write their own names?

Driven to frenzy

The Tamilians of the early 1800s found themselves in the margin of their continent without past glories. But the ensuing discoveries of classical authors and ancient empires made their history full of incident and achievement. The educated elite was quick to take pride in it. They then proceeded to educate and mobilise the masses, thus ushering in what's come to be known as the Tamil Renaissance or Revival. This took decades to gather momentum in India and it was not a single monolithic movement. Rather, it encompassed numerous initiatives, organisations and programmes, some literary, some religious and some – especially at a later stage – political.

Intellectuals passionate about Tamil's literary heritage edited and published ancient texts, founded academies and magazines, taught classes in the classical language, ran libraries and pressed for the use of Tamil in all forms of education, from primary school to university. They tended to be purists, trying to replace loanwords with indigenous alternatives, either old or newly coined. While this is a common endeavour in movements striving for language recognition, the Tamil community was somewhat exceptional in its belief that their language was the oldest on earth, with a history

Ancient glories: a Tamil inscription in Brahmi script, found in Tamil Nadu. It dates from the Sangam period (3rd century BCE - 3rd century CE).

stretching back at least 50,000 years – some would even say millions. (This idea, implausible to begin with, was nonetheless still defended as recently as the 1990s by otherwise serious intellectuals.)

Revivalists of a religious bent were mainly concerned with a reform of Hinduism based on Tamil scriptures, returning to what they considered a more rational, monotheistic strand of India's major tradition. While Shaivism, the special worship of Shiva, has a long history throughout South Asia, this Tamil strand placed its origins in an idealised Tamilian past, untainted by caste differences, gender inequality and polytheism. Such flaws were held to be of later date, introduced by the Sanskrit-speaking Aryans. And Neo-Shaivian rituals could never be performed by Brahmins (the priestly caste), as these were seen to be Aryan interlopers. The literary revivalists held Tamil to be the noblest and most ancient of tongues, but the Neo-Shaivists aimed higher: Tamil was the language of the divine.

How did these literary and religious revivalists get their message across to the Tamilian masses? Given that most people were illiterate, the medium had to be oral. As for the style, high-flown rhetoric was the customary mode. A common trope was the personification of Tamil as a beautiful woman. The scholar, author and activist Mudiyarasan (1920–1998) wrote in a poem: 'If you reject me, how can I endure this life? / Is it not your sweet passion that drives me to frenzy? / O delicious language of mine! Gather me up and embrace me!' His prose may be terser than his poetry, but it doesn't hold back either: 'I consider Tamil as god.' Various others poets rhapsodised about the language's 'glowing face', 'lustrous lips', 'glorious golden body', 'abundant breasts' and 'narrow waist'. The poet Bharatidasan (1891–1964) takes the eroticism to its logical conclusion: 'Even the pleasures that woman alone gives do not compare to our great Tamil!'

There's a gory streak running through these odes, too. To quote Bharatidasan once more: 'Our first task is to finish off those who destroy our glorious Tamil! / Let flow a river of crimson blood!' Or this one, by the radical scholar and writer Pulavar Kulanthai (1906–1972): 'I will chop off the head of Mother Tamil's enemy,

Bharatidasan remains a key figure in South India's Tamil culture – praised here in a dance video of his songs.

even if my own mother prevents me.' More self-destructively: 'If any evil befalls you, my glorious Mother Tamil! (...) to put an end to your suffering, I will give up my life.' Writing at the age of twenty-seven, Kannadasan (1927–1981) relishes the prospect of a good Tamil death: 'Even in death, Tamil should be on our lips. Our ashes should burn with the fragrance of Tamil.'

And some went beyond rhetoric. In 1964, a young schoolmaster became the first to practice what the poet had merely preached: he reduced himself to ashes, with Tamil on his lips. Even as he died a painful martyr's death, Chinnasami yelled, 'Death to Hindi! May Tamil flourish!' An avid reader of the ancient texts, Chinnasami was partly inspired by literature, but his final act firmly places him in the political strand of the revival movement. Such martyrs and political revivalists aimed at returning Tamil to what they considered its legitimate place in society: after centuries of oppression, it should once more become the dominant language of public life, used as a matter of course in administration, education and the media.

In fairness, not everyone involved in the Tamilians' political struggle was so obsessed with language. Indeed, the movement's most influential figure, E. V. Ramasami (1879–1973), also known as 'the patriarch' or 'the great', had little patience with Tamil fundamentalists, seeing the future in speaking English. He would publicly say things such as, 'I do not have any devotion for Tamil, either as mother tongue or as the language of the nation. I am not attached to it because it is a classical language, or because it is an ancient language, or because it was the language spoken by Shiva.' And even, 'Speak with your wives and children and servants in English! Give up your infatuation with Tamil ... Try and live like human beings!' If he could nonetheless become and remain a credible leader, it was because he tirelessly campaigned against Hindi, a language that to him was a tool of Aryan, Brahmin, Sanskritic, North Indian imperialism.

Up until the 1960s, the political wing of the revival movement in India was divided on a crucial issue: should the Tamilians seek independence or merely linguistic rights within the country? Different political parties gave voice to their demands in radical and often violent ways, while at the same time participating in elections. If the literary and religious revivalists prepared the ground by inspiring devotion to the language, it was the political wing that spearheaded the protests and, after decades, reaped the harvest.

Enthroned without a keyboard

So what has this harvest been? In 1947, India gained independence – a nationwide achievement, of course, but one in which Tamilians played a role beyond their numbers. Nine years later, the federal government made a huge concession that Tamilians and several other peoples had long been pushing for: the whole country was reorganised along linguistic lines. The state of Madras, which had been multilingual so far, was reduced to those areas where the main language was Tamil, and soon it was duly declared the official state language. 'All our troubles have now ceased as *Tamilttāy* [Mother Tamil] reclines in royal style on her auspicious throne,' one elated member of the legislative assembly declared.

If Mother Tamil could sit back and graciously enjoy her reign, the state government certainly couldn't. Implementing the measure proved tough and took years. Administrators would frequently find themselves at a loss for words – literally. Swearing to die for Tamil or waxing lyrical about her delightful body was one thing, but expressing all sorts of modern bureaucratic and legalistic subtleties was quite another, and borrowing the jargon from English or Hindi would have been a humiliation. It took a while to develop the required vocabulary. Nor did the problems stop there. Even something as mundane as typing had to be reorganised: typists were not accustomed to using a Tamil keyboard and had to be retrained, which in turn was impossible until a standard keyboard had been devised. Yet these annoyances were merely teething problems, and nowadays the administration goes about its business smoothly, almost exclusively in Tamil.

Another milestone came in 1965. The central government bowed to violent protests in the Dravidian South, Madras state in particular, and did not declare Hindi India's sole official language, in spite of having planned to do so for more than fifteen years. Back in 1949, a leader of the Congress Party had declared: 'I can say to my friends

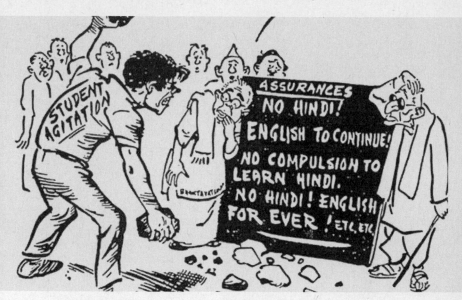

A cartoon from the 1960s showing the anti-Hindi protests in Tamil Nadu. The backing for English in order to keep the Hindi-speaking North at bay was a significant tactic.

in the South that it would be in their best interests to learn Hindi as early as possible, because if they do not learn Hindi quickly enough, they will be left behind.' It was this sort of attitude and the ham-fisted policies derived from it that made Chinnasami and others lay down their lives for Tamil. The Dravidian South insisted on maintaining English as a second official language: partly because they wanted a level linguistic playing field for all Indians, partly because they resented northern dominance as symbolised by Hindi.

At the state level, 1967 saw a political turning point. Nationalists won the elections in Madras and came to power. They have dominated the state government ever since. This feat, unique for India, has enabled them to realise much of their agenda. Within a year, they made Hindi an optional rather than obligatory school subject. This was in clear defiance of the nationwide three-language formula, which expects every citizen to study English, Hindi and (where applicable) their regional language. In 1969, Madras state was finally renamed Tamil Nadu or 'Tamil land', a long-standing nationalist policy that the previous, more Delhi-oriented state government

South India has a thriving Tamil film industry – this is a poster for *Narayan*, one of the most successful Tamil films, based on *The Godfather*.

had consistently refused to implement.[*] Other nationalist measures included 'purifying' textbooks of Sanskrit words and naming numerous streets and public buildings in honour of language devotees, including many 'martyrs' such as Chinnasami.

That is not to say that half a century of nationalist government has left the Tamil devotees fully satisfied. Central government institutions based in Tamil Nadu, such as the military, the railways and the post, continue to conduct their business mostly in Hindi. Even the Institute for the Propagation of Hindi in South India, founded by Mahatma Gandhi in 1918, is still based in Chennai (the new name of Madras). There is a thriving Tamil-language film industry – 'Kollywood' (after a district of Chennai) – but Hindi films and songs are highly popular among Tamil speakers, and increasing numbers of people learn Hindi today.

---

[*] In 1996 the capital city of Madras was renamed Chennai. The choice seems to rest on shaky linguistic foundations. The etymology of neither name has been ascertained, but it's quite possible that Madras is of Tamil origin, whereas Chennai is more likely Telugu.

But perhaps the biggest disappointment has been this: even though Mother Tamil has reclined 'in royal style on her auspicious throne' for a long time, 'all our troubles' have not ceased. Compared to other Indian states, Tamil Nadu does not do too badly in social and economic terms, but it's by no means a haven of wealth, equality and tranquillity. As a matter of fact, neighbouring Kerala does considerably better. Culturally speaking, this is another Dravidian area, but ideologically speaking it is dominated not so much by nationalism as by good old-fashioned communism. When it comes to parenthood, it looks as if Tamil is less caring and effective as a mother than Karl Marx is as a father.

Tiger tongue: Tamil in Sri Lanka

Sri Lanka's population of just over 20 million is tiny compared to India's, but its problems since Independence in 1948 have been just as intense, with conflict rooted in language and culture. When the British withdrew, they left English as the official language. It was a situation that papered over the country's ethnic, religious and language divisions. The majority – nearly three-quarters of the population – were Indo-Aryan, Sinhala-speaking Buddhists, while most of the rest were Dravidian, Tamil-speaking Hindus.

Sinhalese nationalists, almost from the lowering of the British flag, began discriminating against the Tamils, making it hard for them to gain citizenship, and deporting large numbers 'back to India'. Then in 1956 the nationalist prime minister S.W.R.D. Bandaranaike introduced the Sinhala Only Act, which replaced English with Sinhalese in the civil service and all official business. It forced Tamils (who had occupied perhaps 60 per cent of the civil service jobs) out of employment, and often out of the country. And it led, initially, to non-violent protests from the Tamil political parties. These were met by violence and riots, with hundreds of Tamils massacred by Sinhalese mobs. Two years later, the illogically named 'Sinhala Only, Tamil Also' compromise was struck. Even though Tamil's position remained that of a second-class language, the Tamilians went along with it.

Unfortunately, it did not end the majority's overbearing folly. In the succeeding years, they expatriated more than 300,000 Tamils to India. They discriminated against Tamils sitting university entrance exams. They banned the import of Tamil media. In the new 1972 constitution, they gave 'the foremost place' to Buddhism, the religion of most Sinhalese, at the expense of Tamil Hinduism. In other words, the Sri Lankan government did all that lay within its power to create a monster.

Such a monster duly appeared: the Tamil Tigers, a separatist movement that fought a cruel civil war for over a quarter of a century (1983–2009). In the late 1980s, Tamil was declared *an* official national language, alongside Sinhalese as *the* official language – the devil can be in the article. Obviously, it was too little, too late for the Tamil Tigers.

In the end, the Tigers were defeated on the battlefield, and in its aftermath many Sinhalese felt there was no longer any need to accommodate the Tamils, with the former Tiger territories in the north, known as Tamil Eelam, brought back under central government control. Some hope of reconciliation emerged with the 2015 political defeat of the Sinhalese nationalist Rajapaksa (who had brutally ended the war) by a more conciliatory leader, Sirisena. At independence day celebrations the following year, the Tamil version of the national anthem, *Sri Lanka Matha*, was sung for the first time since 1949 at an official government event. But the accord is fragile and beset by Sinhalese Buddhist nationalists, for whom Tamils and Buddhists are, at best, guests in 'their' country.

17

Turkish

TÜRKÇE

90 million speakers

About 78 million native speakers and 12 million as a second language. Turkey and Northern Cyprus are the predominantly Turkish-speaking areas; both include significant second-language speakers. Substantial Turkish-speaking minorities live in the Balkans as well as Western Europe, especially Germany, France and the Netherlands.

Turkish

SELF-DESIGNATION TÜRKÇE, TÜRK DILI.

FAMILY Turkic, which comprises some 30 living languages spread across a huge area, ranging from southeast Europe all the way to northeast Asia. Within Turkic, Turkish belongs to the Oghuz group, along with Azeri and Turkmen. These have a fairly high degree of mutual comprehension.

SCRIPT Turkish is nowadays written in the Latin alphabet with some additional letters: ç, ğ, ı, ö, ş and ü. The capital i has a dot: İ.

GRAMMAR Turkish has no gender. The word for 'she', 'he' as well as 'it' is o. Very few nouns – mainly kinship terms – have separate female and male forms. The grammar is highly agglutinative, which means that words can take long strings of suffixes. For instance, on the basis of BAŞAR, 'succeed', it can create BAŞARISIZLAŞTIRILAN, meaning 'that which is made unsuccessful'. Consisting of a whole series of suffixes (BAŞAR-I-SIZ-LAŞ-TIR-IL-AN), this is a perfectly natural, unforced word that any Turkish speaker may casually use.

SOUNDS Turkish has vowel harmony. The last vowel of a word influences the vowels of suffixes attached to the word. For instance, the plural suffix will take the form -LER if the preceding vowel is an *e, i, ö* or *ü*, but -LAR if it's an *a, ı, o* or *u*.

LOANWORDS Traditonally from Persian, Arabic, French, Greek, Italian; nowadays English.

EXPORTS *Hummus, yogurt, baklava, pasha, fez, minaret, jackal, lilac, tulip, kiosk, divan, harem* and many more (some have even deeper Persian or Arabic roots – see main text).

LEARNER'S LICENCE If you're interested in learning a non-Indo-European language that won't have you tearing *all* your hair out, Turkish is an excellent choice. It's profoundly different from what we Indo-Europeans are used to, which makes it far from easy, but at least its grammar and spelling (in Latin letters) are very regular and it has no tones.

17: **Turkish**

Irreparably improved

FOR CENTURIES, the elite of the Ottoman Empire spoke and wrote an exceptional language. It was Turkish in name, but hardly in nature. A Turk could spend his or her whole life in Istanbul or Ankara without ever mastering it, indeed without understanding much of it. It took schooling to do so. However, in the first half of the twentieth century, Ottoman Turkish became to all intents and purposes a dead language, replaced by – by what? The vernacular? Far from it. The Turkish Republic developed a new standard that was very different from both Ottoman and traditional spoken Turkish. Before we examine this strange beast's nature, let's look at the history of the imperial hybrid it replaced.

I: From Old Turkish to Ottoman

With a vocabulary mostly borrowed from, and a grammar clearly influenced by, Persian and Arabic, Ottoman Turkish reflected over a thousand years of Middle Eastern history. We're about to cover that whole period in a handful of pages – so buckle up.

Until the early seventh century, Turks, Persians and Arabs had not entered into significant contact with each other. Then, in 632, the year after Muhammad's death, the Arabs go to war against the Persian Empire. To contemporary observers it must be an utterly baffling turn of events: some desert tribes of dubious manners, spurred by a new religion, taking the field against a powerful and in many respects more sophisticated empire – and winning one battle after another. In 643 the job is done: Persia has fallen (and so has Egypt).

But subjugating a sophisticated enemy is not without its risks. Before you know it, you become like them – ask the Germanic rowdies who captured Italy, France, Spain, North Africa and Italy once again in the centuries just before the Arabs start their conquering spree. Granted, the latter are a few cuts above the illiterate Germanic hordes in terms of refinement but even so, while they manage to defeat the Persians and convert them to Islam, trying to Arabise them proves a hopeless task. And though the Persians borrow some Arabic words, that is as far as it goes. Their language and culture remain resolutely Persian.

In 750, a new dynasty of Arab caliphs comes to power in the Islamic world – with Persian support. From then on, Persian cultural influence begins to grow, with Persians in many key positions and an increasing appreciation for their language and their writers. Arabic-speaking Damascus loses its status as the imperial capital, which instead passes to a new city on the Tigris river, purpose-built on the site of a Persian village. It is given an Arabic name (MADĪNAT AS-SALĀM or City of Peace), but this never catches on. Even today the world knows it under the Persian name of the old village: BAGHDAD or 'God-given'.

Arabic, the language of the Koran, continues to play first fiddle, but Persian will for a long time play an important role in the Islamic world, especially in the Middle East and South Asia. As a result, it is no longer just a case of Persian borrowing words from Arabic – it's also the other way around, albeit to a lesser extent. Many of these loans have remained in use up to the present day. The Arabic words for 'crown' and 'cup' (TĀJ, FINJĀN) are of Persian origin, while the Persian words for 'theology' and 'trade' (ELÂHIÂT, TEJÂRAT) derive from Arabic.

The Turks do not yet live in the Middle East, but are further north, on the Asian steppe. In the eighth century, one Turkish tribe, the Oghuz, settles to the east of the Caspian Sea, in an area now known as Turkmenistan, bringing them into neighbourly contact with the Persians. If, in an earlier period, the Arab desert tribes were no match for the Persians in terms of cultural refinement, this is even truer now for the Turkish steppe dwellers, and they are keenly aware of it. They copy and adopt all the elements of Persian civilisation that they can find a use for: first new foods and urban conveniences, later the Islamic faith. Since their language evidently does not have names yet for all these novelties, they introduce the Persian words along with the concepts. Some of these loanwords are of Arab origin, so that through Persian a few Arabic words enter the Turkish language quite early on. This is also the time when the Turks replace their Runic-looking Old Turkic form of writing with the Perso-Arabic script. In summary, between the ninth and the eleventh century, a mixed Turko-Persian culture begins to arise.

In the eleventh century, some Turks work their way up to positions of power in Persia, effectively taking over the empire. Yet they do not declare Turkish the new language of administration – they can hardly expect all those poor Persian officials to learn a new and very different language. Persian does adopt a fair number of Turkish words though, mostly related to government and warfare. In cultural terms the Turkish and Persian traditions blend even more than before, with Arabic elements mixed in to boot. But we are still a long way off from the Ottoman Turkish language that started this chapter.

The eleventh century also sees the beginning of the slow Turkification of Anatolia (which roughly equals most of modern Turkey). It's important to realise, though, that for many centuries Anatolia will remain an ethnic and linguistic mix, with Turks, Greeks, Armenians, Jews, Kurds, Roma, Assyrians and others living alongside each other.

We'll skip a nasty period now – the one where Genghis Khan and other Mongols spread death and destruction throughout the Middle East and beyond, creating the largest contiguous empire in history. Let's pick up the thread in 1359, when a series of leaders descending from Osman I, a local prince in northwest Turkey, expands their territory in all directions at a breathtaking pace. Three hundred years later, their Ottoman Empire controls not only all of Anatolia and the Balkans, but also practically the entire Arab world. The Ottoman sultans are soon considered the new caliphs, and in 1517 they are officially recognised as such. The word *caliph* literally means 'successor' and is usually interpreted as 'successor of Muhammad'. From an Islamic perspective, the Turks have now captured the big prize. But once again, they do not impose their language and culture upon the empire's other peoples. On the contrary: this is when Ottoman Turkish, the empire's elite and literary language, reaches its fullest hybrid magnificence, thanks to strong Arabic influence. The ten-century process is complete.

So far I've made it sound as if Ottoman Turkish has only borrowed Persian and Arabic words, but this is far from the case. Greek, Latin, Italian, Armenian and other words have also trickled in. And in the nineteenth century, when the empire, by now crumbling and weakened, attempts to modernise itself, the language is flooded with vocabulary from Europe's leading language of the day, French.

The Ottoman language was artificial and its calligraphy highly artful, as in this manuscript depicting historian Talikizâde Mehmed (on the left) dictating.

Ottoman Turkish was very much an elite language, spoken and written by the cultural and political upper crust of the multi-ethnic empire. Even the elites grew up speaking some other tongue: Arabic or perhaps Persian (though Persia itself had broken away centuries ago), Greek, Bulgarian, Kurdish, Aramaic, Armenian, Albanian – or Turkish. Yes, Turkish as well, because besides the Ottoman variety, there was still the vernacular, referred to as 'raw Turkish'. This too had borrowed liberally from other languages, but not to the same extreme degree as Ottoman, and grammatically it had been much truer to itself.

What is remarkable about this long process is that for so many centuries, the Turks were quite modest about their language and culture. They seem to have looked up to the Persians and Arabs, much as the Romans of antiquity looked up to the Greeks. It wasn't until the establishment of the Turkish Republic in 1923 that the Turks shook off their inferiority complex and became proud of all things authentically Turkish. And when they did, they did it with a vengeance.

II: From Ottoman to modern Turkish

In 1927, President Mustafa Kemal, today better known as Atatürk, addressed a political congress on six consecutive days, speaking for thirty-six hours in all. This was so monumental a speech that even today it is simply referred to as NUTUK – '(the) speech'. But if a twenty-first-century Turkish politician gives a speech, people will no longer call it a NUTUK; they'll use the word SÖYLEV instead. That isn't because they've decided to reserve the other word for Atatürk's mammoth monologue. It's just that SÖYLEV has become the normal everyday word for 'speech'.

Why is that? It would be natural to think that this must be one of those chance changes that continuously occur in every language. But that's not what happened in this case. The shift from NUTUK, which was an Arabic loanword, to SÖYLEV, which is based on Turkic roots but didn't exist as such back in 1927, reflects something else entirely, namely a radical transformation of the Turkish language during roughly the middle fifty years of the twentieth century.

By 1963, the text in Ottoman Turkish as spoken by Atatürk was full of terms that the new generation could no longer understand and had to be translated into modern Turkish. But the translation itself contained neologisms that never caught on, so a new translation had to be published in 1986. To young people in Turkey today, the 1927 version sounds about as alien as a scholarly seventeenth-century tract sounds to a young English-speaker. In a mere two generations, Turkish underwent the sort of evolution that took four centuries for English.

Evolution? Revolution, more like it. And that is indeed a better translation of what the Turks themselves call it: DİL DEVRİMİ, literally a 'language overthrow'. According to the dictionary, DEVRİM is a 'quick, radical and qualitative change'. Sounds like revolution to me. But for some reason, in English, the process has acquired the rather more bloodless name of 'language reform'.

Written Turkish was in desperate need of a change. In the mid-nineteenth century, all books and newspapers were still in Ottoman Turkish, the mixture of Arabic, Persian and 'real' Turkish that had come about in centuries of close cultural contact. The average Turk trying to read a newspaper – assuming they were literate, which was unlikely – would find it as opaque as legal documents are to most of us. In the late nineteenth century and in the years before the First World War, this began to change somewhat. Authors and journalists gradually incorporated more common Turkish words into their writing. Also, they began to use fewer grammatical constructions of Arabic and Persian origin.

To give an example of the latter, an Ottoman writer would use for 'natural sciences' the words ULÛM-i TABİİYE.* ULÛM ('sciences') is an Arabic plural; the singular would be iLiM. TABİİYE is an equally Arabic feminine adjective, even though Turkish as such has no gender. The -i after ULÛM is a so-called *izafet*, a grammatical device of Persian origin that serves to connect the adjective to the noun before it. However, in authentic Turkish, nouns come *after* adjectives and no izafet is required. Claiming that ULÛM-i TABİİYE is Turkish makes as much sense as pretending that SCIENCES NATURELLES is not only

* This is a transcription into Modern Turkish; hence the dots on the capital i's.

French but also English, even though English rarely places adjectives behind nouns and never declines them for gender or number.

In the early 1900s, many writers would no longer use ULÛM-i TABiiYE, preferring TABîî İLiMLER instead. Grammatically speaking, this is perfectly Turkish: adjective first, plural in -LER, no Arabic gender or Persian izafet nonsense. Should an Istanbul street vendor have had occasion to speak about 'natural sciences', these were undoubtedly the words he would have chosen. The words themselves are still Arabic loans, it's true, but what of it? After all, the English words *natural* and *sciences* are also loans, from French and ultimately Latin. Does anyone object?

During the war years 1914–23, with Turkey's political survival at stake, the language issue faded into the background, only to gain centrestage surprisingly soon after the establishment of the republic. The first radical step was the 1928 HARF DEVRiMi or 'letter revolution'. Practically overnight, Atatürk replaced the Perso-Arabic script with a tailor-made variety of the Latin alphabet, henceforth obligatory in all public and official writing. This constituted a symbolic U-turn in the country's cultural allegiance, away from the Middle East, towards the West. The following year, Arabic and Persian were removed from the school curriculum and replaced by European languages. This loosened the cultural ties between Turkey and the rest of the Middle East still further. While Turkish conservatives have lamented this effect to this day, they don't deny that the change of alphabet has made writing and reading Turkish a great deal easier.

With the script fixed and the written language slowly moving in the direction of normal Istanbul speech, Atatürk could have left it at that. But he was not a man to leave things alone – and certainly not the language, which was something of a hobby of his. Atatürk deeply resented the fact that Turkish, even as spoken by humble peasants, factory workers and shopkeepers, was packed with Persian and Arabic loanwords. 'The Turkish nation must liberate its language from the yoke of foreign languages,' he wrote in 1930. In July 1932, the Turkish Language Society (TDK: Türk Dil Kurumu) was established, and later that year, it launched its 'word-collection mobilisation'. The TDK's central committee distributed

Kemal Atatürk teaching the Roman alphabet in Constantinople (Istanbul), c.1928.

to army officers, government officials, schoolteachers and doctors throughout the country a booklet explaining how to go about collecting typical regional words, along with slips of paper to write them down on. Within a year, more than 35,000 different items were collected. Moreover, nearly 90,000 other words were found in old texts and dictionaries of closely related languages such as Azeri and

Turkmen. After a rather cursory inspection, these two collections were merged, along with some minor sources, into a work known as *Tarama Dergisi*. This was intended as a source for experts to draw on when proposing new vocabulary. But enthusiastic purists took it as a reference work and ran with it. In doing so, they plunged Turkey into linguistic chaos. 'For a while, Babel set in,' as Geoffrey Lewis, a prominent authority on Turkish language policy, puts it.

This was not without its farcical elements, such as the new employment opportunities for 'substitutors': specialised copy editors, whose only job it was to replace every word of foreign origin with one of the native alternatives listed in the *Tarama Dergisi*. But since this book often suggested several alternatives, sometimes dozens of them, and every substitutor could freely take his pick, the poor readers' best hope was that he'd choose something they were able to understand – where 'understand' often amounted to translating the neologism back to the Arabic, Persian or French word that had been supplanted in the first place. It was during this turbulent period that, according to an oft-repeated anecdote which may or may not be apocryphal, a Turkish writer was asked how many languages he spoke. 'It's all I can do to keep up with Turkish,' he's said to have replied.

This anarchy was not the sort of freedom Atatürk had had in mind when he declared that the language should be 'free and as independent as the Turkish nation'. Moreover, he didn't care much for the resulting language, known as *Öztürkçe*. When, at a banquet in late 1934, he gave a speech that a particularly zealous substitutor had cleansed of all but five loanwords, the result sounded almost foreign. According to witnesses, Atatürk's delivery was awkward. (And let's spare a thought for the poor interpreter who had to translate the president's words for the benefit of the Swedish royal guests at the banquet.) Clearly, this language thing had got out of hand. But how to backtrack without losing face?

It undoubtedly came as a godsend when in 1935 Atatürk received an unpublished forty-one-page article from Vienna, written in poor French by the Orientalist Hermann Feodor Kvergić. A Bratislava-born Serb, Kvergić argued that Turkish was the mother of all human languages. Never mind what he based his claim on, for it is too preposterous to dwell on – something to do with prehistoric man seeing the sun and uttering a cry of admiration, which became humankind's first syllable, hence the name given to Kvergić's proposition: Sun-Language Theory. The salient point here is that if all words of all tongues were of Turkish origin, there was no longer a need to purge the Turkish language of imported elements. Atatürk immediately saw this potential, according to a distinguished TDK member: no sooner had he finished reading the document than he said, 'That's it! I've found what I wanted!'

Historians are divided on whether Atatürk truly believed in the theory or merely saw it as an expedient to rein in what had got out of control. We have reliable information that his linguistic aides were encouraged to come up with Turkish etymologies for words that had hitherto been considered Arabic, Persian, French or Greek. The word ELEKTRİK, for instance, was 'proven' to have Turkic roots: the word YALTRIK in one Turkic language, Uyghur, means 'gleam, shining'. If French had the word ÉLECTRIQUE too, it must be because it was borrowed from Turkish! To quote one more example: POLİGON was derived from BOL, meaning 'abundant', and GENİŞ, 'wide', so a polygon is a thing 'of abundant width'. Of course, all this was bogus. There was no earthly reason to doubt the traditional etymologies of ELEKTRİK and POLİGON, as their Greek roots are obvious and can easily be proved. Revising them was fact-free politics *avant la lettre*, and few people outside Turkey took it seriously.

The theory's brief reign did put a temporary stop to the purist enthusiasm, as far as the general language was concerned. In the field of scientific terminology, however, Atatürk continued to support the reform, and with good reason. Whether it was mathematics, medicine, geography or physics, the majority of technical terms were Arabic. Of course, Arabic too was an offspring of Turkish, at least according to the Sun-Language believers, but in practice, that didn't make these terms any easier to learn. Moreover, many were still clearly Ottoman, with Arabic word order and Persian izafet (see the example of ULÛM-i TABİİYE above), to which young people were no longer accustomed.

This had to be changed, Atatürk felt, and he himself led the way by writing a book called *Geometri*, published anonymously in 1937, in which geometrical terms were replaced with purisms or sometimes – as can be gleaned from the title itself – European words. Many of these have caught on. To resume our earlier example: for 'polygon', which used to be called KESİRÜLADLÂ, he chose not POLİGON, which would only substitute a French-Greek loanword for an Arabic one, but ÇOKGEN. This is a compound of ÇOK, meaning 'many', and GEN, meaning ... well, officially GEN was derived from a Turkish word for 'wide', as we saw just now, but it seems likely that the resemblance with GON (as in POLİGON) was no coincidence.

Again, as in 1928, a level-headed approach seemed to be winning the day. Purism was being applied to areas where it was useful, while a *laissez-faire* policy allowed the everyday language to develop gradually and naturally. But the advocates of radical purism were still waiting in the wings to press ahead if the opportunity arose. And when Atatürk died in 1938, they seized the moment. Arguing that they merely intended to continue the great man's work, the purists set out to cleanse the language as it had never been cleansed before. The pace at which they introduced new words may have been somewhat slower than in the chaotic mid-thirties, but this was more than compensated for by the length of the period they were allowed to continue doing so: the best part of the 1940s and then again in the 1960s. A statistical analysis of vocabulary in newspapers proves that the purist movement had a huge impact: the proportion of authentically Turkish words grew from 35 per cent in 1931 to 61 per cent in 1965. The proportion of Arabic, Persian and 'Ottoman' words put together sank from 59 per cent to 31 per cent. Words of 'other' sources, mostly French, Greek and more recently English, fluctuated between 4 per cent and 8 per cent, rising towards the end. What these figures obscure is the fact that many Turkish words changed their meaning, sometimes temporarily or more than once.

This transformation of the language left many Turks disgruntled. Some of them were conservatives who felt that the golden days of the Ottoman Empire had been besmirched. Many more simply had their linguistic sensitivities wounded, and it's easy to sympathise. The purists undeniably overshot their original aim of minimising the differences between the written and spoken languages, and by a wide margin. Even that might have been halfway acceptable if they had done so expertly and gracefully, but they did not. And who could expect grace and expertise from people who applied themselves to cooking up bogus etymologies a few years earlier – or as Lewis put it, 'who unblushingly delivered themselves of such drivel in public'.

Not *all* novelties were flawed, to be sure. Many were perfectly clear coinages on the lines of *birdlore* for 'ornithology' or *foreword* for 'preface' – which were indeed nineteenth-century English purisms, the latter successful, the former not. Others were not new creations, but revivals of words long fallen out of use. On a modest scale, this has happened in English as well: the word *sibling* was reintroduced in 1903 (as a handy translation for the German word GESCHWISTER), after centuries of absence from the language; the original meaning was 'relative', 'kinsperson'. Nobody today objects to *foreword* and *sibling*, and no Turkish speaker objects to similar cases in their language.

But a large minority of the new Turkish words were formed carelessly, even arbitrarily. Turkish loves suffixes, so there is no objection to using them in order to create new vocabulary. But it would have been nice, to say the least, if these suffixes had been applied with a degree of consistency. In English, we assume that if *-er* or *-or* is added to a verb, the new word refers to someone or something performing the action expressed by the verb. When earlier in this chapter I used the word *substitutor*, you knew that this person's activity was to substitute some thing for some other thing. You would be baffled if this person were to be called a *substitute*, a *substitution* or a *substituting*. Or to give another example, you understand immediately that something *rehydratable* can be rehydrated, and you could rightly accuse me of playing fast and loose with your beloved language if I were to impose something like *rehydratesome*, *rehydratory* or *rehydratesque* in its stead, not to mention *rehydratal*.

Yet this is exactly what happened in Turkish. To give one example: since the root YAZ means 'write', it is clear to anyone that YAZIM, YAZIN and YAZIT must be semantically related. But there is just no way of telling that they mean 'spelling', 'literature' and 'inscription' respectively. The suffixes are arbitrary. These and many more examples are among the main reasons why Lewis's book about the language reform has the subtitle *A Catastrophic Success*: the reform substantially harmed the language. Of course, new generations growing up with it will take the new words for granted without realising they are new until they turn to older literature. But anybody who learnt and loved Turkish while the reform was in full swing would have gone through a long period of confusion and anguish.

Linguistic resistance

The first half of this chapter, about Ottoman Turkish becoming a beautiful mongrel, describes a process that many languages have gone through, one of them being English. But the second half is more exceptional: it is rare for purists to be as successful as they have been in twentieth-century Turkey (and even rarer to make such a sloppy job of it). It's a remarkable story, and it raises an interesting issue about the feasibility of linguistic intervention.

When grammar pedants, semantic nit-pickers, pronunciation correctors and other idealistic language lovers protest that linguists don't try hard enough to stop the 'degeneration' of English, German, French or any other language, linguists' knee-jerk response is they cannot purposefully steer language in any direction. Academics generally believe that 'science is about how things *are*, not how they *ought* to be' but linguists go one better and claim that trying to interfere is utterly pointless. The community of speakers is autonomous, they argue, and will not follow.

The Turkish experience seems to contradict the idea that linguistic resistance is futile. Today's Turks may not speak exactly the way the TDK wanted them to, but there's no gainsaying that this official busybody has had a huge impact. Especially in the field of vocabulary, the TDK's effect on the language, whether one likes it or not, has been enormous and enduring.

I can offer two explanations for this contradiction.

When the new republic was founded on the ruins of the multi-ethnic, multilingual Ottoman Empire, a new Turkish nationalism had to be designed. A more 'purely Turkish' language, with fewer borrowed words, became one of the crucial elements of this nation-building project. In other words, there was considerable enthusiasm for the language reform right from the start. This may have seemed strange to twentieth-century speakers of English, French, German et cetera, but the fact is that their languages went through a similar stage several centuries ago. These were not always purist in nature, but certainly as prescriptive. People in Eastern Europe, where many languages didn't go through this stage until the nineteenth century, might understand more readily.

Another partial explanation may be that the Turkish republic has from the start been rather authoritarian. It went without multi-party elections for the first quarter century of its existence and has seen several military coups. For many years, the government controlled radio and later TV; all textbooks were subject to official approval. In recent years, the democratically elected president has developed an increasingly totalitarian style. In such an environment, exercising authority over the language may well be more feasible than in a society where market forces are paramount and few politicians dare go against their constituents' preferences. Indeed, President Erdoğan in May 2017 made the first official attempt in a long time at purging the Turkish language: he ordered his minister of sport to replace the Latin word *arena* with *stadyon* – of French origin, but apparently perceived as somehow more Turkish – in the names of all football stadiums.

So Western linguists are probably right: they have no means of steering the course of language. But this is correct in a certain place and time; it's not a universal truth.

16

Javanese

BASA JAWA

95 million speakers

Javanese is spoken in Central and Eastern Java, almost exclusively as a first language. Millions of Javanese now live in other Indonesian islands, while smaller groups have migrated to Malaysia, Suriname, the Netherlands and Saudi Arabia.

Javanese

SELF-DESIGNATION BASA JAWA, colloquially CARA JAWA ('the Javanese way').

FAMILY Austronesian, literally 'of the southern islands'. Nearly all family members, including Javanese, belong to the Malayo-Polynesian branch. The languages are mostly spoken in Indonesia (except New Guinea), the Philippines, Malaysia and throughout the Pacific, with Madagascar as an outlier.

SCRIPT The Latin alphabet has largely replaced the Javanese and Arabic scripts. The former was developed in Java around the ninth century, inspired by the Indian scripts of Hindu and Buddhist religious literature (see chapter 6). The Arabic was introduced by Muslims from the thirteenth century on.

GRAMMAR Nouns and verbs are not inflected for case, number, gender or tense. However, prefixes, infixes and suffixes are used for several other grammatical purposes, such as forming the passive tense. Reduplication (that is, full or partial repetition of a word) fulfils several roles, including the formation of plurals and derivation of nouns from adjectives. Contrary to the more common pattern, Javanese has *lost* its definite article.

SOUNDS Six vowel phonemes. Since four of these can be realised in two different ways, depending on their position in the word, ten distinct vowel sounds can be heard. There are twenty-one different consonants, some of which are so unusual for an Austronesian language that many linguists believe them to be the result of Sanskrit influence.

LOANWORDS Principally Sanskrit. Also Arabic, Dutch and Malay. Examples are BASA (language), KAUM (group of people), AMTENAR (civil servant) and BERITA (news).

EXPORTS Few, and mostly for local cultural phenomena such as *gamelan*, *kris* and *wayang*.

HOME BASE Of the twenty Babel languages, Javanese has the smallest home base in geographical terms: at less than 100,000 km^2, it's roughly the size of Hungary or Wyoming. Java is very fertile and densely populated, with well over 1,000 people per km^2.

16: **Javanese**

Talking up, talking down

WHEN A SCHOLAR WRITES an article for a scholarly journal, we don't expect him to use harsh language. Yet that is exactly what the Dutch philologist Jan Brandes did in 1889. In his discussion of Javanese, he referred to 'a pathological phenomenon', 'an excrescence', that to his mind was 'highly affected' and 'contrived through pedant schoolmastery'. Strong stuff, then as now. But what drew Brandes's ire wasn't Javanese in its entirety. It was a particular style, or, as it's also called, one 'register' of the language – the formal one, known as *krama*. A formal register can be a thing of beauty if speakers are free to employ it as they see fit. But unlike English and most other languages, Javanese isn't so liberal. Numerous social settings positively require the use of krama. Brandes was keenly aware of that, and it infuriated him.

One might be inclined to be wary of a European who writes in scathing terms about the culture of a country that has been subjugated and exploited by his compatriots. Brandes, however, seems to have been on to something. For one thing, he was generally appreciative of the basic, informal register of the Javanese language. And his contempt for krama has been echoed by non-colonial observers. In 1980, the historian, political scientist and Indonesia expert Benedict Anderson called it 'an extreme linguistic development', adding that 'we would not be wrong ... to adopt in large measure the view of Brandes'. Many people in Indonesia itself are ill-disposed towards Javanese, and krama is one of the things that make them so. A Javanese movement seeking nothing less than the abolition of krama emerged as early as the mid-1910s. It was short-lived and unsuccessful, but its aversion to the formal register would leave its mark on Indonesia's language policy.

Nuances of formality

So what's the matter with krama? Why has it annoyed so many people so intensely for so long?

There is nothing special of course about Javanese *enabling* its speakers to choose between levels of formality and politeness. All languages do so. In English, there's a well understood distinction between, for example, *I beg your pardon?* and *What?* or *Huh?* You might address the same man as *Mr Jones*, *Trevor* or *mate*, and informally reduce the words *is not* to *isn't* or even *ain't*. In most European languages, the word for 'you' (especially in the singular) has at least two varieties, one more formal, polite or reserved, the other less so.

These things have been taken a lot further in most of Southeast and East Asia. Here, the many shades and tones between the rude and the courteous have been set in linguistic codes much more strictly than Westerners are used to. In Japanese, for instance, a slew of suffixes and verbal conjugations can express respect or humility, politeness or formality. Korean too is as layered as puff pastry: the verbs code for seven levels of formality, five of which are in everyday use, with the remaining two still common in literature and drama. And as we saw in chapter 1, Vietnamese personal pronouns have status-related meanings such as 'older sister', 'younger sibling', 'friend' and 'grandfather'. Whether it's Thai, Khmer, Burmese or pre-revolutionary Chinese, all of these languages display nuances of formality that put the French *tu* versus *vous* to shame – and English doesn't even have that. 'None of them, however, has developed a system as extensive as that of Javanese,' according to the expert and native speaker Soepomo Poedjosoedarmo.

So there's an exceptionally extensive formality system – what of it? Many languages have hugely complex systems of some sort. Tsez, spoken in a remote corner of South Russia, is said to have a system of sixty-four cases, and nobody seems to mind, even though it's at least as compulsory as krama. Why the commotion in Indonesia?

Let's take a closer look at the Javanese system. At the heart of it is this: every single word in the lexicon belongs to one of five groups. Four of these five convey various levels of formality or politeness, the only exception being *ngoko* (pronounced with an /ng/ sound as in *singer*). Ngoko is the core of the Javanese language. It's what every child learns, it's what every speaker knows, and it's capable, in principle, of expressing any thought. The anti-krama activists of a century ago only ever spoke ngoko, and they were perfectly intelligible and articulate – not to mention shockingly irreverent to the ears of their fellow Javanese.

That isn't to say that ngoko words are informal in the way *bloke* is informal for 'man' or *boob* for 'breast'. The overwhelming majority are impeccably neutral and can be used freely in any conversation.

Formality rules: this nineteenth-century Javanese lady would address her servant with one vocabulary, and be answered with another– and note the body language too.

In this respect, ngoko is like everyday English: we say *cat*, *read* or *near* and no one bats an eyelid. In Javanese, however, around one thousand of these ordinary words have a formal synonym, and it's these that are collectively called krama. To be formal, you *must* use them. In English we may replace *cat*, *read* and *near* with *feline*, *peruse* and *in the proximity of*, but even insufferable snobs do not take exception to the more common terms, because these words in themselves do not make a text informal. Therein lies the difference with Javanese. In a formal situation, such as in a law court, you are simply not allowed to use any ngoko words that have krama synonyms. And it's not just in special settings such as a courtroom that ngoko words are taboo. Krama is the style of choice in any conversation between strangers.

In Javanese dictionaries, all words that are not strictly neutral are labelled according to their style. On the first few pages, for instance, we find ABANG, ADOH, ADOL and AGAMA ('red', 'far', 'sell' and 'religion', respectively) tagged as *ng*, for ngoko. Their krama counterparts are indicated in parentheses: ABRIT, TEBIH, SADÉ and AGAMI. When we turn to the entry ABRIT, we find 'red; *kr* for abang'. Note, by the way, that some ngoko-krama couples are quite similar (AGAMA – AGAMI), while others are completely different (ADOH – TEBIH).

In between ngoko and krama, there is a third, intermediate level called *madya*, literally 'middle'. (The three styles are often referred to as High, Middle and Low Javanese.) While this is for the most part a mixture of krama words and ngoko endings, it also has thirty-five unique words. Dictionaries mark these as *md*. Under AMPUN, for instance, we find not only its meaning, which is 'don't', but also '*md* for AJA'. The entry for AJA in turn tells us that the krama version is SAMPUN. So there are no fewer than three words that mean 'don't', one for each style. From low to high, these are: AJA – AMPUN – SAMPUN.

The other two stylistic categories are 'high krama' (*krama inggil*), which includes nearly 300 words, and 'humble krama' (*krama andhap*), which has only about twenty. In spite of their names, these two categories of vocabulary can be used not only in krama, but at any of the three levels of formality (ngoko, madya, krama). Using high

The traditional Javanese script known as Aksara Jawa is still kept alive in Indonesia. Here a child in Yogyakarta is being taught the letters on a pad handed out on the streets.

krama words implies respect for a person mentioned, no matter whether he or she is the addressee or some third party, present or absent. It's not only the respectable person who must be referred to with a high krama word; equivalent honour is lavished upon their deeds, aides and goods. Thus, if we talk (in Javanese) about their 'bathing', we shall not use the ordinary verb ADUS; the high krama verb SIRAM is called for instead. Likewise, the 'servant' hurrying in to dry, powder and dress the august bather is not a mere BATUR (the ngoko word) and not even a RÉNCANG (which would be krama), but an ABDI, for that is the only correct high krama term. Linguists refer to this category as 'honorifics' – words bestowing honour.

Humble krama, finally, could be described as the functional mirror image of high krama. The job of these so-called 'humilific' words is not to show respect for His or Her Grace, but to emphasise the insignificance of the speaker and other underlings. Think of it as a way of saying, as Catholics do before communion, 'Lord, I am not worthy to receive You' – continuously.

An intimidating language

Whenever you speak Javanese to somebody you're not familiar with, you have to use formal words: krama, or sometimes madya. Whenever you speak to *or about* someone in a superior social position (older, for instance), protocol requires that you use respectful words (high krama) in relation to them and, for contrast, submissive words (humble krama) in relation to yourself and others of inferior rank. And there is more to formality and respect than just the careful choice of words: many aspects of non-language behaviour too are more strictly regulated than Westerners are accustomed to. Krama is associated with a complicated etiquette that dictates how to sit, stand, walk, point, hold your hands, direct your eyes, greet people, laugh and dress – an example of this being the photo on page 87.

Even for the Javanese, the observance of these various codes is not an easy thing. The cultural fundamentals may be ingrained, but using all the correct synonyms while maintaining an easy flow of speech is an art not mastered by many. It requires a great deal of training and is a strong indication of a person's social class. Fluency in krama traditionally was, and in some places still is, a cultural asset which accords the speaker considerable prestige – somewhat like consistently observing the *who / whom* distinction in English, but a hundred times more so. Lacking good krama skills, many less-educated Javanese barely dare speak in the presence of their social superiors. Even in Indonesia, not exactly a nation of impetuous loudmouths, the Javanese are considered shy and timid. (The neighbouring ethnic groups who speak Sundanese, Balinese and Madurese share the same reputation, and their linguistic systems of formality are nearly as elaborate.)

Krama, then, not only reflects the hierarchical nature of Javanese society, it also reinforces it. And that's exactly why Indonesian intellectuals resented it a century ago. Here's a characteristic quote from 1918: 'Now that the Creator has brought light to the slumbering Orient, it is no longer appropriate to continue living under intolerable conditions of irrelevant inequality ... it is not only desirable but even necessary to jettison krama.' Two years earlier, a prominent independence activist stated that, in order to change 'the psyche of the Javanese people', their language had to be changed. Perhaps it even had to be killed, he added as an afterthought.

Fabricated ersatz

Many bewildering linguistic phenomena emerge spontaneously in the course of a language's development. This is not the case with krama. If this formal register and its compulsory usage reflect and reinforce Java's social hierarchy, that's because it was designed for such purpose by those who had a vested interest in the hierarchy and who were aided and abetted by an external force keen to maintain the status quo.

In the fourteenth and fifteenth centuries, the island was home to a powerful and culturally refined empire, named Majapahit, whose sphere of influence included most of the Indonesian archipelago as well as the Malaysian peninsula. After 1500, a steep decline set in. Endless wars and massacres led to famines and migration. The Dutch East India Company did its bit to exacerbate the chaos and profited handsomely from it but, in fairness, they were neither the first movers nor the only ones to commit atrocities. Java was ravaged so thoroughly in this Dark Age that today we depend on documents found mostly in neighbouring islands for information about the previous Golden Age. Locally, very little survived.

In the mid-eighteenth century, the island was in a sorry state: politically subjugated, economically destitute and culturally impoverished. The great empire of yore was forgotten, as was its literature, written in a language that we now call Old Javanese. The court elite had been stripped of their power by the Dutch colonisers, but in spite of their impotence, or more likely because of it, the courtiers and other aristocrats attached great importance to being treated deferentially by the plebs. It was this need for respect, decorum and protocol that resulted, not in a revival of the classical language, which was no longer available, but in the creation

Traditional Javanese script is also used by mermaids and winged horses – or at least in popular art, such as this painting by O'ong Maryono.

of krama and the other registers. This was an ersatz revival of an erased tradition; not genuinely archaic, but merely archaising, like the faux Middle English of *Ye Olde Tea Shoppe*. The Javanese elites pulled off the trick splendidly: krama caught on and became 'the new old', so to speak.

How could that happen? Why did the Javanese commoners go along with this charade when their indigenous elites had become mere colonial puppets? Part of the answer is that a special style to express formality and respect is expected rather than exceptional in the culture of Java and Southeast Asia generally. However, as we saw before, krama is extreme even by regional standards. It's doubtful that it could have reached these heights (or depths) if there hadn't been a colonial administration. As long as the Dutch were well pleased with their local stooges, the latter had nothing to fear and could make the most outlandish demands on their subjects – including the use of krama. The colonial rulers, eager to keep their useful allies happy, actually seem to have encouraged them to do so.

Brandes's claims that krama was 'pathological', 'deformed' and 'affected' seems to be fair enough. But if he ever realised that his own countrymen had contributed to its emergence, he doesn't seem to have remarked on it.

Level playing field

It's seventy years since the Dutch left Indonesia. The island of Java dominates the country in many ways: politically, demographically, economically, culturally – but not linguistically. Even though Javanese is easily the country's most widely spoken mother tongue, the independence movement at an early stage chose Malay, restyled as Indonesian (*bahasa Indonesia*), as the national language. The question as to whether that was a wise decision will be taken up in chapter 9, but one of the considerations underlying the preference for Malay is relevant here: it was felt that the complexities of krama made Javanese unsuitable for the job. If it was a hurdle for native speakers, it would be like a high-jump bar for other Indonesians. Malay, which has nothing resembling krama, was thought to guarantee a level playing field

As a result, Javanese today is on the way to being endangered. It may seem preposterous to worry about the future extinction of a language with 80 to 100 million speakers, but long-term survival does not depend on current numbers – it requires routine transfer to the next generation. And that's where Javanese is in trouble. In the early 2000s, only 12 per cent of middle-class mothers spoke Javanese to their children. These children are unlikely to acquire full native competence in the language. When asked why they prefer to speak Indonesian in the family, women reported feeling that it allows for closer relationships. Lacking ngoko, krama and the rest, Indonesian is perceived to be more 'relaxed' and 'participatory'. Small-scale studies and observations suggest that in rural areas a swift shift from Javanese to Indonesian is likewise taking place. Other studies come to a different conclusion. But while the jury is still out on the fate of Javanese, the use of krama is definitely very much on the wane, in cities and villages alike. The elderly and the middle-aged still speak it, but most of those born from the 1980s onwards do not, or only in a watered-down version. If Javanese manages to survive, its distinctive formality levels seem to be doomed. Brandes would be dead chuffed.

15

Persian

فارسى

fārsī

110 million speakers

Most of the 80 million Iranians speak Persian, just over half of them natively, as do about half of Afghanistan's 35 million inhabitants, while most of the 9 million Tajikis speak the Tajik variety of Persian. There are scattered Persian-speaking communities in Oman, the UAE and Persian Gulf, and substantial Tajiki speakers in Uzbekistan (estimates vary from 1.3 to 10 million). There are 2 to 5 million expatriate Iranians abroad, who left mainly after the revolution of 1979, and millions of Persian-speaking Afghan refugees, mainly in Iran and Pakistan. Perhaps a quarter of a million Tajiki speakers live in Russia and other former Soviet republics. Around 40 to 50 million speak Persian as a second language.

Persian

SELF-DESIGNATION Farsi, written as فارسى (fārsī) or Форсӣ (forsī). The variety spoken in Afghanistan is also known as Dari (درى, darī); the one found in Tajikistan as Tajik or Tajiki (тоҷикӣ, тоЈIКӢ).

FAMILY Persian is the largest of the Iranian languages, which form a group within the Indo-European family. As they are linguistically and historically close to the Indo-Aryan languages of South Asia, the two groups are often clustered under the name Indo-Iranian.

SCRIPT In Iran and Afghanistan, the Arabic script is used, with four additional consonant letters. The same was true for Tajikistan up until 1928, when Soviet policy forced the Latin alphabet on Tajik; in 1939, the Cyrillic alphabet was introduced. Depending on their political views, Tajiks prefer to maintain Cyrillic or readopt the Latin or Arabic script.

GRAMMAR See main text.

SOUNDS Six vowel and 23 consonant sounds. Syllables cannot start with more than one consonant; at the end, there may be two.

LOANWORDS Arabic is the most important source by far. In recent centuries, some borrowing from French (DEMOKRÂSI, MUZIK, TEORI, FÂBRIKE for 'factory') and English (KÂMPYUTER, MÂRKETING) has taken place.

EXPORTS Hundreds of English words of Southwest, South and Southeast Asian origin have passed through several languages, often including Persian, before reaching Europe. Actual words of Persian origin include *baksheesh*, *pyjamas*, *tulip* and *caravanserai*. The Tajik variety has adopted not only the Cyrillic script, but also numerous Russian loanwords in the fields of socioeconomics, government and modern technology: PROLETARIAT, DEMOKRATIYA, MOŠIN (car).

JIDI For over 2,500 years, there has been a Jewish minority in the Persian-speaking world. It developed its own dialect, Judeo-Persian or Jidi, written in the Hebrew script. There's a substantial literature in this variety, most of it over 500 years old and religious in nature. Today, Judeo-Persian is still spoken by tens of thousands in Israel and a few thousand in Iran.

15: **Persian**

Empire builders and construction workers

This chapter will sing one language's wondrous adventures that caused it to be learnt by the unlearned, to change beyond recognition, expand against all odds, be conquered and hybridised, then spread even further and rise to political and literary heights, only to fall from grace and be reduced to a shadow of its former self. In short, it will relate the triumphs and travails of Persian. It will do so by making one-thousand-year leaps through history, acquainting us with a handful of the many kings who spoke this language.

Hold on – 'Persian'? Isn't it 'Farsi', or 'Iranian'?

Depends what you're talking about. *Iran* is the name of a country we hear a lot about. Its inhabitants are called *Iranians* or sometimes *Iranis*. That's common knowledge. Less well known is the *Iranian* group of languages, which is sometimes, and perhaps more clearly, called *Iranic*. They are spoken well beyond Iran's borders and those who speak them may be referred to as *Iranian* or *Iranic* peoples. But while *Iran* has always been the endonym of the country, the name used locally, Western languages used to call it *Persia*, which is an exonym, a name that is not used locally. Since 1935, Iran has preferred to be known by its endonym. But when talking pre-1935 history and culture, *Persia* is still the usual term in the Western world, as in *Persian Empire* and *Persian rugs*.

And in direct answer to your question: the language is still called *Persian*. It's true that the Persian word for Persian is FĀRSĪ, but the speakers are fine with us saying *Persian*. And you could argue that it's the same word anyway: they're both derived from *Pars*, an old name for a certain region of Iran. So there's no need to say *Farsi* in English any more than we need to say *Español* instead of Spanish.

Okay, got it. Bring on the first king you promised. The first *Persian* king.

Before I do that, let's take a peek at the distant past. In the centuries around 1500 BCE, the Iranians were nomadic herders living farther north than the modern country of Iran, in the steppe to the east and northeast of the Caspian Sea. After 1100 BCE, the Persians – and some other groups or tribes or nations-to-be if you like – split off from the rest and moved south, gradually settling an area centred on today's Iran but roughly twice as extensive. Some of them had names that are still familiar to us today: not only the Persians themselves, but also the Medes and Parthians, both of biblical fame, and the Bactrians, who kept Bactrian camels – the ones with two humps. While these Iranian people moved south, other Iranian groups, lumped together as Scythians, remained in the steppe, spreading across ever larger parts of it, including today's Ukraine and Kazakhstan. In later centuries, they would be swept away or assimilated by Huns, Turks and Mongols, who spoke other languages, so that was the end of those Iranians, culturally speaking. With one exception: the small Ossetian language, today no longer spoken in the steppe but in the Caucasus, is a remnant of those days. But the Iranian peoples flourished farther South, where they established a whole series of empires, some of them huge.

Roman Empire-sized?

Absolutely, but many centuries earlier. As a result of this empire-building, fascinating things happened to the Iranian languages, and to Persian in particular. Therefore, let me now introduce the first king.

Darius, King of Persia, 522–486 BCE

'Darius' – that rings a bell. Who was he again?

Does it help if I call him Darius the Great? He was the third king of the Persian Empire. Or, as the Persians put it, the third 'king of kings', XŠĀYATHIYA XŠĀYATHIYĀNĀM. That's because he ruled over lesser, regional kings, also known as *satraps*.

Wasn't he the bloke beaten at Marathon?
That's right – the Battle of Marathon, 490 BCE. After the carnage, a Greek messenger famously ran all the way to Athens to report the outcome before dropping down dead, which is what today's marathon is named after. The battle wasn't quite as big a deal as we've been led to believe though, at least not for Darius. He was a highly successful imperialist both before and after this setback.

Did great things, did he?
He's nicknamed 'the Great' for a reason. He enlarged the empire into today's Pakistan, western Egypt, northern Greece and across the Black Sea, as well as quashing a series of domestic revolts. And that's just the half of it – in terms of administration and policies, he was pretty effective too.

And I guess Darius ran his empire in Old Persian?
That's what you would expect, but as it happens, he didn't. Darius and his fellow Persians *spoke* Old Persian all right, which was an Indo-European language with all the usual frills: three genders, a whole series of cases in pronouns and nouns and adjectives, complicated verb endings, odd vowel changes, et cetera. It was rather like Sanskrit, the classical language of India, and not unlike Latin and ancient Greek.

So the Greeks and Persians at Marathon could have hurled insults at each other?
Neat idea, but no, they weren't that similar. The two languages had started to grow apart thousands of years before. In fact, the ancient Greeks had enough trouble understanding the dialects of some fellow Greeks.

But Darius didn't govern in Persian, you said. So what did he use instead?
Aramaic.

Ah, the language Jesus spoke – or rather would speak, centuries later.

Correct. Under Darius's predecessors, the administration had used a language called Elamite; the shift to Aramaic was his own idea. Neither of those was anything like Persian – nor like each other, for that matter.

But why on earth didn't he just go with his own mother tongue?

Elamite was spoken in what's now southwest Iran by a people the Persians had conquered early on, even before establishing a serious empire. Unlike the Persians, they had a tradition of writing down their language, which is why, when the kings needed scribes, they hired Elamites. These scribes were fluently bilingual. They would take dictation in Persian and read the document aloud in Persian, but what they wrote down would be in Elamite. That practice went on for centuries, and the only change Darius made was hiring new scribes to write Aramaic instead of Elamite.

That's weird. And why did Darius shift to Aramaic rather than ... I don't know, what else was there? Hebrew perhaps, or Babylonian, if that's a language?

Babylonian is a language all right: it's a form of Akkadian. But he chose Aramaic because it was understood by lots of people in the empire, in regions that the Persians had conquered a few decades earlier. Those regions were more prosperous and more highly developed than Persia proper at this point in time.

Still, if ever there was a moment to switch to Persian ...

Not quite. Persian speakers were a small minority: one million or so in an empire of some 25 million. And there was still no tradition of writing it.

And nor was there ever going to be, if they didn't just do it.

You have a point. But then, look at medieval Europe. In many places, Latin was used for official purposes, and that was partly because there wasn't much of a *tradition* of writing official stuff in German,

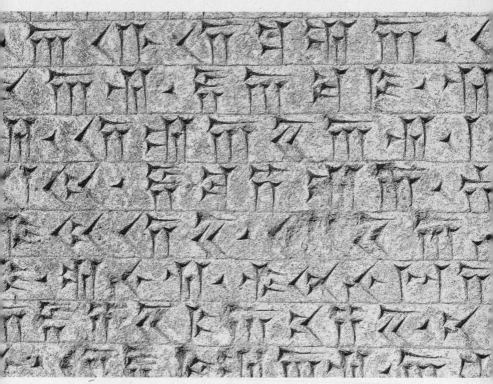

The Behistun Inscription, supposedly authored by Darius himself, describes his ancestry and deeds in grandiloquent style, in Persian, Elamite and Babylonian.

say, or Spanish. In Darius's empire, Persian was written sometimes, but not for the nitty-gritty of administration.

Maybe deep down the king of kings was ashamed of his own language?

Not a bit of it. He *spoke* Persian all the time, and that in itself gave it prestige. And he did have it written on certain grand occasions. The most famous text is the monumental Behistun Inscription, a boastful and rather unreliable account of his ancestry and exploits, chiselled into a highly visible cliff along a well-travelled road. It's still there today. It's trilingual in Persian, Elamite and Babylonian. No Aramaic though. As the language of day-to-day business, that was too mundane, it seems.

Right, enough about Darius. Who's number two?

Just one last thing: he also started an ambitious building programme. We know from written sources that lots of labourers came to Persia proper, from places like Greece, Egypt and India. These people of course spoke all sorts of different languages. As a result, Persia became more of a Babel than Babel itself, which incidentally was also part of the empire – hence the Babylonian text at Behistun.

Do I really want to know about all this building?

You do. You'll see why in a bit. Something to do with our next king, whose name is:

Bahram V, King of Persia, 420–438 CE

Who's that? Never heard of him.

I daresay you haven't, but he's big in Iran. Fondly remembered he is, as well as being the hero of several famous books written centuries after his death. Persian history has had seven King Bahrams, but if many Iranian men are called Bahram to this day, it's because of number V. He cut taxes, which may have earned him much of his good reputation. Also, he reigned at a moment in time when the empire was unusually large. On the other hand, historians hold him responsible for the ensuing decline.

Ensuing decline or not, it seems remarkable that, nearly a thousand years on from Darius, there was still a Persian empire.

Not 'still' so much as 'again'. You seem to be overlooking Alexander the Great, the Macedonian superstar who, a century and a half after Darius, wrought political havoc on half the civilised world, from Egypt and Greece all the way to India. In his seething wake, Persia became part of an empire whose elites were Greek in culture and language. Next in line was an empire led by Parthians, who were Iranian like the Persians but with a distinct language. It wasn't until five centuries after the fall of the First Persian Empire, in 224 CE, that a new one arose, aptly called the Neo-Persian Empire – or Sasanian, if you prefer. That's where we meet King Bahram.

Much of that is news to me. All except Alexander.

It all happened a long way back and a long way off. And since the Persian empires competed first with the Greeks and later with the Romans, Westerners have mostly heard the versions of history told by these rivals. As a result, we tend to think of Persians as the enemy, part of the Orient, that mysterious region where fanaticism and despotism are rife. That's highly unfair, but it's sort of engrained in our thinking. And it's particularly hard to rethink nowadays, now that the West and Iran are none too matey.

If this Bahram of yours headed the Neo-Persian Empire, may I deduce that he spoke Neo-Persian? Or New Persian perhaps?

The variety he spoke is actually known as Middle Persian. But if you compare it to Old Persian, it does indeed seem brand new, because it had been transmogrified to an incredible extent. In Darius's inscriptions, it was just a run-of-the-mill Indo-European language; in Bahram's documents, it was anything but.

Documents! So, the Persians had finally come around to writing their language, had they?

Correct. The state machinery hummed along in Persian now. As before, Aramaic was more widely spoken, but Persian had spread a good deal too – spread and changed. To give you an idea of how different it was from the old version, take this term 'king of kings'. It used to be XŠĀYATHIYA XŠĀYATHIYĀNĀM, but in Middle Persian, it had been reduced to ŠĀHĀN ŠĀH – a mere three syllables instead of nine. This isn't really a fair comparison, as most words did not shorten so dramatically. But if you know what to pay attention to, the example does show two of the essential changes.

One is that the case system practically disappeared – same as would happen in English a few centuries later. Whenever this happens in a language, it usually starts to make heavier use of prepositions and compulsory word order to do the same job (the job, that is, of specifying the grammatical roles of words in a phrase). Persian, like English, did just that. The -ĀNĀM ending of the old title was a genitive in the plural, the possessive case you might say, and there's no trace of it left in the new title. What we do see is an -ĀN ending, which merely indicates a plural, like the -s ending in English, without any overt case marking. Moreover, it's on the first word, not the second, so apparently the word order has changed too: no longer 'king of kings' but 'kings king'. Word order now does the job the case ending used to do.

So that's one: case system shut-down. What would be the other 'essential change' you mentioned?

Plurals got a lot more *regular*: just as ŠĀHĀN is the plural of ŠĀH, so most other words got this same -ĀN ending. There were several other changes, though we can't see them in these two words ŠĀHĀN ŠĀH. For instance, gender went out of the window: no more feminine tables and masculine chairs. As did dual.

Bahram Gar – Bahram V – depicted hunting on a camel, on a gold plate from the period of the pre-Islamic Sasanian Empire.

As did what?

Dual. That's a special plural form for indicating there are exactly two of something. Also, the verbs got reorganised a good deal, which greatly reduced the number of different forms. And certain Indo-European tricks with vowels disappeared – something English has retained, such as when it turns *come* into *came* rather than *comed*. Long story short, if Old Persian was like Sanskrit or Latin, Middle Persian was rather like English: no cases, no gender, no dual and highly regular plurals. In appearance, Persian is nothing like English, but under the bonnet, the similarities are striking.

How did that happen? Was it a general Iranian thing?

No, the other Iranian languages such as Kurdish and Pashto have maintained their Indo-European ornateness to this day. Persian is an anomaly that requires an explanation. The reason *may* have been internal to the language. It's been argued that the stress on the first syllable was so heavy that the endings became ever less sonorous and clear and therefore increasingly useless. But frankly, I don't buy it: German has that sort of stress and while it's true that German case endings have no sonorous vowels left, only weak uh-sounds, the German case system is in annoyingly good health. I'm much more inclined to believe the alternative, or perhaps additional, explanation, which attributes the changes to non-native speakers. This is where Darius's extensive building programme comes into the picture. Large numbers of stoneworkers and carpenters and carriers were contracted from other parts of the empire, outside Persia proper. They learnt Persian as adults, which is to say poorly. And they were so numerous, indeed a majority of the population for a while, that their broken Old Persian went on to become the standard Middle Persian, in which great literature would be written. So thanks to these foreigners, Persian relieved itself of plenty of dead weight.

But those builders had arrived many centuries earlier. Why did it take until the Neo-Persian Empire for the change to kick in?

Good point. We can safely assume that the process of change, in spoken language, set in as soon as all these migrant workers arrived.

That is, the vernacular began to change, the speech of the streets and the building sites. But you wouldn't expect a king of kings to have his feats publicly praised in some migrant-mangled lingo, would you? Darius insisted on the purest and most old-fashioned style that his writers could manage, and in doing so he set a standard for his successors. Then, after Alexander the Great had killed off the empire, Persian was marginalised for six centuries. By the time the scribes of the Neo-Persian Empire got to work, the old language had been forgotten. They began with a blank slate and had no qualms about writing the way people of their day actually spoke. They'd shed the burden of tradition, and good riddance too.

A clean break, eh? Never heard anything like it.
It's not unheard of, though. Much the same thing happened to English after going through two centuries of hardly being written. In the aftermath of 1066, England's new Norman elite wrote in Norman French. When, in the thirteenth century, writers found their English voice again, they no longer bothered with the intricacies of Old English. Those intricacies had vanished from the spoken language centuries before 1066, thanks to the Vikings, who as adult learners simplified English just as the foreign builders had simplified Persian. However, like Darius's Persian writers, the Anglo-Saxon literati before 1066 had kept those intricacies alive on the page.

Why should they do such a thing? Use this outdated style, I mean?
Writing was a rare and revered skill in those days, bordering on the mystical. People didn't go about jotting down the trivial stuff they said in the trivial way they worded it. If something was worth being committed to vellum, it was worth being worded in a stately manner, using the same words and phrases the ancestors had used – in a literary dialect, you might say, a well-preserved old form of the language reserved for writing. We may not go to such lengths any more, but writing does still bring out a conservative impulse. Even today, we write many a dead letter.

Like the *b* in *debt* you mean?
Well yes, that too. But I was speaking a bit more figuratively. What I mean is: in writing we often retain words and bits of grammar that earlier generations may have used in spontaneous speech, but we certainly don't. Things like *the person whom I saw*.

Ah, I see. So Middle Persian spread far and wide across Bahram's empire.
Yes, but not only that: it was also expanding as a trade language. Persian traders travelled south along the African coast all the way to Zanzibar and east to what are now Sri Lanka, Malaysia and south China. Few records have survived, but experts believe that the buyers and sellers would communicate in some sort of Persian. This went on for a very long time, even after the Persians themselves had stopped being involved in the trade. A telling detail is that some maritime place names are of Persian origin, such as Zanzibar in Tanzania, meaning 'coast of black people', and many cities in South and Southeast Asia, Oman and Somalia are called Bandar-something, in which *bandar* is the Persian word for 'port'. For instance, the capital of Brunei is Bandar Seri Begawan.

Can't say I knew that.
It's a small town, I must admit, but it's still the capital of an independent nation. And it's 6,000 kilometres from Iran. Goes to show how far Persian spread back then.

Impressive. And did it spread even further later on?
Not further in a geographic sense, because as a lingua franca around the Indian Ocean it was eclipsed by others, including Portuguese. But spread it did. Let's move on to the third and last of our three Persian kings, accompanied by two of his contemporaries and neighbours:

Ismail I, King of Persia, 1501–1524
Selim I, Sultan of the Ottoman Empire, 1512–1520
Sikandar Lodi, Sultan of Delhi, 1489–1517

Why three of them?
Because they have some fascinating things in common. The three of
them spoke Persian at court. Indeed, the three of them wrote poetry
in Persian. And yet, none of them were native Persian speakers.

You're kidding.
No, seriously. The Ottoman sultan was, as you would expect, a Turk.
He ruled over an empire that encompassed much of North Africa
and southeastern Europe. Sikandar – Persian for 'Alexander' – was
a speaker of Pashto, a language found in today's Pakistan and
Afghanistan. His Sultanate of Delhi covered much of today's North
India, Nepal and Pakistan. Finally, Ismail, though King of Persia, was
not born into a Persian family: his father was Kurdish, his mother's
parents were Azerbaijani and Greek. The dynasty he founded, the

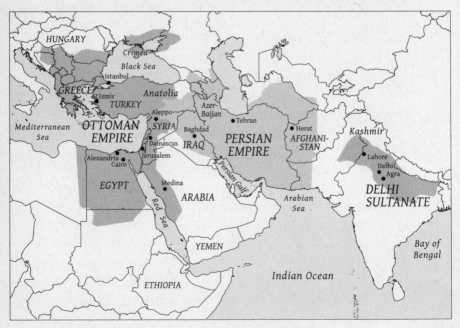

Ottoman Empire, Persian Empire and Delhi Sultanate, c.1520.

Safavids, lasted until the eighteenth century. Together, the three men illustrate how Persian had become a language of culture, and to a lesser degree also of state, and one that had detached itself from its ethnic roots.

So how did *that* come about?
A lot happened between our previous stop and this one. The most momentous event was the rise of Islam, brought to Persia by the Arabs in the seventh century.

But surely the Arabs didn't sponsor the Persian language?
They didn't mean to. But since the Persians had thousands of years of urban life and empire-building under their belt, whereas the Arabs at the time were ...

Desert yokels?
That's definitely overstating it, but in terms of *savoir-vivre*, they were at the time no match for their new subjects. Within a century, the Persians began to put a heavy cultural stamp on Islam. Arabic remained the language of religion, but Persian very much became the language of fine culture throughout the Middle East and South Asia. They influenced each other deeply, and when Turkish later became a regional language of power, it would in turn be altered a great deal by both of them, becoming Ottoman Turkish in the process. As for Persian, it was Arabicised in two main ways. One: it adopted the Arabic alphabet, to which it had to add four consonants that are absent from Arabic but important in Persian. And two: it adopted loads of vocabulary. It is estimated that half the Persian dictionary today consists of Arabic words, and if you take an average Persian text, about one in four or five words is of Arabic stock. Once more, that's reminiscent of English, isn't it? We've adopted comparable numbers of Romance words.

So Persian became a different language once more.
Yes, in terms of script and vocabulary it did; grammatically, it remained comparatively stable. The language of this period is called New or Classical Persian, and modern Iranians are still extremely fond of

their Classical Persian poets, such as Ferdowsi, Hafez and Rumi, in much the same way that English speakers still dote on Shakespeare.

Then after the advent of Islam, the region was sort of quiet?
Anything but. The thirteenth century was the era of the Mongols, with Genghis Khan as their infamous first leader causing bloodshed and devastation on a barely imaginable scale. The Muslim world was particularly hard hit by Mongol imperialism, all the way from

The period of Classical Persian produced poets that are revered even today. These Iranian schoolgirls are paying their respects to the tomb of Ferdowsi (c. 940-1020).

Turkey to Pakistan and Central Asia. But the Persian character of the Middle Eastern elites was so deeply entrenched by now that it survived even the Mongol onslaught – indeed, the Mongol rulers themselves got Persianised soon enough. Their domination was fairly short-lived, and after a period of smaller states, new empires emerged. It took Persia a while to wrestle itself free from foreign domination. Our King Ismail I was actually the first Persian in a long time to rule the country – for he did identify as Persian, in spite of his Azeri-Kurdish-Greek roots.

That's a complex story. What's the take-home message?
It's this: during the late Middle Ages (to use a European term), the Middle East was a bit of a mess, mainly due to the Mongols and their aftermath. Towards 1500, things calmed down. But all the while, Persian remained the elite language throughout the region.

Thanks. And after 1500 we get these three Persian-speaking kings and sultans who were great pals and wrote poems for each other.
Not at all. They were arch-rivals who fought battles and didn't like each other's religions. King Ismail made Shia Islam official in Persia; Sultan Sikandar in India on the other hand was a fanatical Sunnite; while Sultan Selim is considered the first Ottoman caliph, that is to say leader of the Islamic world. The three men never visited each other, unless we count as a visit the battle of Chaldiran in 1514, when Selim beat Ismail. Culturally, however, all three belonged to the so-called Persianate culture, which would continue for another couple of centuries. Its literary heritage has long been considered one of the world's richest, not just by Persian speakers, but also by Westerners including Goethe, Nietzsche, Voltaire and Emerson, and by modern literary scholars.

At the introduction of this whole story, you had those poetic-sounding lines about Persian's adventures. Something about triumphs and travails.
I think I've made good on that. I claimed that the language was learnt by the unlearned and changed beyond recognition: that was when Darius's builders picked it up at work and made it simpler.

I said that it expanded against all odds, and so it did: it had few native speakers, especially compared to Aramaic, but kings spread it across their empires and traders spread it along the coasts of Asia and Africa. It was conquered and hybridised: that's what the Arabs and Arabic did to it. It then expanded even further and rose to political and literary heights: as the cultural language of Islam, it attained high station from Turkey all the way to Bengal.

But I still owe you an explanation of how it fell from grace. The thing is, in modern times, no political elite an afford to be perceived as preferring a foreign language. Therefore, Turkish and South Asian leaders no longer care for Persian. And as for literature, the position of contemporary Persian writing is no loftier than that of, say, Turkish, Korean or Japanese. Yet even as a shadow of its former self, Persian is still sufficiently widely spoken to figure in our Top Twenty Babel Languages, unlike some other former languages of empire, such as Greek, Aramaic, Mongolian and Quechua.

14

Punjabi

ਪੰਜਾਬੀ

125 million speakers

110 million native speakers are concentrated in the Punjab region, straddling the Indo-Pakistani border. Roughly two-thirds live in Pakistan, one third in India. Around 15 million Punjabi speakers live outside South Asia, principally in Britain, the US, Canada and the Arab countries on the Persian Gulf.

Punjabi

SELF-DESIGNATION ਪੰਜਾਬੀ (Pajābī), پنجابی (Panjābī). Whatever the spelling, the first syllable is best pronounced with the 'a' of *palm*, not the 'a' of *man* or the 'u' of *put*.

FAMILY Punjabi belongs to the Indic or Indo-Aryan branch of the Indo-European family, along with Hindi-Urdu, Bengali and many other languages of South Asia.

SCRIPT In Pakistan, Punjabi is mostly written in the Shahmukhi alphabet, a variety of the Arabic. In India, Sikhs prefer the Gurmukhi alphabet, which is related to other Indian scripts. Hindu Punjabis tend to write in Devanagari, India's most widely used script. The names Shahmukhi and Gurmukhi mean 'from the king's mouth' and 'from the guru's mouth' respectively. In this chapter, I will (sparingly) use the Gurmukhi script.

GRAMMAR Punjabi puts the verb at the end of the sentence. It has postpositions rather than prepositions. It has two genders, a fairly limited case system and a complex verbal system. Most other Indo-Aryan languages are similar in these respects.

SOUNDS: Punjabi is sometimes claimed to be 'the only Indo-European tone language'. See the main story for more on this.

LOANWORDS From Sanskrit, Arabic, Persian, English.

EXPORTS *Tandoori* (from Punjabi or Urdu), *bhangra* (musical style).

CORNERSHOP The British band included a Punjabi version of the Beatles song Norwegian Wood on their successful album *When I Was Born for the 7th Time*.

14: **Punjabi**

The tone is the message

Here's a short dialogue in English about a man or a woman with the given name Daljit, which is common among Punjabis:
'Who did it?'
'Daljit.'
'Daljit?!'
'Daljit.'
'Oh no, not Daljit...'

Now, please read it out loud: the first two lines neutrally, the third with dismay, the fourth with sympathy and the last line as a desperate groan. Try to listen to the four instances of the name Daljit the way a musician would. Your four 'Daljits' probably come out something like this:

Daljit   Daljit   Daljit   Daljit

As you can hear and see, the tones of 'Daljit' vary between the four utterances. By altering the pitch, the 'tune' if you like, you do far more than just repeat the person's name.

This phenomenon, intonation, is common to all spoken languages. It differentiates questions and exclamations from neutral statements but it does much more than that: it conveys a surprising amount of other information, including emphasis, irony and emotion – just think of the range of meanings that a simple 'Yeah, right' can have, depending on intonation. This is so central to our speaking that its inevitable absence on the page is something we need to make up for. It's one of the reasons why in writing we need to choose our words so much more carefully and unambiguously, and also why we use punctuation, italics and, these days, emoticons and emojis. (Other reasons why we need all of this in writing include the absence of body language and the impossibility of checking whether the person addressed is understanding us.)

Intonation proves that English speakers pay close attention to what we might call the music of each sentence. Something that doesn't get attention, however, is the musical character of separate words or syllables. Single words in English do not usually carry intonation.

In many other languages, they do. Vietnamese is one: we saw in chapter 1 how a single-syllable word could have as many as six meanings, depending on its 'tune'. That's because Vietnamese is one of the world's many tone (or tonal) languages. The exact number of

As a tonal language, even spoken Punjabi has some melody to it – and all the more so when it's actually sung, as here, by the late, great qawwali singer, Nusrat Fateh Ali Khan.

tones in a language varies: the Vietnamese set of six is impressive, but it's far from a world record. Two dialects of a language called Hmong, spoken in China but unrelated to Mandarin, have twelve tones each, and some languages are rumoured to have fourteen or fifteen. Hmong people with a tin ear must have a serious problem.

Chinese and Punjabi horses

This is the point in stories about tone where *ma* usually gets a look-in. *Ma* is the boilerplate example of tone. *Ma* is a Mandarin word, or rather a group of words, with different sets of meanings depending on tone. Typically, the meanings are given as 'mother', 'hemp', 'horse' and 'scold'; they are written in Latin script as *mā*, *má*, *mǎ* and *mà*, respectively. (If you want to hear the difference, go to bit.ly/ma4tones.) There is nothing extraordinary about *ma* in this respect. The main reason why it has become so popular in books about tone and about Mandarin may well be that one of its meanings, 'mother', is easy to remember – though Mandarin speakers nowadays usually say *māma*.

As this is a chapter about Punjabi, I will now leave Mandarin's mothers and mares behind. Punjabi, unlike the languages of China, is not a poster child for tonality. Tone is a historically recent phenomenon here,[*] and surrounded by some controversy. Linguists disagree as to whether the language has two, three or four tones, while few native speakers are aware that their language is tonal. On the other hand, linguistically minded Punjabis who are aware of the tones have been known to proudly claim that this makes their language unique within the Indo-European family.

Research on Punjabi tone is somewhat scanty but the language has nonetheless acquired its own *ma*, so to speak: *kora*. With a falling tone on the first syllable, usually transcribed in the Latin alphabet as *kòra*, it means 'horse'. With a level tone, without an accent on the *o*, it means 'whip'. And with a rising tone, written as *kóra*, it stands for 'leper'. To hear what these tones sound like,

---

[*] The early ancestor language of Punjabi and the other languages of North India is believed to have been tonal as well. This is Vedic Sanskrit, the Sanskrit of the Hindu Vedas, which predates classical Sanskrit. It was spoken over 3,000 years ago.

check the soundbite links on this book's website (at *languagewriter. com*). Having heard the audio, you may be tempted to ask: how can anyone doubt that Punjabi is a tone language? Isn't it glaringly obvious? Have the doubters *heard* the language at all? Yet in fairness, they have their reasons.

One possible explanation is that they're native speakers. In an online discussion, one speaker of Punjabi confessed, 'As for it being tonal, I have read that as well, but frankly I would like someone to explain the difference' with non-tonal languages. There is nothing ignorant about this. Native speakers always have this huge privilege of doing things right automatically, without knowing what they're doing. This is true for any language, including English. For instance, if you're a native speaker, you automatically enunciate the *k*'s in the words *kin* and *skin* differently. When you say *kin*, you add a puff of air to the k (written as a superscript h: /k^{h}in/ – we encountered this before in the Korean chapter); you can even feel it on your, uh, skin if you place the back of your hand in front of your mouth. In *skin,* you don't do that: you just say /skin/. Native English speakers follow this rule whether they know it or not; hardly anyone does and again, there's nothing ignorant about this. Being a non-native speaker myself, I've had to learn it, and I suspect I often do it wrong even now.

So now let's put ourselves in an ordinary Punjabi's shoes. All our life, ever since we were so high, we've been talking this language of ours, and now suddenly we get told that we do a thing called 'tone' and it's highly unusual for a South Asian language. How do we respond? And remember: Punjabi, unlike Hindi or Urdu, is not a high-prestige language. Saying that something is 'unusual' about it may well be an underhanded sneer. So we might respond with denial.

Forget writing

But there are also other, more substantial reasons for doubting that Punjabi is really a tone language. One is that the meaning of so few words depends on it. It does in the case of *kora*, *kòra* and *kóra* ('whip', 'horse' and 'leper'), and other examples can be found. But the typical Punjabi word has just one meaning, regardless of tone; it's not very common for two meanings to be distinguished by tone

Punjabi's Gurmukhi ('from the guru's mouth') script was created by and named after the second Sikh guru, Angad Dev (1563–1606). It's the Punjabi script mostly used by Sikhs.

only, and three is extremely rare. So even if you can't carry a tune, people will still easily understand you; they'll just think you have an unusual accent. Even if you mix up the three *koras*, confusion is unlikely as long as you're not talking about leprosy patients flogging their horses. Actually, some varieties of Punjabi get along without tone: certain dialects do, and so does the speech of some second-generation migrants in the Punjabi diaspora.

However, none of these facts disqualify Punjabi as a tone language. Indeed, it's quite common for languages to display such variation. The Swedish minority in Finland speak their language without tone, but Swedish as a whole is still considered to be tonal. In both Swedish and Punjabi, tone matters to *most* speakers and differentiates between *some* words. That's enough to make them tonal.

By the way, if Swedish is a tone language, how can Punjabi be unique in the Indo-European family? It can't, and it isn't, unless one loosely interprets the word 'unique' as 'very special'. It may be the only Indo-European tone language spoken in Asia, but certainly not the only one in the whole family. In Europe, there are several: Swedish and Norwegian, Latvian and Lithuanian, Slovene and Serbo-Croatian and finally a group of regional lingos (including my own mother tongue, Limburgish), sometimes collectively called 'West Central German' and spoken in contiguous parts of Germany and the Benelux countries.

Returning to the reasons why Punjabi might not be a tone language after all, we find some linguists claiming that it's better to call it a pitch language. And in a way, they're right, but only if we make that distinction in the first place. Some specialists do: they reserve the word 'tone language' for those that rely very heavily on tone, such as Mandarin, Vietnamese and many African languages. But the distinction is more confusing than helpful, given that the concepts of tone and pitch are nearly identical. A good modern handbook on the subject states that 'a language is a tone language if the pitch of the word can change the meaning of the word'. That makes Punjabi a tone language, full stop.

There's one more reason why some people think Punjabi should be denied access to the tonal club. Tone is *audible*, they'll admit, but since it's consistently triggered by certain letters in certain positions, it's a side effect of something else rather than a 'thing' in its own right. For instance, if a word starts with the letter ਘ, pronounced as /k/, a falling tone is bound to follow. This is not unlike the English habit of puffing a little air after each (word-initial) *k* that is directly followed by a vowel, a phenomenon known as *aspiration*. Aspiration is just a quirk of English pronunciation. It's literally meaningless. If I mispronounce *kin* as /kin/ or skin as /skʰin/, as I sometimes will, the meaning doesn't change one bit. Aspiration is irrelevant to the English sound system. And some people claim that, similarly, tone is irrelevant to the Punjabi sound system.

Except that in fact it isn't, for there's a catch, and it changes everything. Punjabi words that start with a k *sound* can be spelt with either of two Punjabi letters, ਘ or ਕ. The former makes the

भारत विश्व का विशालतम लाकतन्त्र दश
आपका हार्दिक स्वागत करता है।

INDIA THE LARGEST DEMOCRACY IN
THE WORLD WELCOMES YOU .

ਭਾਰਤ, ਸੈਸਾਰ ਦਾ ਵਿਸ਼ਾਲ ਗਣਤੰਤ੍ਰ ਤੁਸਾਂ ਜੀ ਨੂੰ,
ਜੀ ਆਇਆ ਆਖਦਾ ਹੈ।

A welcome to India in Hindi, English and Punjabi at the Pakistan border.

tone of the following vowel fall, but the latter doesn't, leaving it level instead. We've seen the examples already: *kòra* begins with one Punjabi letter that stands for /k/, *kora* with the other. And /k/ is not the only consonant sound to have these contrasting effects: /p/, /ch/ and two kinds of /t/* do exactly the same thing. They too cause a falling tone in one spelling, but not in another. (If you feel that /k/, /p/ and /t/ sound somehow similar, you're right: they're all known as voiceless stops. 'Voiceless' because they don't set the vocal chords humming, and 'stops' because before their release, the airstream is briefly interrupted. The consonant /ch/ *begins* with a voiceless stop.)

---

* One type of /t/ is called retroflex, the other dental, the difference being in the position of the tip of the tongue. You can hear the sounds here: bit.ly/t1-retro and bit.ly/t2-dental.

But doesn't all of that confirm rather than refute the idea that tone is predictable? Not at all. Punjabi tone is related to certain written letters, to spelling. But the part of linguistics that we are discussing here, phonology, is all about sounds. Writing counts for nothing. And with good reason, because we learn the phonology of our native tongue as young children, well before we learn to read and write – if we are schooled in these skills at all. Historically, of course, most people weren't, and in South Asia literacy cannot be taken for granted even today. In *spoken* Punjabi, as we've just seen, there's nothing predictable about the tone of a word; only spelling makes it so. Yet illiterate people know perfectly well how to use just the right tones, saying *kòra* when they mean 'horse' and *kora* when they mean 'whip'. To them, tone is meaningful, and therefore it is not a mere side effect. It's the illiterate Punjabis who prove to linguists that tone is a 'thing' in their language.

From meaningless to significant

Why does Punjabi have tone if Hindi-Urdu, Bengali and its other Indo-Aryan relatives do not? How has tone emerged or, to put it geekily: how has its *tonogenesis* played out?

First of all, remember that tone is not exceptional. While tone languages are concentrated in three regions – East and Southeast Asia, Sub-Saharan Africa and Mexico – they occur elsewhere as well. And while tone seems to run in some families, such as Sino-Tibetan and Niger-Congo, other families have just a few of these musically gifted members. It's very common even for close relatives to be dissimilar in this respect: Norwegian and Swedish have tone, but Danish doesn't; most Bantu languages do, but Swahili doesn't; Vietnamese does, but its sibling Khmer doesn't. Punjabi being the only Indo-Aryan language to have tone is therefore not a startling rarity.

So where does tone come from? Even in languages without tone, such as English, it's natural, almost inevitable, for certain consonants to slightly raise or lower the pitch of the surrounding vowels. The resultant pitch created in this way is not only very subtle, but also meaningless, and neither the speaker nor the listener takes any notice of it. But now assume that for some reason – and this is something that languages do all the time, at the slightest provocation – some consonants begin to change: the th-sound merges with the d-sound, say (which happened in German at some point), or the /g/ goes silent in some positions (which has happened in lots of English words). Yet even after this change, the neighbouring vowel or vowels may maintain their characteristic pitch: a bit above par, or a bit below. Indeed, the change may even enhance this tendency, inducing an ever so slightly high-pitch vowel to rise a bit further, or a low-pitched one to fall some more. This more intense tone compensates for the loss of information caused by the consonant change. And so it is that at some point both speakers and listeners begin to pay more heed to these pitch differences – not consciously perhaps, but certainly as a matter of routine.

In most cases, this process can be reconstructed only by studying historical sources, or not at all. This is where Punjabi is exceptional. Its tones are so recent that their origin can be deduced from spelling, which was designed in the sixteenth century. As we saw above, there are five consonant letters that trigger tone, whereas five others don't, even though today they're pronounced in exactly the same way as their tone-triggering counterparts.

And here's the thing: a simple comparison with related alphabets shows that the consonants that do trigger tone were previously pronounced differently than they are at present. In the sixteenth century, the letter ਘ, the tone-triggering type of k we met above, represented /g^h/, that is, a /g/ with a puff of air. Apparently, this /g^h/ caused a somewhat higher pitch at the beginning of the following vowel. When at some point the /g^h/ morphed into a /k/, that higher pitch didn't just go away (thought it might have – these processes are unpredictable). Rather, it became more pronounced, literally and figuratively. A change in the enunciation of some consonants lent more music to the Punjabi vowels.

Whispering, singing and admiring

Tone is a fascinating aspect of some languages, but it also raises an awkward question: how do these languages deal with situations in which the required pitch cannot easily be produced?

One of these situations is when we whisper. Whispering makes it impossible to vary the pitch of our voice – if you doubt it, try singing in a whisper. This problem shouldn't cause too much awkwardness in Punjabi, which after all remains intelligible when pronounced 'flatly', as witnessed by the toneless dialect and diaspora speakers. But how about Chinese, Vietnamese and other such heavy users of tone? Research suggests that the answer varies from one language to the next. In some, whispering indeed seems to be impossible, and people just don't do it (or they do it ineptly). But the Chinese do whisper, so the question is: how? It turns out that each tone in Mandarin comes with subtle differences other than pitch, such as duration and loudness. The falling tone, for instance, is distinctly shorter than the other three.

If the whisperer exaggerates these secondary features a bit, a competent listener can interpret the toneless words, though slightly less accurately than under normal circumstances.* Actually, something very similar goes on in English. When we whisper, we can't help muddling the contrast between voiced and voiceless consonants: /z/ will sound like /s/, /b/ like /p/, et cetera. But while the main difference between these pairs is that one has the vocal chords vibrating and the other doesn't, which becomes indistinguishable when whispered, there are again subtle secondary differences. They rescue enough of the contrast to keep whispered English understandable – though as with whispered Mandarin, the risk of mishearing is somewhat higher.

A second intriguing question is, how do people sing in strongly tonal languages? If both the language and the melody have tones, how can singers juggle the conflicting demands? Surely if they sing the right notes, the lyrics become incomprehensible, whereas if they utter the words correctly, the melody sounds off? Again,

---

* The game 'Chinese whispers' owes its English name not to the presumed impossibility of whispering in Chinese, but to the perceived incomprehensibility of this language as such. For the same reason, the game is called 'Arabic telephone' in French.

part of the solution is in retaining and emphasising those other features – duration, loudness and more – that come with tone. But more importantly, the singers are helped by the lyricists. In both Vietnamese and Cantonese (and probably other tone languages, including Punjabi, but these are the two for which there's research available), the words are chosen in such a way that they do not counteract the melody too much. So when the melody goes up, the lyricist chooses words whose consecutive tones either rise or stay level; words with progressively lower tones would be a bad fit. When the melody goes down, the reverse applies. Simply put: music and language must rise and fall in approximate accordance with each other. This may seem hard to achieve, but look at it this way: in English, songs require a fairly neat correspondence between musical and linguistic accents, with stressed syllables on the strongest beats and unstressed syllables on the weaker ones or between them. This comes as second nature to us; lyricists writing in tone languages may find their job equally easy.

London's Punjabi heartland – a good place to set out to learn your tones.

And finally, let's get back to a subject I brought up at the very beginning of the chapter, as an introduction to the concept of tone: intonation. I mentioned that this is a phenomenon common to all languages, which raises the question: how do tone languages manage to squeeze in intonation *as well*? The answer is: they do both at the same time. The compulsory tones of each of the words in a phrase get overlaid with an expressive, spontaneous layer of intonation that runs across the whole sentence. So if a word has a low tone and intonation requires a high tone, the result will be somewhere in the middle; if intonation requires a low tone too, the word will come out even lower. Only a listener who knows this tone language really well will be able to tell the two layers apart.

Recognising intonation in a tone language is the acoustic counterpart of estimating the depth of snow cover on low hills: in order to know where it's deep and where it's shallow, you need to remember what the terrain looks like in summer.

13

Japanese

日本語

nihongo

130 million speakers

Practically all 127 million inhabitants of Japan speak Japanese as their mother tongue. Around 2.5 to 3.5 million people of Japanese origin live elsewhwere, mainly in Brazil and the US; not all have retained the language.

Japanese

FAMILY Many attempts have been made to place Japanese in a family (Altaic, Austronesian, even Dravidian), none ultimately convincing. The language may be a mix of those spoken by the archipelago's original inhabitants, known as Jōmon, and by the newcomers who arrived in the first millennium BCE, named Yayoi.

SCRIPT Japanese uses a baffling trio of scripts – hiragana (the main alphabet with forty-six characters), katakana (with extra syllables for foreign words), and kanji (Chinese characters) – as well as romaji (Roman script). There is more on this in chapter 2b, following the chapter on Chinese characters.

GRAMMAR Japanese words can take strings of suffixes. This 'agglutinative' character was a major reason why it was placed, along with Turkish, Korean and many smaller languages, in the Altaic family (a now discredited idea). Japanese has no grammatical gender, no plural and no articles. Verbs are conjugated, but not for person (I, you, et cetera). Adjectives are not a separate word group; some behave like verbs, others like nouns.

SOUNDS Vowels can be short or long, but never appear in diphthongs. Syllable structure is very simple. The duration of syllables and words is measured in *moras*, a typically Japanese concept (though the word is Latin). Tone is relevant for word meaning, but in a limited way and varying between dialects.

LOANWORDS Traditionally from Mandarin and other Chinese languages; today English.

EXPORTS *bonsai*, *emoji*, *anime*, *judo*, *jujitsu*, *karate*, *karaoke*, *sake* (liquor), *sushi*, *wasabi*, *futon*, *geisha*, *gingko*, *go* (board game), *hara-kiri*, *kamikaze*, *haiku*, *manga*, *sumo*, *origami*, *tempura*, *koi*, *shogun*, *kimono*, *tofu*, *tsunami*, *samurai*, *tycoon* and many more. Mandarin has borrowed more words from Japanese than from any other language.

DUTCH Japanese has a surprising number of loanwords from Dutch due to the Netherlands being the only European nation allowed to trade with Japan from 1641 to 1858, making it Japan's gateway to Western culture and knowledge. Examples include BURIKI 'tinplate' (from Dutch BLIK), KARAN 'tap, faucet' (from KRAAN), SUKOPPU 'spade' (from SCHOP) and ZUKKU 'canvas' (from DOEK).

13: **Japanese**

Linguistic gender apartheid

Do women and men speak the same language? The obvious answer seems to be 'yes': people speak whatever language they are born into, irrespective of gender. Alternatively, the answer switches to 'no' if you interpret *language* as 'things people say' or 'the way people talk'. Women and men do not speak in quite the same manner, sociolinguists and psychologists have taught us, and though the twain love to meet, they don't have an easy time of it.

But there is a third answer, and it comes from Japan. On the one hand, it's hardly an overstatement to say that all Japanese speak Japanese – the country is exceptionally monolingual. On the other hand, linguistic differences between women and men go well beyond the level of 'things people say'. The language has two varieties, one for each gender – with *gender*, for once in this book, not referring to a grammatical phenomenon, as in 'German has three genders, Arabic has two'. In Japanese, it's all about *human* gender; about people's sex as seen from a social rather than a biological perspective.

Human gender matters in many other languages. If you're Spanish and you wish to say so in Spanish, you'll put it as SOY ESPAÑOLA if you're a woman and as SOY ESPAÑOL if you're a man (and if you don't gender-identify, some linguistic compromise or creativity is required). That's because in Spanish and quite a few other European languages, your grammatical gender is determined by your social gender (or, in a more traditional view, by your biological sex). On that basis, you choose the corresponding forms of adjectives, nouns, pronouns and sometimes verbs.

Japanese is different. Grammatical gender is for all intents and purposes non-existent. What we find in Japanese is that women and men are expected to speak slightly different 'genderlects' – varieties based on gender. This is not some marginal phenomenon, not one

おんなことば

女言葉

Onna Kotoba

0:18 / 8:13

This YouTube video will have you speaking Onna Kotoba – Japanese women's language – in no time.

of those surprise nuances that linguists sometimes discover after diving deep into the inner workings of any language. In Japanese society, ONNA KOTOBA, JOSEIGO or FUJINGO – all three words translate as 'women's language' – is considered a separate part of the national language, and the cultural establishment sets considerable store by maintaining it.*

So what has history been up to here? How has it produced a special women's variety? What distinguishes this variety from – well, from what actually? From men's language? Or is there also a neutral, ungendered variety?

To begin with this last question: most of the language, indeed nearly all of it, is considered neutral. (This puts us in mind of *ngoko*, the basic register of Javanese, most of which is neither polite nor impolite.) But beyond this, there are separate varieties, both for women and for men. Yet there is an important difference. Men's language, which has a rude, forceful ring to it, is nearly entirely

---

* This is how I interpret the first sentence of a book by sociolinguist Momoko Nakamura, titled *Gender, Language and Ideology*. The original reads: 'Women's language is a socially salient linguistic concept and a hegemonic cultural notion in Japan.'

optional, and boys will not be *taught* to speak it. Rather, they pick it up, much like children elsewhere may pick up street slang. Women's language, on the other hand, is not so optional, and parents and teachers will do their best to make girls toe the linguistic line. But that implies that the 'ungendered' Japanese is in fact no such thing: part of it is the reserve of men, who, moreover, have a special register at their disposal that is particularly masculine. Women's individual options are limited to either conforming to the appropriate genderlect or attracting social censure – in other words, they have to obey or pay the price. Collectively, of course, they have an additional option: once sufficient numbers are willing to flout the rules, the whole concept of women's language will become less rigid. And this is exactly what has happened in recent decades, as we will see later.

Luncheon is on the tableon

Let's get down to brass tacks. What makes women's Japanese different from men's? For starters, women are more likely to use slightly longer versions of words to make them – and consequently themselves – sound polite. Think of it as not only using the archaic word 'luncheon' instead of the workaday 'lunch', but making the difference systematic by also saying 'tableon' instead of 'table' and 'flowereon' instead of 'flower'. In Japanese, this politeness syllable is added not at the end, but at the front: thus HANA ('flower') becomes OHANA (both in speech and in writing).

Next, women and men will use different pronouns to refer to themselves: while WATASHI is a word for 'I' or 'me' that both genders can use (though it sounds rather formal when a man says it), ATASHI is clearly a women's word, while BOKU is for men that are – or want to come over as – young.[*] Indeed, ATASHI and BOKU are what Japanese-language textbooks teach (young people) for the first person singular, just as English-language textbooks teach *he* and *she* in the third person. Similar differences exist in the case of the second person pronoun, 'you'.

---

[*] 'Young' men? Yes, or 'boy', even. The Japanese language differentiates not only between the genders but also, to some limited extent, people of different ages.

The verb 'to be', DA, is differentiated along gender lines as well. In a sentence like 'this is a spider', men will use it, but women will omit it. In other words, men say something like 'this is a spider', whereas the same sentence in women's Japanese is more like 'this a spider'. The point is not that the latter sounds strange in English – a sentence like 'this a spider' is perfectly fine in many languages, including Russian (see chapter 3). What matters is that women and men apply different grammar here.

They will also use different 'little words' of the kind that don't have clearly definable meanings, but suggest the speakers' attitudes. These words are highly frequent in Japanese, adding all sorts of

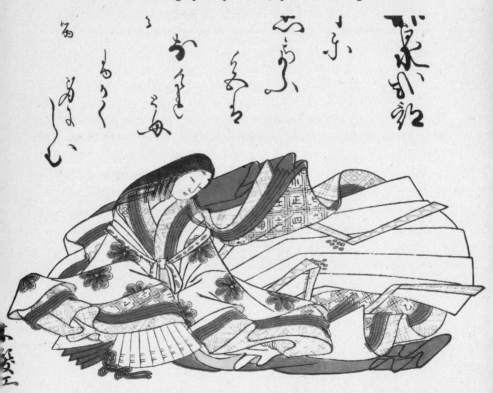

Japanese women didn't always use deferential language. This is Izumi Shikibu, one of the great poets of the Kyoto court, who wrote a series of passionate love poems in the early eleventh century.

subtexts, ranging from 'please agree with me' and 'we both know' all the way to 'I'm positive, damn it'. Both men and women can use Ā for 'oh', as in 'oh, how beautiful', but only women may also choose ARA or MĀ. To express 'I wonder', women will say KA SHIRA, whereas KA NA is more neutral. A particularly well-known example is the feminine WA, which expresses admiration or emotion; men are highly unlikely to use it.

Some assorted items of more straightforward vocabulary are strongly associated with women (IYĀN meaning 'no') or with men (MESHI for 'meal', DEKAI for 'big'). Synonyms for these words (IYA, GOHAN and ŌKII for 'no', 'meal' and 'big') can be used by either gender.

Finally, pronunciation too may occasionally differ: men may reduce the vowel sequence /ai/ (which rhymes more or less with English *lie*) to /ē/ (rhyming with *lay*), whereas it would be unladylike for a woman to do so.

Speakers do not exactly break a hard-and-fast grammar rule when using elements normally used by the opposite gender, but they certainly break a social convention: they bend both a rule and their gender. Imagine if a female school principal insisted on being referred to as 'headmaster': she'd raise eyebrows, even though the difference is arguably insignificant – *headmistress* and *headmaster* both mean 'person with the greatest responsibility for the management of a school'. Or more remarkable still: imagine a male principal insisting on being called 'headmistress' – the tabloids would have a field day.

But perhaps this is not the best comparison, because at its heart the difference between women's and men's Japanese is about refinement, about coming across as either polished and graceful or a devil-may-care force to be reckoned with.

Over twenty years ago, my English teacher told me that I'd better not emulate her habit of saying 'Oh my gosh', as it somewhat undermined my gender credibility. While that seems to have changed now, it's still the case that 'foul' language is something that men get away with more easily than women – it's hard to envisage a woman winning a presidential election after saying 'grab 'em by the dick'. In other words, English too has certain variations depending on gender. But in Japanese, these differences are rather more marked: they comprise more aspects of speech and are more strictly codified.

Virtuous muttering

Many Japanese believe that 'women's language' is an ancient phenomenon, that it was formed by the way women actually spoke and that it is a natural reflection of what they all have in common, i.e. their femininity. Modern scholarship has persuasively challenged all of these assumptions.

Certain differences between women's and men's varieties of Japanese can be traced as far back as the Heian period (794–1185). Women at the time were expected to avoid Chinese borrowings and use words of domestic origin instead. So were children and young men, which meant that only mature men had the prerogative of using Chinese vocabulary, which, like Latinate words in English, lent a ring of intellectual class to their speech. This avoidance of Chinese words would remain a recurring theme in treatises about women's language for a long time. Using such words would suggest more knowledge than was thought proper for a woman.

Another important difference had to do not so much with vocabulary or grammar, but what we might call linguistic or communicative behaviour: women in the Heian period were encouraged *not* to be articulate. Ideally, they would mutter to themselves in unfinished sentences.

Over the next four centuries, known as the Kamakura and Muromachi periods (1185–1333, 1336–1573), conduct books for the higher classes – dealing with both etiquette and morality – began to proclaim a new norm: better for a woman to speak as little as possible, or in a small voice if it was absolutely necessary for her to speak. This was in accordance with Confucian ideology, which held that it behoved women to obey men and that a woman, by speaking, might easily destroy the proper order of the family and society as a whole. So the evidence shows that these speech patterns were a *norm* rather than a description of untaught behaviour. No one claimed that women spontaneously tended to be silent; it was just thought to be in everybody's best interest if they learnt to be.

It was during this period, and especially from the fourteenth century on, that there arose at the imperial palace a new phenomenon that would be of great importance in centuries to come. Noblewomen serving at the palace ('ladies-in-waiting' might be a good European equivalent) gradually developed a peculiar jargon among themselves in which many words, especially for domestic items, were changed radically or even replaced by new coinages. To give a few examples, MANJŪ (bun) was shortened to MAN, SHINPAI (worry) became SHINMOJI and KŌ NO MONO (pickle) was shortened and then reduplicated to give KŌ-KŌ. Other words were replaced by a basic sensory feature of the object, preceded by O-, a suffix of respect: cold water (MIZU) was referred to as something we might translate as o'cool (OHIYA), sea bream (TAI) as o'thin (O-HIRA) and adzuki beans (AZUKI) as o'red (O-AKA; also AKA-AKA). Again, Chinese words were avoided, so that for instance KAJI (fire) was replaced with AKAGOTO (literally 'red thing'). There are several theories as to why the ladies serving at court did this – for the sake of secrecy, classy indirectness, or communication between speakers of different dialects – but the fact of the matter is that from the imperial court, their jargon gradually trickled down to the shogun's palace and the samurais' mansions.

The jargon was also adopted by the noblemen, and while it's called 'court-ladies' speech' today, for a long time it was more a mark of class than of gender. In the literature of the period there are numerous examples of men, including monks and warlords, speaking in this style. Elsewhere, male characters from the lower classes would mock and parody this elite speech. Only later did conduct books begin to criticise men who employed this style, with one book calling it 'disgusting' yet 'often observed'.

Don't talk reason

This quote from 1687 brings us to the next phase in Japan's history, known as the Edo period (1603–1868), when the country was closed to most of the outside world. This is when the elite speaking style gradually came to be associated with gender instead of class, especially in the eighteenth and nineteenth centuries. Non-elite women became acquainted with the linguistic dos and don'ts through hundreds of new conduct books, which now circulated among all social classes, laying down rules that were more restrictive and complex than ever before. Silence and the avoidance of Chinese words remained *de rigueur*. But even certain non-Chinese words had to be shunned, such as SHIKATO (certainly) and IKIJI (pride), presumably because certainty and pride were deemed to be unfeminine. Moreover, women were expected to sprinkle their language with the O prefix and the MOJI suffix that we saw above, as these were now felt to have a softening effect, making the language more feminine: plain GUSHI (hair) sounded too harsh, so OGUSHI should be uttered instead; instead of SONATA (you), women should address people with SOMOJI.

Modern and traditional – is Japanese gender language on the wane?

Gendered language reached a new stage from the late nineteenth century, when the country underwent rapid modernisation after opening itself to the outside world. One element of this was the standardisation of the language, which had so far been characterised by huge dialect variety; another was the introduction of the concept of equal rights between women and men. However, this was interpreted as 'equal but innately different', and the new national language was no less gendered than the old. Indeed, an 1879 imperial edict specifically promoted its gendered nature.

When universal primary education was introduced, in 1886, it applied to both girls and boys, but the official textbooks were different. Here's a quote from one for girls (from 1893): 'Restrain yourself from speaking. Intentionally androgynous speech is indecent. Direct speech is snobbish. A woman's good speech should not jar one's ear, but should be soft and lovable, and should not talk reason ... It is especially disgusting to see a woman speak knowingly and cleverly.'

In terms of vocabulary and grammar, women's language came to be influenced by a variety known as schoolgirl speech, a style that emerged among elite students in secondary schools. Though decried as being vulgar in the late 1800s, it gained wide acceptance within decades and has been considered feminine and proof of a solid education ever since. It offered a home-grown innovation that seamlessly fitted into the older linguistic gender-division, and Japanese society soon came to regard it as a venerable, ancient part of the language, though in fact it was no such thing. Never before had Japanese women's language been formalised in grammars and textbooks, and many of its modern characteristics were recent (schoolgirls') inventions, whereas many older (court ladies') elements had fallen by the wayside.

Alive and elegantly kicking

In recent decades, the Japanese language has become decidedly less gendered. US-based linguist Yoko Hasegawa has noticed a sea change in the language used by female characters in Japanese films, TV dramas and theatrical productions in the last twenty-five years:

their speech now has a much more masculine character than before. The reason for this can't be that women wanted to appropriate a form of speech that was more highly regarded *culturally*, because superior cultural status was traditionally accorded to the female variety of the language. But socially, economically and politically, Japanese men have always been dominant. The conquest of male linguistic territory is about power rather than prestige.

Less rigid though the code may have become, speakers of Japanese are as keenly aware as ever that the genderlects exist. 'Ignore [them] and at some point you will wind up sounding like a little Japanese girl – or a guy – when you didn't intend to,' *The Japan Times* wrote in 2009. Novelists cleverly use the conventions to convey their characters' genders, and readers pick up on the signals without missing a beat – even if many of them are actually outdated. Translations are not exempt: Angelina Jolie is made to speak women's language in an interview with a Japanese newspaper, as is Hermione Granger in the Harry Potter books and films – even though at the beginning of the series this is unrealistic for her age.

But at least those incredibly sexist 'conduct books' have disappeared – or have they? Well, they have changed, but when the sociolinguist Momoko Nakamura searched an online bookshop using the keywords JOSEI (woman) and HANASHIKATA (way of speaking), she got seventy-three results. She analysed the first seven, and they all emphasised 'that a woman can improve her attractiveness by changing her way of speaking, and by speaking feminine women's language, she can be elegant, wise, beautiful, happy, and loved'. These books and their success prove that women's language is alive and kicking, she concluded.

12

Swahili

KISWAHILI

135 million speakers

Estimates for native Swahili speakers vary from 3 to 15 million; most of the 135 million speakers use it as a second language. Swahili is the main lingua franca of Kenya and Tanzania and is widely spoken in Burundi, Rwanda, Uganda, the eastern half of Congo (DR) and parts of neighbouring countries. In Oman, whose sultan used to rule Zanzibar, the 'capital of Swahili', the language is still said to be spoken by a significant number. There are also Swahili-speaking migrants in the UK, US and Gulf states.

Swahili

SELF-DESIGNATION Kiswahili. Also used in English.

FAMILY Swahili belongs to the large Bantu branch of the Niger-Congo family. Bantu languages are spread across Central, East and Southern Africa. The rest of the Niger-Congo family dominates a smaller area, mostly in West Africa.

SCRIPT Swahili today is written in the Latin alphabet. Before Europe's 'scramble for Africa' around 1900, the Arabic script was used.

GRAMMAR Swahili nouns fall into a range of different noun classes, somewhat comparable to the genders that most European languages have. Each of these classes has its own prefixes, one for singular, one for plural. Other words – verbs, adjectives, even prepositions – assume different forms depending on the class of the noun.

SOUNDS Swahili is highly exceptional for a Bantu language in not having tone.

LOANWORDS Around 30 per cent of the Swahili vocabulary is of Arabic origin, with English a distant second at about 10 per cent. Swahili developed in the contact between East African coastal dwellers and Arab clove farmers, traders and (later) rulers, particularly from Oman.

EXPORTS The most common English loanword from Swahili is *safari*, which has Arabic roots. The name of *Kwanzaa*, a week-long festival celebrated mostly by African-Americans, is derived from Swahili *matunda ya kwanza* or 'first fruits'. The colonial *bwana* for 'master' was another Swahili word. While not loans exactly, several of the names in the film The Lion King are of Swahili origin, including that of the main character: *Simba* means 'lion'. And yes, *hakuna matata* really does mean 'no worries', or literally 'there are no problems'.

YOUTH The oldest known documents in Swahili are from the early eighteenth century: letters from 1711 on and a long poem dated 1728. This makes its written literature easily the youngest among our twenty Babel languages.

12: **Swahili**

Africa's nonchalant multilingualism

As I don't know you personally, I could be wrong, but my considered guess is that in terms of language-learning you are, well, shall I be frank? – a dunce. A dunce, I hasten to add, compared to Jonas from Jilve.

Not that you're to blame, mind you.

If you grew up in a country like Britain or the United States, chances are that English was the language that your parents spoke to you as a child. So did the telly, so did the babysitter. As you grew up, you discovered that the outside world too was awash with English: neighbours and shopkeepers spoke it, teachers and classmates, priests and politicians – the language was everywhere, as far as the ear could hear. Later on, you and your companion probably shared the same old language. And so it's likely to remain for the rest of your life: from your first word to your last breath, you rarely need anything but the language of William Shakespeare, Oprah Winfrey and Homer Simpson. You may have learnt a foreign language, or even several, but barring migration you're unlikely to ever *need* them (as opposed to using them recreationally).

As the world's linguistic powerhouse, English is rather extreme in this respect. However, if you grew up in, say, France, Spain, Mexico, Brazil or Korea, your story is likely to be more or less the same, because throughout Europe, the Americas and East Asia, substantial portions of the population lead largely monolingual lives.

But not in Africa.

Africa is where we find people like the aforementioned Jonas. I can't tell you Jonas's family name, because it was very properly withheld by Leslie C. Moore, the American linguist who met him

141

during her research. But we know that he was born around 1980 in the village of Jilve in Cameroon's northern Mandara mountains; that, unusually for his village, he completed primary school and even went to secondary school; and that his life is about as far removed from being monolingual as can be.

Jonas's linguistic saga started at home, where he acquired not only his mother tongue, Vame, but also a 'father tongue', Wuzlam. So he was bilingual at the tender age of four, albeit in languages with just a few thousand speakers each. Next came Wandala, the region's lingua franca (language of interethnic communication), spoken by a few tens of thousands and the favoured lingo of the school playground. Vame, Wuzlam and Wandala are quite closely related, belonging as they do to the Central branch of the Chadic family, but they're not mutually intelligible. Also in primary school, Jonas had to come to grips with French (language number 4), which is the main official language of Cameroon and the medium of education in most of the country. A few years later, he was also formally taught English (5), the country's other official language.

While in secondary school, Jonas began to court a girl named Gogo, and even though the two of them spoke Wandala and Wuzlam, he decided to learn her mother tongue, Mada (6). No doubt he did so for the reason famously cited by Nelson Mandela when asked why he studied the Afrikaans of the apartheid regime: if you speak to a person in their own language, your words go straight to their heart. Schmaltzy, perhaps, but true.

Secondary school, which was situated outside the Wandala-speaking area, brought two further lingua francas into Jonas's life: Zulgwa (7), yet another Central Chadic language spoken in the neighbourhood around the school, and Fula (8), spoken by the majority of both students and townspeople.* This last addition to Jonas's repertoire was a highly useful one, as it enabled him to

---

* Confusingly, most of the African languages mentioned here, and many others, have more than one name. In some cases, speakers of different dialects prefer different designations. Elsewhere, colonial administrators or foreign linguists are to blame for the confusion. In Jonas's repertoire, the aliases are as follows: Wuzlam is also known as Uldeme (spelt Ouldémé in French), Vame as Pelasla, Wandala as Mandara or Mura, Fula as Fulfulde, Fulani, Pular or (in French) Peul, and Zulgwa as Zulgo-Gemzek. Only Mada has just the one, except that it's sometimes spelt Mada to distinguish it from an entirely unrelated namesake spoken some 500 kilometres to the west.

communicate with some 25 million people spread across twenty or so countries, mostly to the west of Cameroon. But it wasn't easy to learn: belonging to the Niger-Congo family, it is as unrelated to his other African languages as English is to, say, Hungarian.

A billion Jonases?

Truth be told, this story is exceptional, even by African standards. Partly, this is because Cameroon is a hotspot of linguistic variety: the country has around ten languages for each one million inhabitants – 250 languages in all. Another reason is that Jonas's community of Wuzlam speakers belongs to a multilingual ethnic group called the Montagnards (French for 'mountain dwellers') or Kirdi, in whose culture language-learning is particularly valued. And then there's Jonas's individual biography: thanks to his many years of education, he was exposed to a greater range of languages than his peers, both in the classroom and in the street. Being a Montagnard, he happily learnt whatever seemed useful to him. Most other Africans in his situation might have chosen not to spend energy on the town's Zulgwa nor on the girl's Mada, wooing her in Wuzlam instead. But even Africans less voracious than Jonas would still have learnt the other six – and not given it another thought.

This chapter focuses on Swahili, which is spoken in East Africa: mostly in Tanzania and Kenya, where it originated, but also in Uganda, Burundi, Rwanda, the eastern half of Congo and smaller parts of Mozambique and other neighbouring countries. Even in Southern Africa, people are more likely to learn Swahili than, say, Amharic, for the same reason Europeans would sooner learn Italian than Romanian: Swahili and Italian yield a better return on one's investment.

The Swahili region doesn't bubble, churn and gurgle with linguistic plenty in the way Cameroon does. Kenya and Tanzania, at the historical heart of the Swahili region, have two languages per one million inhabitants; in the rest of the region, the number is nearer one per one million, perhaps even less.

While Swahili will be the main star in this chapter, it will have to share the limelight with its relatives and neighbours. That's because

I want the story to be about sub-Saharan Africa as a whole (hereafter called Africa for short), as its linguistic landscape is markedly different from that of other continents. A practical consideration is that we won't get a second chance to visit it, as Swahili is the only African language in this book.

Perhaps the most crucial similarity between East Africa's Swahili region, West Africa's Cameroon and Africa generally is this: when daily life throws a new language at them, people are unfazed and willing to learn it (as in 'start speaking it', not 'take a course'). The main difference between the Swahili region and the rest of the continent is precisely the presence of this friendly giant called Swahili. To give an idea of how exceptional that is: the language has at least twice, perhaps three times as many speakers as Africa's number two, Hausa. Small wonder that several intellectuals, most famously Nigerian Nobel literature prize winner Wole Soyinka, have made the case for Swahili as a continental lingua franca. And when the Ghanaian historian K. A. Kumi Attobrah launched an Esperanto-like auxiliary language for Africa in 1970, he based it on Swahili and named it Afrihili.

If Africans don't dread tackling a new language when it seems useful, how *many* do they end up learning? As we saw in Jonas's case, that depends on their personal circumstances and on local cultural values. But as a broad generalisation, the answer would be three: a mother tongue, a lingua franca and what I will call a 'VIL' – a Very Important Language. One of several factors to muddle this neat picture is that many languages can appear in two of these roles simultaneously and a few, including Swahili, even in all three. Still, mother tongue, lingua franca and VIL are three serviceable poles (think tent poles, not magnetic poles) for the basic framework; real-life complexity will be added later.

'VIL' may be a playful term and you won't find it in other texts about African linguistics, but I think it does a good job of representing a range of different situations. Typically, the VIL is the country's official language as well as the medium of instruction in all education beyond primary school; typically, it's what the urban higher classes speak and what journalists and literary authors write in. Typically, it's those things – but not always all of them. A country may have several official languages or none at all, education may be multilingual, some famous authors may prefer to write in their mother tongues, et cetera. Nonetheless, in nearly every African country it's obvious which is the VIL.

Also in nearly every African country (as in the Americas), the VIL is of European origin. Both English and French are Very Important in roughly twenty countries; Portuguese is a distant third with five. In three countries (plus North Africa, not considered here), the VIL is Arabic, which similarly was introduced from outside, but centuries earlier. In several countries, such as Zimbabwe, one or more languages of African origin are 'officially official', but in practice they play second fiddle. Countries where African languages have risen to VIL status are few: Tanzania, Ethiopia and Somalia.

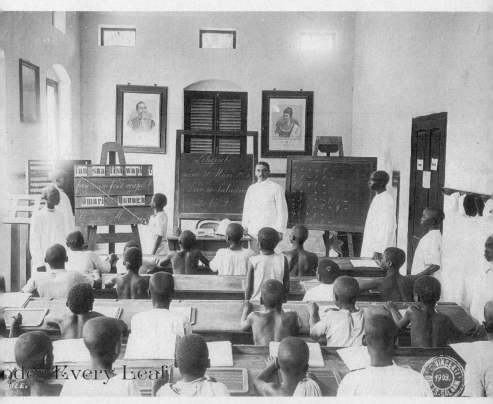

Even back in German colonial times, before the First World War, Swahili was taught in Tanzanian schools.

Even Swahili is still struggling to attain the role that an innocent outsider would expect this giant to fulfil as a matter of course. Only in Tanzania has it indisputably come out on top. In Kenya it's as widespread as in Tanzania, but in both formal status and social prestige it lags far behind English. For a long time its legal position was that of 'national language', which throughout Africa is a polite term for 'officially irrelevant'. Only in 2010 did it become Kenya's second official language. In Uganda, where Swahili is less widely spoken, the government chose English at independence (1962), then added Swahili as an official language ten years later, only to abandon it in 1995 and to change its mind once more ten years after that. Last time I checked, Swahili maintained its official status, but English still had more prestige and Luganda more speakers. Outside Tanzania, Kenya and Uganda, Swahili is merely a lingua franca.

What people speak...

Africans speak three languages, I claimed: a mother tongue, a lingua franca and a Very Important Language. But including the VIL in this triad may be considered an exaggeration. In most countries where a language of European origin has this status, it is spoken by only a minority of the population. On the other hand, English, French and, above all, perhaps surprisingly, Portuguese are making considerable headway, especially in cities, so maybe the above claim is not so much exaggerated as premature.

While most Africans do not at this stage speak their national VILs, many have mastered more than one lingua franca, bringing the average per person close to three again. That's because it's not uncommon for there to be several lingua francas spoken in close proximity to each other. Jonas, you'll remember, first acquired one lingua franca as a young kid and then two more as an adolescent: one local, the other spoken throughout West Africa. In Uganda, two lingua francas – Swahili and Luganda – are fairly widespread and people who have use for them will not hesitate to learn both. Congo has four important lingua francas, including Swahili, and again, it's not as if speaking one stops anybody from learning another if the need should arise.

Finally, and obviously, Africans have their mother tongues, of which there are over one thousand, two thousand or three thousand, depending on who you ask.* As a result, it's by no means rare to find spouses with different mother tongues. Their children may well grow up bilingually, speaking what in the case of Jonas I've labelled a mother and a father tongue. (To be exact, he learnt his 'mother tongue' not from his mother but from her relatives, as local culture prescribes that she speak her husband's language to the children. That's the sort of real-life complexity that I promised.)

Many mother tongues have a very limited reach: they're the local lingos of just one clan or a few villages. Others are spoken by large ethnic groups spread across several countries. The larger mother tongues may at the same time be lingua francas for native speakers of smaller languages: Jonas learnt Fula as a lingua franca, but it's also spoken natively by over 20 million. Swahili goes one better by fulfilling three different roles: VIL in Tanzania, lingua franca in a much larger area, and mother tongue for several million people in the Zanzibar archipelago and along the Indian Ocean coast. In some African cities, the European languages too are widening their functions: from VIL to lingua franca, and in some elite families even to the status of mother tongue.

...but don't write

VILs have a crucial feature to distinguish them from the other two categories: they are *written* much more. Some African languages have been committed to paper for centuries and today many of them have standardised spelling systems, whether in the Latin, Arabic or Ethiopic alphabet (also called *Ge'ez* – ግዕዝ). In practice, however, only a few of them are written to any great extent. Many African authors prefer English, French or Portuguese for the same reason that made me choose English for this book rather than my native Dutch: it gives them (us) access to the international market. But in their case, that can't be the whole story: even African works of

---

* Linguistics, like other sciences facing the problem of classification, has splitters and lumpers. By emphasising differences, the former raise the language count; the latter, seeing similarities, lower it.

purely local interest are mostly published in one of the European languages. There is an additional reason beyond the commercial one for writers to prefer these to their mother tongues: readers, even those who are staunch speakers of African languages, find it easier going. Reading a language they're not used to seeing in print feels to them much like reading the dialect dialogue in *Huckleberry Finn* feels to us: we get slowed down by the unfamiliar appearance of the words.

Journalism too is written mostly in European languages (and to a lesser extent in Arabic). Even in Tanzania, Somalia and Ethiopia, with their African VILs, English is highly visible in print and online media. For several other countries, my online searches didn't turn up a single news magazine in an African language. This can't be for economic reasons only, since far more people understand the lingua francas than English or French. Rather, it would seem that roughly half a century after independence, readers and writers still have a preconception that African languages cannot fulfil the 'modern' roles that colonial languages have played for several generations. Swahili proves them wrong, if proof were needed.

Normal folks, not prodigies

Unless you grew up in the same continent as Jonas and his fellow polyglots, you may be beginning to feel that in language-learning, as in long-distance running, you can't compete with these Africans. They're just too good at it. Something in their build, one assumes; something genetic that makes the rest of humanity look like hopeless laggards. When it comes to running, there's something to that: East Africans, and Kenya's Kalenjin in particular, are more likely to be blessed with certain physical qualities that are ideally suited to long-distance running. But as ever, genes are far from the whole story. It took a few initial successes to kindle the athletic ambitions in a great number of young East Africans, which in turn multiplied the likelihood of latent talents manifesting themselves. Only people who train for and participate in races can ever prove their excellence and become champions. Kenyans have done and achieved just that.

On the menu in Arusha, Tanzania. MENU, CHIPSI, SUPU and ROST are English borrowings, KARIBUNI ('welcome') is of Arabic origin. NYAMA is a very widespread Bantu word for 'meat'. Many Swahili words for abstract concepts have Arabic roots.

How does this work for language-learning? Can African multilingualism too be explained by a mixture of genes and social factors? In the individual case of Jonas, there may be an element of innate talent in the sense that he seems to possess above-average intelligence. But his choosing to learn some languages that were merely useful rather than indispensable has more to do with the culture of his ethnic group, where multilingualism is considered a good thing in itself. Regarding the *average* African, the explanation is even simpler: their personal multilingualism is due to the multilingualism of their societies. If you lead your life among people who speak different languages, you have a reason to learn them – and opportunities for practice.

My own experience confirms this connection between necessity, opportunity and achievement. The only foreign languages that I'm any good at are those that I needed and had ample time to practice. I needed German when, back in my teens, I fell in love with a German girl, which enabled me to practice to my heart's delight. I needed Spanish when as an undergraduate I did research in Peru, where I spoke little else for half a year. Later on, a job motivated me to improve my English. I did, but never having lived in an English-speaking country, my speaking proficiency lags somewhat behind my writing skills to this day and my vocabulary is a tad bookish. My French speaking skills, however, are a persistent embarrassment, even though my father taught the language and I sat through six years of lessons (not his) in secondary school. The reason is that I've never needed to speak it for any sustained period. All my later, mostly curiosity-driven attempts at mastering languages were too half-hearted to bear fruit – remember the Vietnamese fiasco. Putting in the hours is the hard bit in learning.

Taking language barriers by storm

So Africans are not born as linguistic geniuses; it's Africa that makes them so. But having said that, I should add that Africa's linguistic culture is different from Europe's (and to a lesser degree America's) in ways that make it less daunting to tackle a new language.

In Europe, the major languages are policed with a grim zeal that borders on the totalitarian. Most have official academies or councils, spelling laws, grammar books, dictionaries, pronunciation standards, style guides and terminological committees. As a result, they also have spelling dissenters, letters to the editor, spelling bees, spelling refresher courses, Henry Fowlers, Lynne Trusses and other finger-waggers. Self-styled 'language-lovers' insist that everyone, regardless of their station in life and their mother tongue, should spell well, punctuate punctiliously, toe the grammar line and eschew words that are deemed unacceptable. Pernickety pedants, that's what Europe bristles with, and if my impression from afar is not mistaken, so does North America (except they would be called persnickety).

If only we could be Africans! Most people south of the Sahara are much more pragmatic and easy-going in this respect. It's not that they're altogether cavalier about language: their mother tongues are sources of pride and identity, they admire eloquence and verbal swagger as much as the rest of us and vivid story-telling is held in high regard. But knowing that their mother tongue will only take them so far both socially and geographically, they speak other languages too. They don't make a show of their multilingualism: they carry it lightly and nonchalantly. When two Africans run into a language barrier, they will storm it from both sides with all the resources at their disposal, be it fluent Luganda, simple Swahili or broken English – and often a mixture of several. What matters is establishing communication, and finding a common language is the way to do it.

This sensible and pragmatic attitude is not uniquely African. Indeed, it was once shared by Europeans, in the days before national standard languages first emerged. The same sensible and pragmatic attitude once reigned in the British Isles. Anglo-Saxons and Vikings dealt with each other in this way, producing English in the process. It was the same way in the Balkans, Europe's own Babel, until nationalism got hold of the region in the nineteenth century and turned its multilingual mosaic into a Gordian knot. Sensible pragmatism becomes harder to maintain as fluid tongues solidify into regulated standards. Once languages become dominant over a wide area and are widely used in writing, tolerance begins to wane. Perhaps Africa's linguistic pragmatism will crumble if African languages one day attain VIL status across the continent.

Another difference that makes Africa's languages easier to learn than Europe's is the fact that they have smaller vocabularies. I know, this sounds like a dangerous thing to say. Am I suggesting that African languages are somehow simpler, cruder? Most emphatically not. Educated African *people* wield extensive vocabularies. The thing is, they can't do this in most African *languages*, because only VILs (including Swahili) have developed large lexicons. Thanks to being used in modern domains such as government, education, science, technology, finance, art, philosophy, sport and so on, they – and only they – develop the jargons that are needed for these activities, thereby multiplying their lexicons. Moreover, those that have been written for centuries have developed a rich seam of 'fossils': words that are no longer heard in everyday speech but still found in literature and multi-volume dictionaries. No native speaker knows anything like all of these old, specialised or otherwise unusual words, but they do know tens of thousands. The sheer size of its lexicon makes the typical VIL a daunting prospect for the student. Africa's lingua francas are less formidable. They're perfectly useful vehicles for accurate and subtle communication about numerous aspects of life. And not just traditional village life either: many are also used in political rallies, radio news, local administration and primary courts, so they have coined or borrowed the words needed for these areas. But on the whole, their word-hoards are less extensive.

As for grammar and pronunciation, the other two things that language learners have to grapple with, African languages are not simpler – if anything, the opposite. For one thing, most of them have tone, the tricky sing-song quality that we've already encountered in Punjabi. For another, many African tongues have consonant sounds rarely found elsewhere, such as /mb/ (one sound, not two, e.g. in MAMBA, originally syllabified as ma-mba) or the famous click sounds of Xhosa and Zulu. In terms of grammar, African languages tend to be densely inflected, like Latin, Russian or Turkish: words have many different forms reflecting such concepts as number, case, gender, tense and mood. Another common feature, at least in the vast Niger-Congo family, are the so-called noun classes. These are not unlike the genders that make German and Latin so hard for the adult learner, but while genders usually number two or three, noun classes come in gaggles of ten or more.

A wind tunnel of multi-ethnic chatter

How do people master all these intricacies? Part of the answer is that what appears difficult to outsiders may come more easily to you if you grew up speaking an African language. If your mother tongue is a Bantu language such as Nkore, Sukuma or Kikuyu (spoken in Uganda, Tanzania and Kenya respectively), you are already accustomed to noun classes. Swahili will be different in its particulars, but it's clearly a close relative. Compare it to your learning a European language: the plurals may be different and more irregular than those of English, but you have no trouble using them in the right places. To a native speaker of Mandarin or Vietnamese, however, plurality is an alien concept to begin with.

Nor does this mechanism work only between African languages that are related. Even members of different families, say Niger-Congo and Chadic, have converged somewhat. Thus, to give one example, nine out of ten African languages place the numeral after the noun (as in 'I have children three'), whereas the opposite order is more common outside Africa. This sort of convergence often occurs in places where multilingualism is widespread. Multilingual areas are like washing machines running at 60°C or more: laundry of various colours will come out in intermediate hues, though still recognisable as shirts, socks and dresses. A well-studied linguistic washing machine in Europe is the Balkans, where Bulgarian (Slavic) and Romanian (Romance) have in several ways become more similar to Albanian than to their close relatives. Linguists call such similarities *areal features*, shared by a *linguistic area*, also known as *sprachbund*.

Lingua francas as a class are particularly prone to absorb their neighbours' metaphorical colours. And the more franca the lingua, the more this is the case. In other words, the more the second-language speakers outnumber native speakers, the more undistinctive the language will become. It will lose the things that its new speakers find hard to handle, such as irregularities. In chapter 15 we saw this happen dramatically to Persian (and English). To Swahili, it has happened to a lesser extent. In Tanzania, where Swahili as the VIL is widely taught in school, widely used in media and widely written, the spoken language tends to be close to the standard. Moreover, this standard is based on the dialect of Zanzibar, which is part of Tanzania (it puts the 'zan' in the country's name). But the Swahili spoken by people who've picked it up informally and seldom hear it in formal settings, such as in East Congo, is likely to be a far cry from the Tanzanian TV newsreader's gold standard.

One feature that is ubiquitous in languages throughout the region but conspicuously lacking in Swahili is tone. This may be due to the influence of Arabic, the non-tonal mother tongue of the Omanis who used to dominate Zanzibar and the adjacent coast. But another, purely African scenario can also explain the loss of tone. Africans learning the language would have been familiar with tone as such,

That sign is ubiquitous. This one reads 'Keep calm and speak Swahili', unless you follow Google Translate which suggests the more incendiary slogan of 'Slay the master and learn it to be free'!

but their mother tongues, confusingly, would use it differently. Therefore, in the end, they gave up on tone in Swahili altogether. This is very similar to what happened when the Anglo-Saxons and the Vikings mingled in England a thousand years ago: both Old English and Old Norse had case systems, but different ones. The resulting muddled English, later renamed Middle English, had practically no cases left. Tone-free Swahili and case-free English have travelled light and far since.

Between past and future

The linguistic landscape depicted above is in some important ways unique to Africa. Most European countries have one leading lingo that is home-grown (or perceived to be). The same is true in Asia, though the exceptions to the rule – India for one – are more significant there than in Europe. In the Americas and Australia, a few European leviathans dominate the scene: Spanish, English, Portuguese and, to a lesser degree, French. They are both the VILs and the majority's mother tongues in nearly every single country. Only in sub-Saharan Africa are VILs and mother tongues nearly always different.

So how come? What happened? In the broadest of brush-strokes, it's like this.

Pre-colonial Africa never had empires as large, powerful and bureaucratically sophisticated as Asia, so the dominant languages didn't spread as widely as Chinese, Hindi-Urdu, Arabic, et cetera. This explains why so many Asian languages have made it into this book as against just one from Africa. On the other hand, Africa hasn't endured a phase of European colonialism quite as genocidal as the Americas and Australia, so the colonial languages never replaced the indigenous ones as mother tongues. As a result, Africans today still speak a fairly large number of languages, nearly all of African origin. (Perhaps you feel that 'a fairly large number' is an understatement to describe the current situation. But pre-colonial America and Australia were much more linguistically diverse, and a few places still are today. Even Jonas's Cameroon looks like a monoculture compared to the island of New Guinea, which has over sixty languages per one million inhabitants.)

After decolonisation, nearly all African countries continued to use English, French or Portuguese for administration and education, partly because a domestic minority language might divide the nation, and partly because African languages were held to be unsuitable for such lofty roles. However, these VILs of foreign origin have not replaced the older lingua francas, let alone the mother tongues. But even if at some point in the future English, French and Portuguese were to be universally spoken, it's quite conceivable that they will mostly be used for formal purposes, with African languages still preferred for interethnic communication in everyday life. This may sound unlikely to Europeans and North Americans, but it's a common enough pattern in places with an extensive linguistic menu. The clearest example is perhaps Suriname, where alongside a dozen minority languages there are two commonly spoken lingua francas, one perceived to be formal (Dutch, the official language), the other informal (Sranan, originally of the Creole minority).

If, in accordance with the global trend, linguistic diversity is decreasing in Africa, this is due not so much to the VILs replacing the lingua francas, but rather to the lingua francas driving the smaller mother tongues to extinction. Africans may be adept at learning languages, but they don't mind learning fewer languages if that's enough to meet their communication needs. They are pragmatic rather than passionate polyglots.

With some exceptions, of course, such as Jonas. His eight languages were always remarkable, even for Cameroon. Which makes me wonder: assuming that Jonas today has children – not with Gogo, for his courtship was ultimately unsuccessful – how many languages have *they* learnt? Unfortunately, researcher Leslie C. Moore doesn't know. I would love to ask him.

11

German

DEUTSCH

200 million speakers

German has about 100 million native speakers and a further 100 million who use it as a second language. It is native to Germany, Austria, Luxembourg and two-thirds of Switzerland. German-speaking communities exist in most neighbouring countries, Romania, Namibia, the US, Argentina and Brazil.

German

SELF-DESIGNATION Deutsch, Hochdeutsch.

FAMILY As its English name suggests, German belongs to the Germanic branch of the Indo-European family.

SCRIPT German is written in the Latin alphabet. *Ä, ö, ü* and *ß,* while frequent, are not considered separate letters and may be replaced by *ae*, *oe*, *ue* and *ss*. Until 1941, a black-letter or Gothic script known as Fraktur was in general use.

GRAMMAR While Old German and Old English were very similar, German nouns, adjectives and verbs have retained many more of the endings that both languages used to have. Like English, German is fond of making compound nouns; unlike English, it writes them without spaces, resulting in monsters such as the notorious *Rindfleischetikettierungsüberwachungsaufgabenübertragungsgesetz*, which was part of the name of an actual law, repealed in 2013. For more on grammar, see the main story.

SOUNDS Like other Germanic languages, German has a fairly high number of different vowel sounds: fifteen to twenty. The number of consonant sounds, twenty-five, is more average.

LOANWORDS Traditionally from Latin, French, Greek; nowadays English.

IMPORTS *angst*, *bratwurst*, *doppelganger*, *ersatz*, *hinterland*, *kindergarten*, *pretzel*, *realpolitik*, *schadenfreude*, *statistics*, *sauerkraut*, *weltanschauung*, *zeitgeist*. In linguistics: *urheimat* and *sprachbund*.

FAKE NEWS In view of the country's large German-speaking minority, US Congress in 1795 considered the option of having all laws translated into German. The proposal was rejected by an unknown margin. This event has somehow led to the modern legend that German narrowly (by one vote, it is often claimed) failed to become the official language of the US. This never happened.

11: **German**

An eccentric in Central Europe

I heard lately of a worn and sorely tried American student who used to fly to a certain German word for relief when he could bear up under his aggravations no longer – the only word whose sound was sweet and precious to his ear and healing to his lacerated spirit. This was the word damit. *It was only the sound that helped him, not the meaning (it merely means, in its general sense, 'herewith'); and so, at last, when he learned that the emphasis was not on the first syllable, his only stay and support was gone, and he faded away and died.*

THE AWFUL GERMAN LANGUAGE, MARK TWAIN

Of the three foreign languages most commonly taught in British and American schools – French, German and Spanish – German is widely considered the most difficult. A mind-numbing back-breaker, that's how it's looked upon; not so much a brain-teaser as a brain-bully. Nor is it just the English-speaking part of the world that thinks so. The Scandinavians and Dutch do likewise, even though compared to English, their languages are much more similar to German. (I like to call Dutch 'German for beginners', and that's only half in jest.) Indeed, the Germans themselves seem to agree with the outside world, seeing how frequently they say, '*deutsche Sprache, schwere Sprache*' ('German language, difficult language'). Self-flattery may have something to do with it – we all like to believe we excel at something that others can't do – but the wide consensus suggests there must be a certain amount of truth to it.

Could the explanation be that German is very much *unlike* other languages? After all, anything unfamiliar takes getting used to, requires hard work. Different sounds, different words, different grammar: they're all stumbling blocks. So could German simply be an outlier, an anomaly or, not putting too fine a point on it, a weirdo?

Bricks in the WALS

To find out, let's look at an article by American linguist Tyler Schnoebelen, in which he statistically separates the world's weirdos from the average Joes. He does this by using a publicly available database called the World Atlas of Linguistic Structures (*wals.info*). Think of this database as a huge spreadsheet, in which each column represents a linguistic feature – presence or absence of nasal vowels, say, or order of subject, object and verb – while each row represents a language, from Aari in Southern Ethiopia to Zuni in New Mexico. WALS includes 192 features and 2,679 languages, so if we were to print the spreadsheet, it would be truly gigantic. Even if we made the cells just one centimetre wide and half a centimetre high, the whole thing would still cover a two-metre wide wall standing five storeys tall. Unfortunately, it would also be over 80 per cent empty, as most languages have only a few dozen filled-in cells – or bricks in the WALS, as I like to call them.

Schnoebelen does not take all 192 features into consideration, because many of them are logically correlated with each other. For instance, a language with many different vowels (WALS feature number 1) is also likely to have a high vowel-consonant ratio (feature 3), whereas this ratio will be lower when there are few vowels present. Taking both features into account would give undue weight to what is for statistical purposes just one characteristic. There are many cases like this, and they could easily skew the overall picture. (He doesn't entirely avoid this pitfall, as we'll see.)

To that end instead of 192 features, a mere twenty-one are included, spread across grammar, phonology and vocabulary. As most cells in the WALS spreadsheet are empty, very few languages – eighteen to be exact – boast the full twenty-one 'bricks', and since such a small sample would not be representative of the world's linguistic variety, Schnoebelen lowers the bar. By setting the minimum number of bricks per language at fourteen, he gets a set of 239 languages, among which we encounter fifteen of the Babel Twenty; the five that don't make the cut are Bengali, Javanese, Portuguese, Punjabi and Tamil. The next step consists in crunching the numbers, to get a weirdness index for each of the 239, which may range from nearly 0 for outrageously bizarre to 1 for extremely banal. Finally, they're all ranked from 0 to 1: bizarre at the top, banal at the bottom. So just to be clear: low figures reflect rarity, and are placed at the top of the weirdness 'chart'.

Is German a weird language? At least it no longer looks weird – as in this pre-war primer, when Gothic scripts were the norm.

The weirdness ranking for fifteen of the Babel languages*

LANGUAGE	NUMBER OF FEATURES	WEIRDNESS INDEX (WI)
German	20	0.144
Spanish	21	0.211
English	21	0.244
French	20	0.246
Arabic (Egyptian)	19	0.259
Japanese	20	0.264
Vietnamese	18	0.325
Mandarin**	21	0.342
Persian	19	0.351
Swahili	19	0.441
Korean	19	0.546
Russian	21	0.599
Indonesian	21	0.755
Turkish	21	0.786
Hindi-Urdu	17	0.913

* data for the other 5 are too incomplete
** I have corrected one obvious error in the data for Mandarin. In the original article, it was 0.212.
Source: corplinguistics.wordpress.com, blogpost 'The weirdest languages' (published 21 June 2016) and the file weirdness_index_values_full_list.xlsx.

Before we turn to German, let's briefly look at the extremes. In the nether regions, we find not some small, out-of-the-way dialect no-one's ever heard of, but a familiar character – indeed, one of Babel's biggest: Hindi-Urdu. Its index is no less than 0.913, making it fascinatingly uninteresting. Also down there in the boring bottom ten are two languages that may come as even bigger surprises: Hungarian and Basque, considered by most Europeans to be wild, wayward and whimsical rather than plain vanilla.

The top weirdo, with an index of just 0.028, *is* a small dialect, kept alive by only a few thousand people: the Mixtec language as spoken in the Mexican district of Chalcatongo. In spite of its extremely low index, it's not bizarre across the board. Of its 17 features, 11 are entirely unremarkable, attaining the maximum score of 1. It owes its gold medal to three very exceptional features, each with a score under 0.1, and especially to its unique way of turning statements into questions. Of all the 955 languages for which WALS includes information about this feature, Chalcatongo Mixtec is the only one not to make any distinction between statements and questions. For instance, the sentence *ñábaʔaró librúro*, pronounced with the same intonation – same pitch, same volume, everything identical – can mean both 'You have your book' or 'Do you have your book?' It really makes one wonder how do they do it.

The Mixtec dialect is among only 6 languages with an index of under 0.1, nearly all of them small. The only one with more than a few thousand speakers is Eastern Oromo, of Central Ethiopia, which has millions. The first language in the list that might, at a stretch, be called European, is Armenian, in ninth position. And just a nose length behind, its index a mere 0.003 higher, coming in as number ten, we find ... *Deutsch*. So German *is* a weirdo. It looks as if Mark Twain and all the complaining students are on to something.

Seven decisive features

What is so exceptional about German? Remarkably, on ten features, it scores a resounding 1 – perfectly banal, in other words; solidly part of the herd. But it has no fewer than 7 features where it scores lower than 0.33, setting it well apart. Let's take those in turns.

1 Yes–no questions

To make a question out of a statement, German typically inverts the order of subject and verb. A statement such as *wir trinken Bier* in the question form becomes *trinken wir Bier?* As long as you translate the sentence as 'we are drinking beer', this method will appear natural, because English does likewise – 'are we drinking beer?' However, another legitimate translation of the German statement would be 'we drink beer', which as a question of course becomes 'do we drink beer?' If you say 'drink we beer?' you may still be understood, especially if your intonation is interrogative, but it will get you strange looks. In spite of this fairly fundamental difference, WALS places English and German in the same category here, which is that of 'interrogative word order'. This earns both of them a very low 0.023, because changing the word order is an exceedingly rare way of forming questions, except in Europe.

2 Ng

German words can have an /ng/ sound in the middle and at the end of a word, but not at the start: *ring, angst* and *finger* are legitimate German words (meaning exactly what they appear to mean), but there can be no *ngatwurst* to rhyme with *bratwurst*. African and East Asian languages think nothing of starting a word in /ng/ (remember *ngoko* in chapter 16?), but German phonology won't have it. Nor does English phonology, for that matter, so both languages get the same score, 0.319.

3 Rare consonants

Few languages have consonants pronounced with the back of the tongue near the uvula, which is the small fleshy bit dangling from the back of your palate. And even if they do, it's usually a stop (/t/ and /p/ are stops), not a continuous sound, like /s/ and /n/ are (not that any of these are anywhere near the uvula). Thanks to the /kh/ sound of Bach (which is also how Liverpudlians pronounce *back*), German is a member of this very select group: only 11 out of 567 languages have it. This earns it a very low score of 0.026. English too stands its ground fairly well in the funny consonants department thanks to the /th/ sounds of *thin* and *this*, earning it a respectably low 0.089.

4 Always a subject

The subject of a German verb must always be made explicit by the use of either a noun or a pronoun. A noun can be replaced by a pronoun, but this cannot be dropped, except in imperatives and in the most colloquial forms of speech: *Ja, komm schon*, 'Yeah, coming', would be short and very informal for *Ja, ich komme schon*, 'Yes, I'm coming'. This compulsory presence of a noun or pronoun is a rare phenomenon worldwide, since most of the world's languages think nothing of either leaving the pronoun implicit or integrating it into the verb. German earns itself another low score of 0.190 here – and yet again, so does English.

5 Gender in pronouns

German has separate words for 'he', 'she' and 'it': ER, SIE and ES. From a global perspective, that's far less common than we might think. Another low score here for all Germanic, indeed for most European languages: 0.246.

6/7 Complicated word order

Complicated rules for word order play a large part in earning German its tenth spot in the weirdness index. If a main clause does not begin with the subject, it postpones the subject until after the first verb. So while *ich sehe sie* has the same word order as our 'I see her', this changes as soon as you start the phrase with, say, 'there': *dort sehe ich sie* – literally 'there see I her'. And that's not the end of it, because subordinate clauses are different again. Here, the verb doesn't turn up until the very end, invariably hugging the full stop: *ich denke, dass ich sie dort sehe*, 'I think that I her there see'. This may sound like chaos, but it obeys strict rules. German scores a 0.148 here, while English, with its extremely common subject-verb-object order, gets a full 1.0.

Somewhat unfairly, Schnoebelen has also included a category 'placement of negation', in other words: where does a language insert the word 'not' in its sentences? German treats *nicht* more

Germany's new language museum at Bad Hersfeld. Its name, wortreich, means both 'rich in words' and 'empire of words'.

or less as if it were an object (which indeed it once was), moving it about in the way just described: *Ich gehe nicht dorthin; Dorthin gehe ich nicht; Ich glaube, dass ich nicht dorthin gehe* ('I go not there'; 'There go I not'; 'I believe that I not there go'). This lands it an even lower score of 0.043. The reason why I feel this is unfair is because the two features are obviously correlated. It's a case of 'double jeopardy', a lawyer might say.

Three messages

Now admittedly, all of this is not linguistics at its most scientific, nor does Schnoebelen claim it to be: his article is not a peer-reviewed publication in a scholarly journal, but merely an intelligent and well-argued blogpost attempting to answer a popular question, 'which languages are weirdest?' The WALS data, though they're frequently used by reputable scholars, are not always reliable. Also, it's hard to tell if a mere twenty-one features can be truly representative of the full linguistic variety to be found in a wide world full of wonders. Nearly all languages, even German, score 0.9 or more (in other words, 'entirely unremarkable') on most features, so that very low scores on just a few other features make a huge difference for the index and the final ranking. This probably explains why close sisters such as Spanish and Italian are very far apart (23 and 198, respectively), as are Czech and Polish (21 and 112).

But against these caveats, we can point out that Schnoebelen's conclusion does fit a pattern. Another linguist, Michael Cysouw, also delved into the WALS data with a similar question on his mind. And while he went about the exercise rather differently, at least one of his conclusions was very similar: the languages of Northwestern Europe (Dutch, English, French, Frisian and German) are outliers, and none more so than German. Unlike Schnoebelen, he did report on his findings in a scholarly book, aptly titled *Expecting the Unexpected* and published by a highly respectable publisher.

Whether or not the Germanic languages as a group (as well as French, under Germanic influence) really deserve to end up as such weirdos, the whole exercise brings home a few useful messages. First of all, it shows that English, German and the rest of the family have several characteristics that really make them stand out from the global crowd. Hardly ever dropping a pronoun is something that you and I might feel is natural, but in point of fact, it's extremely unusual, and the same is true for reversing the order of subject and verb to ask a question.

Secondly, it turns out that German, while indeed weird, is not much more so than English. Among the Germanic languages included in the sample, English may be the most 'normal' (Schnoebelen puts it in position 33), but that isn't saying much. Spanish is only slightly (-0.033) weirder than English, and French is practically level (+0.002). Some notoriously singular Babel languages such as Arabic (Egyptian Arabic, to be precise: +0.015) and Japanese (+0.020) are in the same league as English, whereas Korean, Russian and Turkish are much nearer the bottom of the list, with indices 0.302, 0.355 and 0.542 higher than English, even though we tend to think of them as strange and difficult languages. The weirdness index of Hindi-Urdu, the most boring one of the bunch, differs no less than 0.669 from that of English.

All of which informs message number three: weirdness, at least as measured in this research, correlates only very weakly, if at all, with difficulty of learning. Partly, that will be because we come to these languages from a Germanic, and therefore from an objectively odd, perspective. But more importantly, some of the things that make languages hard – irregular verbs, irregular plurals, a case system, tone – are not the same things that make them weird.

So why *is* German such a darned hard nut to crack, if it's not due to its weirdness?

Wait, not so fast. The weirdness index *does* help to answer the question. German has just about the weirdest rules for word order

'The Modern Grammar': whatever linguists may say, the real syntax of spoken German is 'subject, predicate, insult, mate (*Alter*)!'

imaginable. That's a major obstacle because whatever you're saying, you always need to put your words in some order. To quote an erudite British author of my acquaintance: 'In English one can embark on a sentence with no very clear idea of the destination, but with German we find we can't really improvise in that way. We have to have a clear notion of what we're going to say before we try to say it, and we have to get the clauses in the right order.' Unquestionably that's what he and most other non-native speakers of German *find* – but it's a very different story for the Germans themselves. In their mother tongue, they can and will ad lib like nobody's business, starting on sentences without having thought them through till the end. That's how humans in most situations talk, and the Germans are no exception. Indeed, they feel that it's *English* that forces them to plan their utterances more carefully, because one must bring to the front parts of speech (such as the subject and the verb) which one would often rather put towards the end. I'm speaking from personal experience here, for while my mother tongue is Dutch, not German, word order is largely identical in the two languages.

Still, *most* of the difficulties of German are unrelated to Schnoebelen's findings. His weirdness index reflects abstract linguistic concepts. Difficulty for learners, on the other hand, is often hidden in the nitty-gritty, the spadework of learning all that unaccustomed vocabulary and all those damnable irregularities – and German is well-provided (or infested, if you like) with both. Take the example of case: roughly equal numbers of languages have and don't have a case system, so there's nothing exceptional about it either way. But even if you're familiar with the case system of your own language, it's still hard work to familiarise yourself with that of another, which is different in its endings and precise application. When learning Russian or German, even Turks suffer. Moreover, every noun in German (as in Russian, Latin and many other languages) has one of three genders, which makes it somewhat harder to master than French and its relatives, which have two.

So is German weird? Oh yes. Is it hard to learn if you come from English? Yes, for a Germanic language, it's remarkably difficult, and probably harder than Spanish and French, with all their familiar vocabulary. But I would say it's not *quite* as hard as it's cracked up to be. Most of the twenty Babel languages would definitely require more effort. The thing is, German has a reputation. To quote the same British author again: 'Endemic anti-Germanism might play a part there.'

10

French

FRANÇAIS

250 million speakers

80 million native speakers, mostly in France, Canada, Belgium, Switzerland and the Caribbean. Second-language speakers number about twice as many, with numbers growing in most former African colonies but declining steeply in Europe.

French

SELF-DESIGNATION Français.

FAMILY A member of the Romance group of the Indo-European family, French displays more Germanic influence than its fellow members.

SCRIPT Latin alphabet. The acute and grave accents are frequent (é, è); the circumflex, diaeresis and cedilla less so (ê, ë, ç). French spelling is notoriously complex.

GRAMMAR As a Latin-derived language, French is fairly rich in inflection, especially of verbs (tense, mood, person, et cetera) and adjectives (gender, number). However, much of this inflection involves silent letters, and therefore can only be distinguished in writing.

SOUNDS French has some twenty consonant sounds and rather more vowel sounds than most Romance languages: around fifteen, including three or four nasals. Word stress is weak. Silent word-final consonants may be pronounced when followed by a word that commences with a vowel.

LOANWORDS Frankish (Germanic), Italian, Greek, Latin (literary borrowings), English.

EXPORTS English has been borrowing from French for a thousand years. Depending on how you count, between a quarter and half of all English words are of French origin.

CAJUN AND ACADIAN Cajun, a shortening of *Acadian*, is world-famous today as a cooking and music style from Louisiana, the US state named after King Louis XIV. But it is also used informally (not by linguists) to refer to the French language natively spoken in the state by over 150,000 people. Originally, *Acadian* referred to the Acadia region in Eastern Canada, from where many French speakers fled to Louisiana in the eighteenth century. Today, Acadian French is still spoken by over 300,000 people in a rather smaller area, most of it belonging to New Brunswick (Nouveau-Brunswick), but including some towns in Maine (US).

10: **French**

Death to la différence!

France is a country of delicious diversity. It boasts about 400 types of cheese, over 300 wines with an *appellation d'origine contrôlée* and a cuisine that distinguishes at least a dozen regional cooking styles. The scenic diversity of its landscapes is broadcast the world over in an annual Visit France campaign cleverly disguised as a three-week bike race. The country's linguistic delights are not to be sneezed at either: its 65 million people speak at least twelve French dialects, about eight other regional languages and dozens of migrant languages – and that's without including the French territories outside Europe.

The French are justly proud of this diversity. In Paris alone there are more than a hundred speciality shops offering a range of cheeses from all regions. The *appellations contrôlées* are implemented by an august *institut national.* When it comes to fine, finer and finest gastronomy, the Michelin guides represent the leading authority.

With languages, though, it's different – linguistic diversity gives many French people the willies. A cheese may stink to high heavens and still be considered a delicacy. A wine displaying tones of tar and hints of hay is admired for it. Serve bull's brain or sea urchins and the guests will lick their lips. A newborn with an Arabic or Breton name, however, triggers a very different reaction.

In the 1990s, a registrar in the Provence region denied French parents of my acquaintance the right to name their baby girl Naïma (of Arabic and Hebrew provenance), which is why she now goes through life under the proper French name of Céline, or so her passport would have us believe. As recently as 2017, parents in Quimper were sued for having registered their son as Fañch, which is a common name in Brittany. The judge could no longer force them to call the little chap François, as would have been standard practice until 1966. But the tilde had to go, he ruled, so the name became Fanch. Why? Because accepting the tilde 'would be tantamount to breaking the will of our rule of law to maintain the unity of the country and equality without distinction of origin', the judge declared. Not that his decision did much for the unity of the country. It was met with disbelief and outrage, showing that his nineteenth-century views are not shared by the whole of France, and was later reversed. Even in *la France profonde*, where babies even today get given names like Jules and Jeanne, few people care for such linguistic fundamentalism.

So who does agree with the judge? That would be the conservative majority of the highly centralist establishment, based in Paris and other centres of power, as well as those aspiring to it. They are the main determining force behind the linguistic culture of France and even the French-speaking world, as reflected in education, serious media and government policy.

Laissez-faire, laissez-parler

The establishment's preoccupation with the national language is of much more recent date than the country's linguistic diversity. In the last centuries before the common era, the major tongue of today's France was Gaulish, a member of the Celtic family. But something akin to Basque was spoken in a large area in the southwest, and a Greek dialect on the south coast, by the same people who planted the first vines on French soil. The island of Corsica meanwhile was a jumble of languages, including Phoenician, Etruscan, Greek and probably some others that are now lost to history, until Romanisation began in the third century BCE.

In the second and first centuries Gaul gradually became a Roman province, enabling the Latin language to conquer Gallic society and Gallic cheeses to conquer Latin cuisine. After the fall of Rome, traditionally dated at 476, the Frankish kings established a power base in the northeast that would gradually expand, but their Germanic language was nonetheless destined to be outdone by (Gallic) Latin. In the northwest, Celtic refugees from England introduced Breton.

Throughout the Middle Ages, regional diversity increased apace. This is true for food and drink – Brie has been produced since Charlemagne's day, Roquefort came soon after and the regional wine styles too can be traced back to this era – and also for Latin, which diverged into a wide range of dialects. Only much later would these cluster into French, Occitan, Corsican, Catalan and Franco-Provençal. The Basques and Bretons were also sticking around, and people living on the borders of the realm spoke Germanic dialects, which today would be labelled German and Dutch.

Within this patchwork, one dialect was favoured by fortune: that spoken in Île de France, the region around Paris. This is where the Frankish king established his capital in the sixth century, and as in several other European countries, the court dialect would lay the foundation for the standard language. This process stretched over hundreds of years, and Latin remained France's official written language until 1539. In that year, King François I signed the Ordinance of Villers-Cotterêts into law. Henceforth, all official documents had to be written *en langage maternel françois* – 'in the French mother tongue'. Or in a French mother tongue, for that's another legitimate interpretation. If the Basques preferred to write (and speak, of course) in Basque and the Provençals in Provençal, well, let them. As long as it wasn't in Latin. And as long as letters to Paris were in something resembling French closely enough for the chancellery to be able to get the gist.

To spot *les ignorans*

This shift from Latin to the vernacular was not uniquely French, but rather a secular trend that spread from south to north, having started in Spain and Italy. French did become exceptional, however, in the seventeenth and eighteenth centuries. From 1610 to 1792, kings Louis XIII, XIV, XV and XVI ruled the country in an absolute, 'l'État, c'est moi' manner. They were one-man powerhouses, the radiant centres of the realm and the standards of good taste in all things, from etiquette to architecture, from haute cuisine to haute couture, from parties to poetry – and also, of course, in *le bon usage*, the correct use of the French language.

But just as courtly manners were not adopted by every French citizen, so the king's French did not spread to all six corners of the country. (France thinks of itself as a hexagon.) Of 20 million people, perhaps a million courtiers, aristocrats, well-to-do *bourgeois*, scholars and literary types knew how to speak according to *la Norme*, the standard. The peasants and craftsmen of the countryside hardly understood this variety, if at all. Their speech was generically labelled *patois*, a word that can be translated as 'dialect(s)', but with undertones of backwardness.

As courtly French became the official language of the realm, it was being strapped into an ever tighter straitjacket of rules. This was yet another Western European trend, but France embraced it with more ardour and determination than any of its neighbours. Or to put it more accurately, the centralist establishment did, for this is the time when it grabbed linguistic control, never to let go again. In 1635 the Académie Française was established and tasked with rendering the French language 'pure and eloquent', and turning it into 'the Latin of modernity' – in other words, a well-regulated language for an international elite.

Ever since, the standardisation of French has been inseparably linked with Vaugelas – Claude Favre de Vaugelas, to use his full name. A founding member of the Academy, he undertook the Herculean labour of composing the first official dictionary. Though the dictionary wasn't completed until 1694, forty-four years after his death, Vaugelas exerted an immense influence on the language through his style guide, titled *Remarques sur la langue française*. As shown by the *Remarques*, Vaugelas's love of regulation was all-consuming.

To give one example, he decided that the dictionary should only contain words that were suitable for conversation at court and in the literary *salons*. A mere 24,000 passed muster; more than 15,000 did not. Many of the *refusés* were considered too specialised, and listed in a separate publication. Others were adjudged to be too colloquial, including ÉPINGLE (pin) and POITRINE for 'women's breast' (for 'chest' or 'animal breast', it was okay). Yet others were felt to be outdated, such as IMMENSE and ANGOISSE (immense, anguish), which even today are not particularly old-fashioned.

The regulator: Claude Favre de Vaugelas of the Académie Française, author of the first French dictionary.

Vaugelas had been dead for a generation and the dictionary's completion was almost coming into view when the Academy was struck by the idea of creating order in the spelling, which had hitherto been a happy anarchy. Unfortunately for today's schoolchildren, the men commissioned with this task felt strongly about adhering to etymology and much less so about rendering contemporary pronunciation. Spellings based on Latin and Greek, one *académicien* unabashedly declared, would help '*distingue[r] les gens de Lettres d'avec les ignorans et les simple femmes*' – in other words, distinguish the elite from the rabble and women. This morbid fascination with dead languages saddled French with loads of silent consonants as in

CORPS (body), TEMPS (time, weather), POULMONS (lungs), PTISANE (herbal tea), TESTE (head) and thousands more. Some words were later simplified (TISANE, TÊTE), but most were not – and some were even made harder (GENS and IGNORANS are now spelt GENTS and IGNORANTS, with silent *t*'s). One result has been that French spelling is now almost as erratic as English.

The Academy set itself up to enforce correct enunciation too. But just as its prescribed spelling gradually changed through the ages, so too did the recommended pronunciation. For instance, should final *l*'s and *r*'s be silent or not? Blithely unconcerned with actual practice, authoritative advice flipped back and forth for a while, leaving a somewhat messy outcome: the final consonant should be audible in FINIR, MINEUR and BEL (finish, minor, beautiful), but it should be silent in MANGER, MONSIEUR and OUTIL (eat, mister, tool). Remarkably, most French speakers today believe that their language has been a paragon of stability ever since the days of the Sun King. That illusion is carefully maintained: whenever a spelling reform takes hold, publishers stock bookshops with new, respelt editions of the classics.

One thing the Academy omitted to do was codify French grammar.* This gap was filled by the *Grammaire de Port-Royal* of 1660, so called after the abbey near Paris where its two authors lived. Or, to give it its full title, the *Grammaire générale et raisonnée contenant les fondemens de l'art de parler, expliqués d'une manière claire et naturelle* (general and rational grammar, containing the fundamentals of the art of speaking, explained in a clear and natural manner.) Like spelling, French grammar has been a minefield ever since. The following is a quote from a letter accompanying the text of a new play, sent by its author to the prominent grammarian Dominique Bouhours: 'I beseech you, my Reverend Father, to take the trouble of reading it, and to mark the errors I may have committed against the language of which you are one of the most excellent masters.' Thus wrote Jean Racine, perhaps the greatest writer of the age (though admittedly only budding at the time).

---

* The Academy wouldn't publish a grammar until 1932, almost three centuries later. It was a dud. The critics shook off their reverence for the institute and lambasted the book as a dismal failure. The Academy has never made a second attempt.

Only the French can properly be said to speak

As the capital of Europe's most powerful and populous country by far, seventeenth-century Paris – and its Versailles exclave – was the unrivalled cultural model for the courts, aristocracies, bourgeoisie, and scholarly and literary circles in much of Europe. The French standard language spread to Brussels, Amsterdam, Copenhagen, Stockholm, Berlin, Vienna and Moscow. It also became the language of choice in European, and later global, diplomacy.

Languages of high prestige can easily be mistaken for being superior languages, exceptionally rich and harmonious or even divine. Many a speaker and writer of Greek, Chinese, Sanskrit, Latin, Arabic and English has fallen into this trap, and those of French haven't managed to avoid it either (nor do they seem to have tried very hard). For one thing, the French elite has loved what it considers their language's outstanding beauty. Bouhours, Racine's grammatical role model, wrote in 1671, 'Of all languages, French has the most natural and sleekest pronunciation. The Chinese and well-nigh all Asian peoples sing; the Germans grumble; the Spaniards holler; the Italians sigh; the English whistle. Only the French can properly be said to speak.' Even today, *la belle langue* is, like *la langue de Molière,* routinely used as a synonym for 'French'.

The French elite attributed yet another trait to their language, one that in this period of Enlightenment was valued more highly than godliness: logic. The claim was perhaps most famously defended by Antoine de Rivarol (1753–1801) on grounds that were both illogical and plain wrong. He argued that the French word order (subject first, followed by verb and then object) is both unique and more logical than any other. But not only is it extremely common among the world's languages, including English, it's also an order that French itself very often does not respect – and these are only some of the more obvious objections. As silly as it is, the notion of 'French as the pinnacle of logic' became another *idée reçue.* The cover of my parents' French dictionary, published in the 1950s (outside France), claimed that the language was 'an unsurpassed creation as a vehicle for the mind'.

Extirpation of the patois

During the French Revolution, very different fates awaited the last King Louis and his illustrious language: one was sent to the guillotine, the other placed on a pedestal. The king, so the argument went, was a relic from the past and had better be removed. The standard language, however, was deemed to be of vital importance for the future of the republic. These were the early days of a new ideology, nationalism, which forged a strong link between three phenomena formerly seen as loosely related at best: state, nation and language. 'In a free people, the language has to be one and the same for all', the revolutionary Bertrand Barère declared. The 'barbaric yammer' and 'rude lingos' of the countryside 'merely serve the fanatics and counterrevolutionaries'.

The new rulers set about tackling the linguistic 'remnants of feudal backwardness'. A survey conducted by Henri Grégoire, a member of the revolutionary National Convention, found that French was the common people's everyday language in only fifteen out of 83 departments, and that only one citizen out of eight was capable of speaking the language, with another one in four being able to understand it. This had to change, Grégoire argued, because only then would 'all citizens (...) be able to mutually communicate their thoughts unimpeded'. In the countryside, he felt, the regional languages were perpetuating the servitude in which the Ancien Régime had kept the peasants. Because 'ignorance of the language could compromise social happiness and destroy equality',* it was imperative to 'annihilate' the patois. The idea that citizens might speak their regional languages *alongside* French is never mentioned – which is very strange, given that this must have been commonplace among the members of the National Convention, who represented every region of France.

On 20 July 1794, some six weeks after the publication of Grégoire's findings, new legal provisions and sanctions were introduced in order to impose linguistic unification. Henceforth, all official documents – contracts, records, regulations, you name it – had

---

* President Charles de Gaulle seems to have considered *any* diversity, not just of the linguistic kind, an obstacle to efficient governance. 'How can one rule a country which has 246 varieties of cheese?' he quipped in 1962.

AUX ÉLÈVES DES ÉCOLES

IL EST DÉFENDU

1° DE PARLER BRETON ET DE CRACHER A TERRE;

2° DE MOUILLER SES DOIGTS DANS SA BOUCHE pour tourner les pages des livres et des cahiers;

3° D'INTRODUIRE DANS SON OREILLE le bout d'un porte-plume ou d'un crayon;

4° D'ESSUYER LES ARDOISES EN CRACHANT DESSUS ou en y portant directement la langue;

5° DE TENIR DANS SA BOUCHE les portes-plumes, les crayons, les pièces de monnaies, etc.;

Voulez-vous savoir maintenant pourquoi ces défenses vous sont faites ? Demandez-le à vos maîtres qui vous donneront les explications nécessaires.

Catch them young. An early twentieth-century prohibition to Breton schoolchildren against uttering a word of their native language. Or putting their pencils in their ears.

to be written in French. Disobedient officials risked dismissal and six months' imprisonment. But this looming *terreur linguistique* never materialised, because just one week later the leader of the greater Reign of Terror, Maximilien Robespierre, was overthrown and beheaded.

In the chaos of the subsequent years, linguistic policy did not figure highly on the list of priorities. Under Napoleon, France shifted its energies to fighting battles across Europe, and as long as soldiers followed orders barked in French, the populace was allowed to speak any patois they liked. What did survive, however, was the nationalist ideology of one country, one people, one language. It was destined to travel far and wide, conquering Europe in the nineteenth century and the world in the twentieth. In some mild form, it's almost certainly an element of your own world-view, especially if you live in a country of long standing.

Speak French, be clean

In the long run, of course, standard French would prevail. Military conscription, introduced in 1872, brought together boys from all over the country, so speaking nothing but patois would no longer do. Compulsory education was introduced in 1882, with the teaching of French to every citizen as one of the explicit aims. Mass media reinforced what had been learnt at school and in the army.

This paralleled developments elsewhere in Europe, but France remained exceptional. Unlike their counterparts in Britain, Italy or Germany, the French establishment campaigned vehemently against the dialects and minority tongues. Publications in languages other than French were officially labelled 'foreign' and regularly banned or seized. In Algeria, which for more than a hundred years was as integral a part of the République as Brittany or Corsica, even Arabic was 'foreign', and hence unwelcome. Schoolchildren were not allowed to speak patois in class or in the playground. In Brittany, they were 'forbidden to speak Breton or spit on the floor', as classroom rules put it. Elsewhere, banners admonished children to 'speak French, be clean' ('Parlez français, soyez propre').

Today's French attitudes towards their language may have lost some of their sharper edges, but they are still curious from a non-Francophone perspective. There is a widespread belief among people speaking French as their mother tongue that they make a deplorably poor job of it.

The seeming paradox of native speakers believing themselves to be inadequate speakers is easily explained. It's an undeniable fact that their everyday speech is at variance with the strict rules of traditional grammar. Elsewhere in Europe, when there's a clash between practice and prescripts, traditionalists put up a fight to defend the latter, but new generations move on and stop paying attention, making it a rearguard battle. In twenty-first-century English, few people get worked up about usages such as 'who have you met?', or replying 'yes, I will' in response to 'will you?', though some will still write letters to the editor insisting on 'whom' and 'shall', respectively. (The same fate will undoubtedly befall my own pet peeves, such as singular 'media'.) But French traditionalists are made of sterner stuff. If official grammar has changed since the Revolution, I haven't been able to find evidence of it. Of course, this constancy hasn't stopped everyday speech from evolving as

Mission civilisatrice – spreading the French language through the colonial lands, in this photo Algeria c.1860.

it does anywhere and any time. Speech and writing have diverged quite substantially as a result.

A few examples may illustrate the abyss. Standard French distinguishes a large numbers of relative pronouns: QUE, QUI, OÙ, DONT and four forms of LEQUEL; colloquial French mostly uses the first three, with a particularly liking for QUE. Standard French turns statements (*Elle est contente*, 'She is happy') into questions by inversion, that is, by changing the order of subject and verb: *Est-elle contente?*, 'Is she happy?', as English does (in some cases anyway). But in an informal conversation, this is passé. Defenders of standard French will, in a lenient mood, grudgingly allow for the use of the phrase EST-CE QUE as a question marker: *Est-ce qu'elle est contente*, 'Is she happy'? While this is indeed commonly used in daily life, it's at least as common to say, '*Elle est heureuse?*' Here the question is marked by rising intonation; in writing down this colloquial sentence, the question mark will do the trick. But standard grammar will have none of it. One last example: French negations typically require two elements, the general negative NE and a more specific negative such as PAS (not), PERSONNE (nobody) or NULLE PART (nowhere). Everyday speech will leave out many of these NE's, entrusting the task of negation completely to the other element. Again, official grammar rejects this – leading to the amusing situation that while English double negatives are rejected for being 'illogical', their French counterparts are considered essential.

Radicalisation at the top

Since the 1960s, much has changed in the linguistic landscape of many Western countries. Our speech and writing have grown more informal, both in private and in the media. The taboo on regional accents has been on the wane. Minority languages have seen a marked revival: speaking Welsh, Scots, Catalan, Low German or Frisian is no longer a source of shame but a source of pride and a badge of identity.

French society hasn't been immune to these changes. Basque, Breton, Catalan, Corsican, Alsatian and Occitan have witnessed a resurgence, and thanks to regional authorities they're now even used and taught in some schools. Regional accents can be heard on national radio and television, especially in sports news, weather forecasts and popular programmes.

That said, France still has its guardians of the language, and they continue to preach, correct and advise. Language has remained an important part of the centralist establishment's identity, and their political and cultural dominance is still strong. Nor is their cultural influence limited to France. It extends to the surrounding 'half countries' (part of Belgium, part of Switzerland, part of the time in Luxembourg) as well as the former colonies, thanks to La Francophonie, the French equivalent of the Commonwealth.

While English, German, Spanish, Portuguese and Dutch are pluricentric languages, meaning they accept somewhat different standards in different countries, all of the French world looks to France for linguistic guidance, and all of France looks to Paris. People speaking with an accent that does not strictly meet *la Norme* may become sports commentators or game show hosts, but not newsreaders or reporters on radio and TV. A young man from Tarn in the South, wishing to study radio journalism, was asked by a member of the admissions committee, 'Did you *really* believe you could make it in this profession with an accent like that?' Québécois journalist Sabrina Myre, who worked hard to minimise her accent while studying in Paris, would be allowed to report on French national radio – but only from Canada. Unfortunately, she was based in Jerusalem, so French radio turned her down. Not the right *appellation d'origine contrôlée*.

In some respects, the conservative centralist establishment has radicalised in recent decades. For one thing, they have enshrined their traditional rejection of regional languages in law. The constitution of 1992 was the first to declare French to be 'the language of the Republic'. These words in Article 2 may sound like a statement of plain fact, but judges have interpreted them in a highly restrictive manner. After President Chirac signed the European Charter for Regional and Minority Languages, the Constitutional Court stopped the government from ratifying it. Recognition of, and support for, other languages would undermine the position of French, the judges argued. Just to put this into perspective: about 3 per cent of the population speaks a (non-immigrant) language that is neither French nor a dialect of it.

When the constitution was amended in 2008, the Senate accepted that the regional languages are 'part of France's heritage', but refused to include this in article 2; article 75 was good enough for them. When a more liberal government in 2015 pushed for another amendment in order to make ratifying the Charter possible, the Senate's right-wing majority voted it down, all the while proclaiming that they were 'in favour of regional languages'. No-one was fooled.

A comparatively new element of France's linguistic culture is the aversion to the language that has stolen its position of global pre-eminence, English. The government (in France and Québec) and the Academy do their best to cleanse French of English words and public space of English-language signs. Due to the same Anglophobia, radio stations have since 1994 been required by law to play French-language songs 40 per cent of the time. If you've ever spent a few hours driving on French motorways, you're likely to have noticed. Also, you're likely not to have been pleased. You weren't alone: the quota is unpopular among listeners (who are now moving to streaming services) and radio stations alike. But hey, they're only the people. They don't get to decide what French culture, linguistic or otherwise, should be like.

9

Malay

BAHASA MELAYU

275 million speakers

At least 80 million native speakers, around 200 million second-language speakers, nearly all in Indonesia, Malaysia, Singapore, Brunei and the southern tip of Thailand, an area known as the Malay realm. Malaysians like to think of all forms of Malay as one language, whereas Indonesians tend to emphasise the differences.

Malay

SELF-DESIGNATION (Bahasa) Melayu ('Malay language'); Bahasa Indonesia ('Indonesian language'); Bahasa Malaysia ('Malaysian language'); Bahasa Melayu Baku ('Malay standard language'). Also called Malaysian (for the Malaysian standard language), Indonesian (for the Indonesian standard), Bahasa (less correctly, as this is merely the Malay word for 'language').

FAMILY Malay is the largest of the Austronesian languages. It belongs to the huge Malayo-Polynesian branch of the family – the only branch to be found outside Taiwan.

SCRIPT Today, Malay is mostly written in the Latin alphabet or Rumi, a name derived from *Rome*. The Arabic-based Jawi script is still used in certain religious and cultural settings, as well as in some conservative regions; only in Brunei is its use somewhat more widespread.

GRAMMAR Pronouns have formal and informal varieties, but only to a limited extent. They're frequently replaced by kinship terms. Nouns, adjectives and verbs have no inflection for case, number, person or tense. However, adjectives and verbs can take numerous affixes (prefixes, suffixes, et cetera) with several grammatical functions, such as passive and transitivity.

SOUNDS Malay has no tone, regular word stress, only six different vowel sounds and nineteen consonant sounds, none of them uncommon and usually appearing alone rather than in clusters. In a word, Malay phonology is simple.

LOANWORDS Sanskrit and Tamil (in the early Hindu-Buddhist period), Arabic and Persian (after Islamisation), Dutch and English (due to colonisation) and Javanese (increasingly since independence).

EXPORTS *Amok, kapok, orangutan, pangolin, sago, sarong, satay*.

DOUBLE DUTCH One major difference between Malaysian and Indonesian Malay are their predominant sources of loanwords: English for the former, Javanese, Dutch and Latin for the latter. This has given rise to doublets like BONET – KAP (bonnet), MAJORITI – MAJORITAS (majority), EMPAYAR – IMPERIUM (empire), JULAI – JULI (July), PLATFORM – PERON (railway platform) and many more. Due to their differences in vocabulary, Malaysians and Indonesians may prefer to talk to each other in English or Cantonese.

9: **Malay**

The one that won

Linguistic diversity is great, except when you're in the business of running a country. Being in power, you want your citizens to understand each other. Or if not each other, at least your orders. However, in nearly all countries on earth, people speak several different languages. Back in the days when being the boss was practically synonymous with collecting taxes, this wasn't a problem – a taxman would have his methods, and words were not of the essence. In the modern world, however, mutual comprehension is essential.

What's more, a shared language creates a sense of allegiance. Social cohesion can be strengthened in many ways: a common enemy, a pervasive religion or ideology, universal conscription, state propaganda, a national myth, unique traditions and so forth. But as identity markers go, few are as potent as a common language. Indeed, marking identity is what language does best: as a means of communication, our speaking and writing can go badly awry at times, but we're all experts in spotting accents, words and other linguistic traits that set people off from our own group. A national language, or even just a national variant (Australian English, Austrian German) works wonders in defining where we belong.

If communication and national identity are potential headaches for every country with more than one language, imagine the problems faced by Indonesia. Its population of 265 million people, spread across nearly a thousand inhabited islands, speak over 700 different languages, more than any other nation in the world except neighbouring Papua New Guinea. But here's a surprise: whatever Indonesia's problems since independence – and they have been both numerous and serious – language has not figured among them to any appreciable degree. Early in the twentieth century, the nationalist movement declared Malay to be the national language, and after independence in the later 1940s, this was accepted without a murmur. Over the past seven decades, it has been learnt by the majority of the population.*

Not all countries have been so blessed by fortune or their leaders' foresight. Sri Lanka, China, Belgium and Pakistan, for example, have seen persistent, even violent conflict along linguistic lines. This is not to imply that language has been the only or even the fundamental issue. In tense political situations, there is always more at stake, such as economic, religious and political antagonisms. What language has to offer is a convenient line along which trenches can be dug. In numerous countries, language has played its nation-building role imperfectly, poorly, or not at all.

Six types of language landscapes

Let's see how countries with various linguistic landscapes and policies have fared in terms of political stability. I'll focus on those nations where at least one Babel language is spoken.

In analysing national populations according to linguistic groups, we can usefully distinguish six types of distribution, illustrated by the pie charts on the right.

1 and 4: In the first and last types, the risk of linguistic conflict is low. Group 1 includes countries such as Bangladesh, Saudi Arabia, North and South Korea, and most Caribbean islands, where the largest language is spoken natively by a majority of over 90 per cent. Linguistic minorities (other than recent newcomers, who unless they come as conquerors or in overwhelming numbers, do not usually cause a country or territory to exchange one official

---

* With one important exception: the western half of New Guinea, also known as Papua (formerly Irian Jaya); not to be confused with independent Papua New Guinea, which occupies the eastern half. The Papuan people are linguistically, culturally and even genetically very different from other people in the archipelago. The territory was not part of the country at independence, but was acquired by Indonesia in the 1960s in a questionable manner. There has been violent conflict ever since, mostly low-level, but sometimes flaring up horribly.

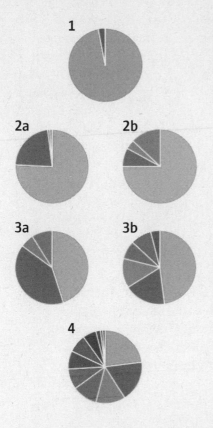

language for another) are small or non-existent.

In the countries of group 4, even the largest language is spoken natively by less than 40 per cent of the population. Here we find many African countries as well as the Philippines, Vanuatu and Papua New Guinea. Any single minority is unlikely to monopolise power for long, as this might induce the others to unite in protest. In most cases, the puzzle of how to communicate nation-wide is solved by picking a former colonial language for official purposes (the 'Very Important Languages' of chapter 12). Tanzania is a rare special case in that it has given this status exclusively to home-grown Swahili.

In the four middle groups, however, things are less clear-cut.

2a: clear majority, large minority. Here, the risk of tensions building up and getting out of hand is often serious. One case in point is Sri Lanka (see chapter 18), where the Tamilian minority was subjugated by the Sinhalese majority, resulting in a quarter century of civil war. Similarly, the Kurds of Turkey suffered severe cultural oppression for decades, and responded violently. The Iraqi Kurds suffered a similar or worse fate under Saddam Hussein, though under the current constitution, Kurdish is an official state language, alongside Arabic.

The treatment of Turkish speakers in pre-partition Cyprus, of Berber speakers in the Maghreb countries and of Russian speakers in the three Baltic states and Ukraine has also fomented conflict.

In the case of the Baltics and Ukraine, it's easy to understand the majority's feelings after 70 years of enforced Russification. But is there really any justice in making citizens suffer for the language they were taught by their parents?

India does not strictly speaking belong to this group, as it has one large *minority* language, Hindi, and numerous smaller ones, which would place it in group 3b. But three-quarters of its population speak one of the Indo-Aryan languages, most of them closely related, while one fifth speaks a Dravidian one. Therefore the situation in India could be said to fit the 'clear majority, large minority' scenario. In general, the Indian government has managed to defuse the situation by reorganising the states along linguistic lines and by maintaining English as an official language, as demanded by the minority.

2b: clear majority, several minorities. Countries in this group have better prospects of keeping the peace. In most of Latin America, Spanish or Portuguese rules supreme, and while indigenous emancipation movements clamour for their official recognition in countries such as Mexico and Bolivia (successfully, in the latter case), language is only a secondary fault line in social conflict. In Vietnam, the majority hasn't made any concessions to the numerous linguistic minorities, all of them relatively small, and discontent over this situation seems to be minimal.

In some other countries, regional linguistic rights have satisfied some, but not all minorities. In China, the increasing dominance of ethnic Chinese people and their language is much resented by Tibetans and Uyghur, giving rise to outbursts of violent protest. In Russia, 35 minority languages are co-official in various regions; the speakers of two of these, Tatar and Chechen, have had serious conflicts. In Spain, after a long history of linguistic oppression by non-democratic governments, the Catalans, Galicians and Basques were granted extensive regional rights in the late 1970s. Nonetheless, the country has seen fervent independence movements, leading to decades of bloodshed in the Basque case, and to the present political paralysis in Catalonia.

Those minorities with a strongly contrasting cultural identity (such as Tibetans and Chechens), a strong economic position

(Catalans and Slovenes), or both (Basques) seem likeliest to revolt. Size matters, too: Tatar and Tibetan may appear like mere puddles set off against the sea of Russian and the ocean of Mandarin, but in absolute numbers of speakers, they're in the same range as Catalan, and Uyghur is spoken by twice as many.

3a: two large groups. A population consisting of two large groups of roughly equal size may sound like a recipe for disaster, but this is not necessarily so. Afghanistan, for example, has two official languages, Persian (Dari) and Pashto, but language does not constitute a fault line in its conflicts. In Paraguay, where Spanish and Guaraní are the official languages, most native speakers of either language also speak, or at least understand, the other. A more complex situation obtains in Singapore: Mandarin and English are the languages most widely spoken in the home, with smaller groups preferring other Chinese languages, Malay or Tamil. English, Mandarin, Malay and Tamil all have official status, with English as the main language and Malay as the national (identity) language. The only language-troubled country in this group seems to be Belgium, but it has stopped short of bloodshed.

3b: one large group, several minorities. We have now reached the category to which Malaysia and Indonesia, the two major Malay-speaking nations, belong.

In Iran, native speakers of Persian make up only slightly more than half the population. Some of the minorities speak languages that are unrelated to Persian, which makes mastering it harder for them. In spite of this, the country's linguistic minorities seem to accept Persian's dominance. Part of the reason may be that, as we saw in chapter 15, Persian's long history as a lingua franca has made it quite learner-friendly. Also, centuries of use by kings, poets and imams have given it high prestige throughout the country.

In Pakistan, which became independent in 1947, the official language has always been Urdu (with English as a temporary companion). Like Persian, it has high historical, cultural and religious prestige (see chapter 4). Unlike Persian in Iran however, Urdu in Pakistan has always been numerically insignificant. Until 1971, it was the mother tongue of a mere 5 per cent of the population, as against some 50 per cent for Bengali, spoken in what's now Bangladesh. Feeling politically, economically and linguistically disadvantaged, the region seceded in a short but bloody civil war. In the new, smaller Pakistan, with Urdu now representing some 10 per cent of the population, the new giant was Punjabi, spoken by at least 45 per cent. However, with a stronger presence in national politics than the Bengalis used to have and a more detached attitude to their mother tongue, the Punjabis have been more accepting of Urdu's pre-eminence.

At first sight, the situation in Malaysia appears to be similar to that in Iran: Malay, here called Malaysian (or *Bahasa Malaysia*), has exclusive official status, yet it is the mother tongue of only a small majority. Also, some of the main minority tongues are unrelated to it. But that's where the similarities end. Under British colonial rule, especially in the late nineteenth and early twentieth centuries, mass

Indonesian first, then English; Chinese, Arabic and Japanese are also represented. A quarter of the Babel languages on one airport sign.

immigration created an uneasy ethnic mixture of indigenous Malays, and Chinese and Indian newcomers. After independence in 1957, political power fell to the Malays – hence the official status of their language. Meanwhile, the Chinese ran most of the economy. Ethnic tensions escalated into riots in 1969, after which the Malays created official privileges, claimed to be temporary, for the BUMIPUTRA ('sons of the soil'), i.e. for themselves and indigenous minorities. The Chinese and Indian minorities, who speak Malay as a second language, became poorer than the majority ethnic Malays, while the government became ever more unabashedly racist, and often pandered to extremist (Malay) Muslims. However, victory for a multi-ethnic coalition in May 2018 – the first political change in decades – offers hope of wiser policy-makers.

Indonesia's linguistic situation, on the other hand, looks like Pakistan's: Malay, the official language (here called *Bahasa Indonesia*) is the mother tongue of a small minority, while the most wide-spread language is spoken by 40 per cent or more of the population. There is a crucial difference however: in Pakistan, a small but dominant minority imposed its language on the whole country, whereas in Indonesia, Malay, a minority language, was given official status not by its speakers, but by the largest and highly dominant minority of Javanese speakers, who renounced linguistic privilege for the sake of national unity.

Beyond the statistics

As we've seen, not all countries with similar linguistic distributions show similar levels of peace and conflict. Numbers, therefore, cannot be the whole story. What else matters?

Familiarity does. Communities that have long been exposed to certain languages – for instance in religious ceremonies, contacts with elites or negotiations with traders – will not perceive these as entirely strange, even though they're not spoken in daily life. The association with places of worship or halls of power will moreover confer status on these languages, as happened in the cases of Persian in Iran and Arabic in the Maghreb countries. Trade languages do not enjoy such prestige, yet the marketplace – the real marketplace, not today's deified abstraction – allows for more equitable interaction than do temples and palaces. In negotiating prices and conditions, buyers and sellers will at the same time negotiate any linguistic barriers, sometimes creating a simplified trade lingo in the process. This is to an important degree what has allowed Swahili to thrive in Tanzania and Malay to burgeon in Indonesia.

Similarity matters, too – though not consistently. Languages that are easily learnt, usually thanks to a common origin, are more easily accepted than those that are more unfamiliar. Again, fortune smiled on Tanzania: most of its people have mother tongues belonging to the same Bantu family as Swahili. And again, it smiled on Indonesia too: nearly the entire population speaks a language closely related to Malay. Many of the disgruntled minorities elsewhere in the world, such as the Kurds, Tatars, Tibetans, Uyghurs, Basques, Berbers and the indigenous peoples of Latin America, are 'linguistic strangers' to the majorities that rule over them. Similarity is not, however, a sure-fire guarantee against friction: Ukrainian is a close sibling of Russian, and so is Catalan of Spanish.

Political and economic history also matters, and has a way of causing bad blood – in both Ukraine and Catalonia, for example, it's in ample supply. At the root of such tensions tends to be a troubled relationship involving conquest, oppression or exploitation. In their absence, history can occasionally create peaceful coexistence, as in the case of the Swiss Confederation: having grown by voluntary accession and cherishing a strong tradition of decentralised government, the multilingual country has never seen any serious language-based hostility. As for Indonesia, it has indeed had its share of conquest, oppression and exploitation: the Dutch were keen practitioners for over three centuries and the Japanese for three years (1942–45), leaving their languages unpopular.

But while all these factors matter and create different baseline situations, eventually it is government policies that determine the outcomes. Sri Lanka's descent into civil war was not inevitable: some moderation on the majority side might have prevented the minority taking up arms. It was unwise for the Turkish leadership to claim, without any factual justification, that the language of the Kurds was a degenerated Turkish dialect, instead of recognising them as a minority. It was hubris on the part of the Urdu speakers to make their language official in all of Pakistan, even though they represented a mere 5 per cent of the population.

Ruling elites do well to handle linguistic minorities with care. Leaving aside all considerations of political expediency, respect for such minorities is simply an ethical imperative. Speakers and writers of all languages should be allowed to speak and write in peace: not doing so is a violation of human rights.

The rise, rise and rise of Malay

As mentioned at the beginning of this chapter, Indonesia has enjoyed linguistic peace ever since independence, in spite of being the world's second most multilingual country. Rather than divide the nation, *Bahasa Indonesia*, the country's standard version of Malay, has helped forge its unity. How was this achieved? Why have this country and its national language fared so much better than many others? A peek into the past is called for.

The documented history of Malay begins in the seventh century, when a Sumatra-based kingdom controlled the Malay peninsula, most of Java and the smaller intervening islands. Thanks to its commercially strategic position as a node between the mainland and the archipelago, it came to dominate a large trade network. Along the coasts of many islands outside the kingdom, traders acquired at least some basic Malay. In this way, the first seeds of the language's modern role were sown, over a thousand years ago.

In the thirteenth and fourteenth centuries, two major changes set in. The first was religious, as contact with Arabian and Indian traders kicked off a long process of conversion to Islam, moving slowly across today's Indonesia from west to east and from the coasts to the inland areas. Then, in the political arena, a new Java-based kingdom shifted the Malay centre of power from Sumatra to the mainland (today's Malaysia). Here, the city of Malacca became the largest city and port of Southeast Asia as well as the capital of a sultanate of the same name. Malacca's fifteenth-century heyday is considered to have been the political and cultural Golden Age of the Malay world. In coastal areas under its influence, which stretched as far east as the Moluccas ('spice islands'), both Islam and the Malay language gained a foothold. Significantly, the association with religion gave this lingua franca more prestige than a mere trade lingo can normally hope to achieve. This second stage thus represents not just a further spread of the language, but also a rise in status.

Next, European colonialism changed the scene entirely. In the seventeenth and eighteenth centuries, the Dutch gradually consolidated their hold over Java and the Moluccas, later extending it to the other islands. For communication with Java's traditional elites, they first tried Javanese. But the status-related sensitivities of this language (see chapter 16) were way beyond these hard-nosed traders and sailors (whose very Dutch virtue of bluntness didn't help either). At the same time, they felt that teaching their own language to the Javanese elites was not a practical option. As an alternative they embraced Malay, a language that they had discovered to be widespread. The interaction between colonisers and subjects gave rise to a simplified form called 'service Malay', in reference to the civil service. From 1865 on, this was the colony's second official language, alongside Dutch. Since Malay has a tradition of informal use as a lingua franca, the elites accepted even this butchered version more readily than they would have accepted a Javanese that lacked the proper finesse.

In the late nineteenth century, the ascent of the native language of Central Sumatra and the Malay peninsula was accelerated when the colonial administration enthusiastically supported the spread of popular literature in Malay. As a result, the language grew in vocabulary, number of speakers and prestige. In 1928, the budding independence movement chose Malay as its official language, a decision reinforced when independence was proclaimed in 1945.

Hindsight may make it look like an inevitable choice, but it was not entirely so. In political circles, Javanese speakers were even more predominant than in the population at large, so it took sound statesmanship to resist the temptation of favouring their mother tongue. Thankfully, they realised at an early stage that Javanese was deeply unpopular on the other islands, both because of its complicated codification of hierarchy and its association with the country's largest ethnic group.

Members of the Indonesian Students Union at the Second Youth Congress in 1928. It was at this event that the historic Youth Pledge was proclaimed, which made *bahasa Indonesia* the national language.

Another option would have been Dutch. This idea was not quite as far-fetched then as it may seem now – indeed, another former colony, Suriname, made just this choice at independence in 1975. The leaders of the Indonesian independence movement were fluent in the language, thanks to the same European-style education that had contributed greatly to their ideas about liberty, equality and fraternity. It's true that a mere 1.5 per cent of the non-European population spoke the colonial language in the 1940s. But then, India decided to maintain English as one of its official languages even though a mere 2 per cent of the population could speak it at the time of independence.

A substantial advantage of Dutch, as of other colonial languages elsewhere, was its wide-ranging vocabulary. After centuries of use in all domains of European life, from administration to science, it had all the words that modernity might require. Malay had been catching up somewhat thanks to being used by the colonial administration, but when the Indonesian leadership made it official, they knew they faced a challenge in expanding the vocabulary to cover all branches of science, economy, government and anything else Indonesians might conceivably need to talk about in any formal setting. The job was handed to a language academy, which went about the job pragmatically, energetically and successfully, creating and defining hundreds of thousands of specialised terms. As a result, Indonesian has been spared the chaos that afflicted Turkish in the mid-twentieth century (see chapter 17).

Bahasa Indonesia has been a success story from the beginning. Soon associated with modernity, 'Indonesianness' and social mobility, it has been boosted by increasing urbanisation and the spread of modern media. In 2010, over 90 per cent of the population claimed proficiency in Indonesian, up from 40 per cent in 1970; at independence, the figure was much lower still.

But the country's language policy didn't privilege Malay exclusively. From the outset, widespread bilingualism was the declared aim: all citizens were encouraged to learn Indonesian for the sake of national unity, but also to maintain their vernacular language. The language academy was tasked to work not only on Indonesian, but also on the other tongues. Of course, like everywhere in the world, Indonesia's smaller languages are today under threat from larger languages, and in the major urban centres, with their mixed populations, Indonesian is taking over the linguistic cityscape. But it's important to note that this is occurring not as an intended consequence of state intervention, but rather in spite of it.

Another sensible aspect of Indonesia's language policy has been to allow the use of vernaculars in the first three years of primary education, rather than force the official language upon young children right from the start, as is the practice in many other countries. As a result, young Indonesians learn to read and write in a language they're familiar with, which is unquestionably the

Sometimes you need to translate the translation – a 'gang' in Indonesian is an alleyway (the word comes from the Dutch).

best way to acquire these skills. If nonetheless they score rather poorly on reading skills in international rankings, this may be due to the rather early shift from their mother tongues to the official language. Most educationalists would recommend a few more years of mother-tongue use in class.

While successful at the national level, the language policy has not served the country's need for international communication equally well. Indonesian is so dominant in all formal sectors of society that knowledge of English and other foreign languages is limited and mostly poor. In this matter, Tanzania has followed a more effective course, in maintaining English in those sectors where international contact is crucial, especially higher education and big business. But ultimately, of course, this is a matter of ideology – of identity versus economy, and of nationalism versus globalisation.

For Malaysia, Malay has been a poisoned gift: its speakers, constituting a very small majority and feeling threatened by more recently arrived but successful minorities, have imposed the language on the whole nation. This is just one of several privileges they have secured for themselves; together, they make the country inherently unstable.

For Indonesia, on the other hand, Malay has been a godsend – almost literally, given its historical association with Islam. As it had been spread by trade, many people were somewhat familiar with the language; its religious association had given it some prestige; it was spoken by a small minority, so it wasn't perceived as a threat; and as it was related to the languages spoken by most of the population, it was easy to learn. In a word, it had all the features of a good national language.

Indonesia's leaders saw the opportunity and seized it. As far as language is concerned, their policies have been among the most sensible and successful in the world.

8

Russian
РУССКИЙ ЯЗЫК
russkiy yazyk

275 million speakers

150 million native speakers, mostly in Russia, Belarus, Ukraine and Central Asia. 125 million speak Russian as a second language, mostly non-Russians across the former Soviet Union and its satellite states in Eastern and Central Europe, as well as Mongolia. As a second language, Russian continues to lose ground.

Russian

SELF-DESIGNATION РУССКИЙ ЯЗЫК (russkiy yazyk). Also called Great Russian. Now obsolete, 'Great Russian' was mostly used to distinguish the language from 'Little Russian' (Ukrainian) and 'White Russian' (Belarusian).

MIGRANTS Russian is spoken by more than a million migrants in Israel and a slightly lower number in the US. In Germany, there may be two million Russian speakers, mostly of German ethnic origin.

FAMILY Russian is the largest of the Slavic languages, which form a branch of Indo-European. They are spoken in a large contiguous area from Poland and the Czech Republic all the way east to the Pacific Ocean, and in the Balkans. Upper and Lower Sorbian are small Slavic languages in Germany.

SCRIPT Cyrillic alphabet.

GRAMMAR Nouns: three genders, six cases, singular and plural. Adjectives agree with nouns in gender, case and number. Verbs come in two varieties, imperfective and perfective, which are always similar but in unpredictable ways.

SOUNDS Like other Slavic languages, Russian is rich in sibilants: /s/, /z/, /sh/, /zh/ (like the s in *measure*), /ch/, /shch/ and /ts/. Most consonants come in two varieties: in the soft variety, the middle of the tongue is raised higher than in the hard one. Words can begin with remarkably long consonant clusters, as in ВЗГЛЯД (VZGLYAD – 'view').

LOANWORDS Historically, words were borrowed from Old Church Slavonic (a classical Slavic language), Turkic languages, French, German, and Dutch; today, the principal source is English.

EXPORTS Most loanwords are directly related to Russian culture: *tsar*, *intelligentsia*, *vodka*, *troika*, *pogrom*, *dacha*, *apparatchik*. Others include *steppe*, *mammoth* and *taiga*.

SPACE Russian was the first language spoken in space – by Yuri Gagarin in 1961.

8: **Russian**

On being Indo-European

Languages, like humans, belong to families. And like human families, they sometimes make you wonder what it *means* to belong. When you come right down to it, what do they have in common? The question seems easy enough as long as you look at close siblings: Spanish and Portuguese are spitting images of each other and have very clearly taken after their mother, Latin. English has no siblings quite as close as that, but linguists unanimously declare that English is snugly embedded in both a nuclear family, Germanic, and an extended family, Indo-European, which includes a language as apparently dissimilar as Russian.

If you compare English with its German relative, things are relatively simple. Trace the languages back and you will find that they become mutually comprehensible around the year 900 CE. English and German people of that time would be hard for modern speakers to understand but they would be reasonably at ease with each other. That's what it means to say that German and English belong to the same family: there was a point in history where one group of people spoke one language which went on to form dialects which in turn became different languages, which finally became English and German. During their multifarious historical adventures, these languages were learnt by great numbers of people who were genetically unrelated to each other. In the case of English, they included Vikings, Normans, Huguenots, enslaved Africans and the tired, poor and huddled masses that migrated to the US, Canada and Australia. German, until the immigration of recent decades, saw rather less 'new blood', with Slavs being the major influx. As a consequence, English has morphed rather more energetically than German, so modern German speakers would have an easier time talking to their ancestors than would English speakers.

In spite of the many changes, though, there remain many similarities between English and German, in terms of both grammar and vocabulary. Take this sentence:

Der Biber und der Otter leben in fliessendem Wasser;
der Biber baut Dämme.

The beaver and the otter live in running water;
the beaver builds dams.

The word order is the same, for starters, which would not be the case in all languages (French and Spanish would have 'in water running' instead of 'in running water') and both sentences contain articles (DER, *the*). In terms of vocabulary, too, there are obviously kindred words: OTTER and IN stand out, but WASSER is pretty close too, and so is BIBER, though more in sound than in looks (if it were an English word, we would spell it 'beaber'). DÄMME looks even more familiar in the singular, DAMM, and even DER and LEBEN have a resemblance to *the* and *live*. All these German words share an origin with their English version in the common ancestor language, Proto-Germanic: in other words, they are cognates (from CO-GNATUS, Latin for 'born together').[*]

If you suspect me of wilfully doctoring the example sentence with the intent of showing a good number of related words, I plead guilty. But in their basic vocabularies, English and German really do have a high proportion of cognates. The two sentences that begin this paragraph are entirely undoctored, and they too contain lots of words that have cognates in German: *if*, *you*, *me*, *of*, *the*, *with*, *show*, *a*, *good*, *words*, *I*, *in*, *and*, *do*, *have* and *high* have direct cognates, while *wilfully* can be taken apart into words with German cognates, such as *will*, *full* and *-ly*.

As with German, so with Russian. But since it's an Indo-European cousin rather than a Germanic sibling of English, the similarities will be fewer and further between; the differences more glaring.

---

[*] 'Born together' is not the same as 'borrowed together'. The word *bank* exists in English, German, Russian and many other languages, but it's not a cognate. *Bank* originated in fourteenth-century Italian, from where it gradually spread across Europe. It doesn't stop many language-teaching publications from calling this and similar cases 'cognates'.

make everything
great again

Always suspected they were natural allies? English and Russian – and Trump's own ancestral German – are all Indo-European relatives.

If we conjure up our linguistic ancestors we will find that communication along the English line collapses much sooner than on the Russian. Go back 500 years and an English speaker would likely find it impossible to make head or tail of anything that anybody's saying, while a Russian speaker could probably communicate with their ancestors going back several more centuries. But the interesting point is that – if English and Russian are indeed related languages, as all linguists know they are* – we can keep going back through the generations and we will eventually get to a point where our English and Russian linguistic ancestors will understand each other. With English and German this was around the year 1000 CE.

---

* All linguists except Nikolay Yakovlevich Marr (1864–1934) and his school of thought. I've written about him in an article about crackpot linguistics. See *bit.ly/Aeon_TalkingGibberish*

But with Russian it takes a lot longer. We cross the point where CE turns into BCE: nothing. We cross the 500 BCE milestone, the 1000 BCE milestone: still nothing. We keep going and going until, somewhere near the 3000 BCE mark, it finally happens: the lines start talking to each other and eventually merge into one – that of the Proto-Indo-Europeans. We have travelled fifty centuries back in time, two hundred generations or so, more than ten times the distance between us and Shakespeare. Just imagine the havoc such a long stretch of history can wreak on the way people – *any* people, no matter who – speak. Or actually, no need to imagine it: just compare English to Russian. The differences between them are exactly that: the result of fifty centuries of havoc wrought on the two of them.

Here is one Russian sentence, first in Cyrillic, then below in transliteration:

Бобр и выдра живут в проточной воде;
бобр строит плотины.

Bobr i vydra zhivut v protochnoy vode;
bobr stroit plotiny.

Once more, we are informed that the beaver and the otter live in running water and that the beaver builds dams.

Commenting on the German sentence, I pointed out three grammatical similarities between German and English: the order of subject and predicate, the order of adjective and noun and the presence of articles. You might observe that here again the subject comes first, which is particularly easy to see in the second phrase: BOBR is the Russian word for 'beaver'. (Admittedly, its resemblance to BEAVER is on the faint side, but having met the German BIBER, we can see it for what it is: an Indo-European cognate.) I should add that the order of subject and predicate in Russian is much less rigidly fixed than it is in English and German, but subject-first is the default.

What about the order of the adjective-and-noun couple in this sentence, 'running water' or, in Russian, PROTOCHNOY VODE? Those too are in the same order as in English and German, and again, the reverse order is possible but secondary. (One doesn't need any knowledge of Russian to guess that VODE, not PROTOCHNOY, means 'water'. Indeed, it is not miles away from the American English pronunciation /wodder/.)

As for articles, they represent a major difference between the two languages, for Russian has none. Most branches of the Indo-European family love using articles (either 'a' or 'the', or both), from Germanic, Romance and Iranian to Greek, Albanian and Armenian. Just three branches tend to avoid them, and Slavic is one of them. But it's not as if the Slavs have carelessly dropped and broken a venerable Indo-European heirloom. On the contrary, the Proto-Indo-European grandmother language didn't have articles.

The otter and the hydra

In the German beaver example, we saw that the sample sentence was packed with Germanic cognates: most words had siblings. Given that Indo-European is much older, the family members have had much more time to lose items from the common vocabulary. Nonetheless, quite a few have stuck around.

An obvious one is BOBR, which derives from the same ancient word as *beaver*, namely BHÉBHRUS. (Modern linguists have given Proto-Indo-European a horrible spelling, taking advantage of its speakers being long dead. It's full of asterisks, numbers and superscript letters. I've dumped all of those.) An even more evident case is VODE, or rather VODA to call it by its unconjugated name. *Water* and VODA are both derived from the Proto-Indo-European WÓDR or UÓDR (w and u are merely spelling variants for the same sound). They are also cognate with the Greek word for 'water', HUDŌR, an echo of which we hear in our modern word *hydrate*. (And if you need to hydrate yourself, it's not wise to drink VODKA, even though the name of the Russian drink consists of VODA for 'water' plus a suffix.)

A third interesting word is VYDRA, which is cognate with *otter*. Not only that, they're also related to VODA and *water*. Some 5,000 years ago, the word for 'water', WÓDR or UÓDR, was accompanied by an adjective UDRÓS or UDRÉH (masculine and feminine respectively), meaning 'watery' or 'aquatic'. Germanic picked the masculine and morphed into OTTER. Slavic took the feminine, which somehow picked up an initial *v* along the way, becoming VYDRA. Speakers of other Indo-European languages, including Sanskrit and Latin, effected similar changes – but not the Greeks, who reserved their HYDRA for a many-headed water monster quite unlike the playful and graceful otter.

Any other cognates in the sample sentence? Yes, two more, but they border on the implausible. According to linguists, the Russian preposition V traces its origin to the same Proto-Indo-European word as our *in*, namely HÉN. The HÉN-IN transition doesn't overly tax our credulity, but the metamorphosis of HÉN into V almost appears like a conjuring trick – albeit an extremely slow one.

The other invisible cognate is ZHIVUT, a form of the verb ZHIT'. Unlikely as it may appear, this is a cognate of *quick*, an English word that used to mean 'alive'. Mind-bogglingly, ZHIVUT and *quick* are also related to *biology* and *revival*. They are all modern reflexes of the Proto-Indo-European words GWEIH and GWIHWÓS for 'live' and 'alive'.

The rest of our sample sentence about the beaver and the otter doesn't present any direct cognates, but there too we can find proof of Russian's Indo-European descent, provided we venture into the Romance branch. The clearest example is the Russian word STROIT for '(he) builds'. In Latin, this would be STRUIT, from the verb STRUĔRE, which has given us quite a few English words, including *structure* and *destroy*. Also note that STROIT and STRUIT have the same t-ending that we saw in German BAUT.*

In PROTOCHNOY, the first syllable looks suspiciously like the Latin prefix that we see in *provoke* and *pronoun* and *pro-choice*. And true enough, they're both derived from the same Indo-European prefix. Interestingly, English also has traces of it (other than those borrowed from Latin), namely in *forgive* and *forgather*. The middle

---

* I'm cutting corners here. The full story is as follows: Russian and the other East Slavic languages used to have a t'-ending. (This *t'* sounds similar to the *t* as pronounced in *tiara*.) Russian at some point dropped this ending. Later on, Russian acquired the t-ending mentioned in the main text, probably as a result of this verb form frequently being followed by the word *tŭ*, an old word for 'this' or 'that'. So the t-ending we now see in Russian is not, strictly speaking, of the same origin as the t's in Latin and German. But Russian did formerly have an ending that was cognate with these, some Russian dialects still do and so does closely related Ukrainian. In a word, I'm lying the truth.

syllable of PROTOCHNOY, which means 'flow, run', also has Indo-European cognates, but nothing we would recognise in English.

PLOTINA (the basic form of PLOTINY) 'dam', is derived from PLOT, a Slavic word for 'fence', plus a suffix, so a dam in Russian is literally something like a 'fenceling' or a 'fencedom'. The old Slavs must have had fences that were 'plaited things', for the word is related to the verb PLESTI, meaning 'plait, interweave', a steadfast Indo-European term whose oldest form was PLEḰ-. The Germanic family has maintained the word as well – German, for instance, has FLECHTEN – but the Old English FLEOHTAN got lost somewhere along the way. Still, the loanword that replaced it, *plait*, from French PLEIT, is another cognate of Russian and German words.

Russian *ushanka* hats were often made from beaver in the nineteenth century, but luckily for the *bobry* they now tend to be rabbit or fake fur.

That leaves us with the smallest Russian word in the whole sentence, I. A word that means 'and' and sounds like /i/ – surely that's cognate with the Spanish word Y? Not so: Spanish Y comes from Latin ET, as in ET CETERA. The Russian I, in contrast, is derived from an Indo-European word, EI, whose further connections in Latin and English would take us into even deeper etymological waters.

Black as *sazha*

We can safely conclude that the above ten-word line of Russian text brings home how closely the language is related to its Indo-European cousins. And the funny thing is, once you become conscious of such parallels, they start cropping up all over the place. This is true not only for numerous Russian words (see the box below for another collection) but also for Russian grammar.

I mentioned that the third-person singular endings of Latin STRUIT, Russian STROIT and German BAUT share a common origin. Now let's look at all the endings:

	LATIN	RUSSIAN	GERMAN	OTHER
1st p sg, I	o, m	u, m	e	Old German: o
2nd p sg, you (thou)	s	sh	st	English, archaic and dialects: st
3rd p sg, s/he	t	t	t	English, archaic: th
1st p pl, we	mus	m	n	Proto-Germanic: maz
2nd p pl, you (y'all)	tis	te	t	
3rd p pl, they	nt	t	n	German dialects: nt

Quite an impressive amount of similarity, I would say, especially between Russian and Latin, but also with Germanic varieties, especially the older ones. English, admittedly, is a bit underrepresented, due to its small number of remaining verb endings.

To compensate, let's look at passive participles, forms such as *thrown* and *bent*. In English they come either with an *n* or with a *t*

SOME ENGLISH-RUSSIAN COGNATES OF INDO-EUROPEAN ORIGIN			
byt'	be	moy	my
den'	day	noch'	night
dva	two	noga *(foot/leg)*	nail
dver'	door	novy	new
golos *(voice)*	call	serdtse	heart
gorod *(town)*	yard	svet *(light)*	white
gost'	guest	tysyacha	thousand
imya	name	ty	thou
materi	mothers	yest'	is
mesyats	moon, month	znat'	know
mnit' *(think)*	mind		

(or a *d* of course, as in *stayed*, which shares the same origin as the t). German has both types too: GEWORFEN and GEBEUGT ('thrown' and 'bent'). Both endings have Indo-European roots, and both are reflected in Russian: the same words translate as BROSHENNY and GNUTY.

Another feature of Indo-European languages is that they change their vowels a lot in ways that most other languages don't. Some of these vowel changes, such as the irregular plural of MAN and WOMAN, are modern: we can't blame the Proto-Indo-Europeans, because MEN and WOMEN only emerged thousands of years after they'd left the scene. But in their day, they had some bewildering vowel changes of their own. A short /e/ – which was an extremely common sound – could under certain conditions change into a long /ē/, a short /o/ or a long /ō/ – or it might disappear altogether. These five varieties (specialists call them 'grades') could occur in both nouns and verbs.

A good example is SED-, a root with the meaning 'sit':

❖ The basic e-variety produced not only English *sit* (why *i* instead of *e*? long-term havoc!), but also Russian SEST' ('sit down') and Latin SEDĒRE ('sit').
❖ The o-variety produced the Germanic past tense, SOT, which in modern English has become *sat*.

213

❖ The ē-variety, SĒD-, resulted in the noun *seat* as well as its Latin cognate, SĒDĒS.

❖ The ŌVARIETY is the origin of English *soot* and possibly of Russian SAŽA (though it more likely derives from the o-variety), the connection being that the black stuff 'sits' on surfaces.

❖ And the vowelless variety SD- has landed in our word *nest*: the Proto-Indo-European word NISDOS refers to a place where a bird sits (SD) down (NI). Russian has turned this into GNEZDO, Latin into NIDUS.

It's not easy to find examples such as SED, where all five varieties have left their mark on English and other modern languages, but the phenomenon as such – variously called ablaut, vowel alternation or vowel gradation – is common as muck. In English, it's the culprit behind such headaches as *sing - sang - sung - song*. In Latin, ablaut produced irregular verbs such as FACERE – FECI – FACTUM, which in turn saddled Spanish with HACER – HICE – HECHO (both mean 'do, make'). In Russian too, ablaut has messed up a few verbal conjugations including BRAT' ('take'), which in many forms adds an *e*, as in BERU ('I take') . Ablaut's main activity in Russian, however, has consisted in creating new words. One example from many are the triplets DUKH, DOKHNUT' and DYSHAT', where the first means 'spirit', the second is slang for 'to die' (to breathe one's last) and the last one means 'to breathe'.

How the other half speaks

So far, I've looked for similarities between English and Russian that stand out. Or rather, that can be *made* to stand out – ZHIVUT and *quick* conceal their common provenance rather effectively until you delve into their respective CVs. However, there are also quite a few things that do not at all strike us as characteristically Indo-European until we compare English and Russian with languages that belong to other families.

For example, phonology. Consider the Russian word STRELA, meaning 'arrow'. Unremarkable, isn't it? You may or may not know the archaic English word STREAL, which has the same meaning. 'Okay, another cognate', you yawn – what else is new? Well, syllables

Moscow's bus terminal. Like the Russian language, the word *avtovokzal* (bus station) is more closely connected to English than it seems: *avto* is a respelling of auto(mobile), *vokzal* is a phonetic rendering of Vauxhall. One of the first Russian train stations was near a pleasure garden of that name.

beginning with three consonants, that's what. We think nothing of them: when I presented Russian STROIT and Latin STRUIT, relating them to English *structure*, you didn't bat an eyelid. But outside the Indo-European family, this is a rarity: fewer than one in ten non-Indo-European languages will have it. (Even inside the firm, some don't like it: Spanish doesn't have 'STRUCTURA', but ESTRUCTURA, where the second syllable begins with a more manageable *tr*.) It's true that Russian takes things a bit further still, as witness words like SKHVATKI and VZGLYAD. But by global standards, STRONG is just as, well, strange.

For a second faint family feature, consider once more the verbal conjugation. We so easily take for granted that both English and Russian conjugate their verbs, but many languages in East Asia don't. Also, they conjugate them mostly with suffixes, whereas many in Africa much prefer prefixes. And finally, the conjugation depends on the subject, never on the object or other parts of the sentence. There are not a few languages – Basque is a European example – where the conjugation can also depend on the direct object, the indirect object or other parties concerned.

Yet another similarity: both English and Russian are much given to using prepositions. You will find them in nearly every sentence. In many non-Indo-European languages, prepositions are much rarer, if they exist at all. Moreover, both English and Russian make their prepositions serve additionally as prefixes, using them to great effect for the formation of nouns, adjectives and verbs. In English, we have *off(spring)*, *over(joyed)*, *up(date)* and thousands of similar cases. Open a Russian dictionary and you'll find similar numbers of words beginning with V ('in'), OT ('from'), OB or O ('about, against'), BEZ ('without'), et cetera. Latin and Greek did the very same thing, as shown by *in(vent)*, *pre(dict)*, *sus(pend)*, *peri(scope)* and *meta(phor)*, words that we borrowed from them. This procedure of turning prepositions into prefixes is not unheard of in unrelated languages elsewhere, but it's far from ubiquitous.

Perhaps more than anything else, it's the contrasts between the languages inside and outside the Indo-European family that show us how similar 'we' are: English and German, English and Russian, even English and Bengali if you look closely enough. And, of course, that may well be just as true for families of flesh and blood.

7

Portuguese

PORTUGUÊS

275 MILLION SPEAKERS

250 million speak Portuguese natively, 25 million as a second language. Speakers are mostly in Portugal, Brazil, Angola and Mozambique, with small numbers in Guinea-Bissau, Cape Verde and São Tomé and Príncipe. The Portuguese have migrated not only to their former colonies, but also to Spanish- and English-speaking countries in the Americas and to Western Europe. In Luxembourg, they represent sixteen per cent of the population.

Portuguese

SELF-DESIGNATION Português.

FAMILY A member of the Romance group within the Indo-European family.

SCRIPT Latin script, with generous use of acute accents, tildes, circumflexes and cedillas (á, õ, ê, ç).

GRAMMAR Portuguese grammar is very similar to that of Spanish and other Romance languages. Even for this group, though, its verbal conjugation is remarkably rich (somewhat less so in Brazil), with forms that have fallen out of use elsewhere or that never existed in the first place.

SOUNDS For a Romance language, Portuguese, like French, has a large set of vowel sounds (about fifteen, five of them nasal), which can moreover be combined into many different diphthongs and triphthongs. There are about twenty consonant sounds.

LOANWORDS Moorish rule in the Middle Ages left numerous Arabic words, though far fewer than in Spanish. Colonialism led to the adoption of Amerindian, African and Asian words. Among modern European languages, French and English have been the major sources.

EXPORTS Portuguese has been the conduit of many Asian and some New World words, such as *mango*, *pagoda*, *tank*, *junk* (ship), *cobra*, *mandarin* and *Mandarin* (Chinese official and language), *piranha*, *jaguar* and *tapioca*. Portugal has also given us *tempura* (via Japan), *caste* (via India), *auto-da-fe*, *marmalade* and *baroque*, derived from BARROCO, a word for an irregularly shaped pearl. From Brazil, English has imported *samba*, *bossa nova*, *caipirinha* and *capoeira*.

DIVIDED BY A COMMON LANGUAGE Differences between Brazilian Portuguese and the European and African varieties are more noticeable than between New World and Old World English or Spanish. Pronunciation is so distinct as to force second-language learners to choose one variety. The grammar of Brazil's spoken language is much more distinctive than that of its written language. But 99 per cent of vocabulary is identical.

7: **Portuguese**

Punching above its weight

Does this book pass over the New World too lightly? Not a single chapter focuses on a language that was born and bred, so to speak, on the American continent. Maya, Navajo, Quechua, Guaraní – none of them gets more than a passing mention, if that. The thing is, not even the most widely spoken Amerindian languages come close to our global top twenty. Quechua, once the lingua franca of the Inca Empire, is today spoken by a mere ten million people, far behind Vietnamese and Korean, the smallest Babel entrants. Even Guaraní, which has official status in Paraguay, Bolivia and part of Argentina, and for which some (perhaps overenthusiastic) sources claim more than 15 million speakers, isn't really in the running.

Then again, one could just as easily argue that this book serves the American continent admirably. From Alaska in the north to Tierra del Fuego in the south, 90 per cent of the population is familiar with Spanish, English, French or Portuguese; for most, one of these languages will be their mother tongue. So if we're talking about the present day, or the relatively recent past, the Americas are well represented; for the deeper past, however, the opposite is true.

The watershed between the two eras occurred in 1492, with the arrival of Cristóbal Colón, aka Christopher Columbus. The man's name could not be more appropriate. His first name etymologically means 'carrier of Christ' – and Columbus did indeed bring about the Catholic invasion of the continent. COLÓN is even more apt: with his voyage of discovery, the age of European colonialism began. He also ushered in the global expansion of colonial languages, a process that will be at the heart of this chapter. I've already mentioned four of these languages, which were taken to all continents by the Spanish, English (later British), Portuguese and French empires. But there was one other major colonising nation: the Dutch Republic.

It even imprinted its language on the Americas, in the small nation of Suriname and on a few Caribbean islands.

The Dutch and their language are mentioned here not because I myself am from the Netherlands but because the story of the Dutch colonies can help to answer the question of why some colonial languages have spread so much more widely than others. English and Spanish have of course been hugely expansive, with French lagging behind. But Portuguese and Dutch are more extreme cases. Among the colonial languages, Portuguese resembles the small-town boy who has cleaned up on a truly impressive scale. No such rags-to-riches story for Dutch: out in the big world, it has proved a dismal failure.

A few figures can illustrate how different their fortunes have been. Around the year 1500, both Portugal and today's Netherlands (then known as the Northern Netherlands) had populations of about one million. Five centuries on, the Netherlands has considerably more inhabitants than Portugal (17 million as against 10 million), but worldwide, Portuguese is almost ten times as widespread as Dutch: 225 million as against 25 million native speakers; 275 million as against 28 million if we include second-language speakers. Or how's this for a contrast: of all Dutch speakers, 98 per cent live in Europe, whereas over 95 per cent of Portuguese speakers live elsewhere.

Comparing these statistics with the other three major colonial languages highlights how extreme the scores are. The European speakers of English and Spanish represent some 10 per cent of their entire language communities, which is more than twice the figure for Portuguese. French comes in at around 50 per cent. These per centages include second-language speakers; in terms of native speakers only, English, Spanish and French score higher still.

Why is it that Portuguese has spread in a way that seems little short of epidemic, whereas Dutch very much has not? Has the former, but not the latter, benefited from determined efforts by the erstwhile empires to teach it around the globe? It can't be that, because neither the Netherlands nor Portugal made such efforts to any appreciable degree. If any colonial power has gone out of its way to culturally integrate its overseas subjects, including by language education, that power is France. And a fat lot of good it

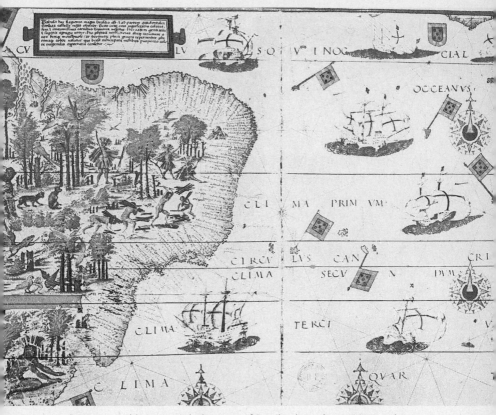

Portuguese ships approach the coast of Brazil, where the natives cut down brazilwood, in this map of 1519 by Lopo Homem.

has done the French language: as we've just seen, the number of speakers outside Europe is comparatively modest.

Neither can the outbreak of Portuguese be explained by some sort of inherent quality of the language that French has less of and Dutch almost none. Such inherent qualities simply do not exist. Difficult or easy, melodious or grating, written or unwritten, any language has the potential to grow into the lingua franca of a great empire: Latin, Arabic, Russian and Quechua all proved it in their day. And English has managed the feat most effectively of all, in spite of its challenging pronunciation and disorderly spelling.

But if neither effort nor inherent quality explain the diametrically opposed fortunes of Portuguese and Dutch, what does? In what linguistically relevant way did their colonial empires develop differently during half a millennium of European maritime imperialism?

A brief history of Iberian colonialism

Christopher Columbus couldn't have made his big voyage of exploration without the numerous smaller ones that went before. Starting in 1420 and inspired by Prince Henry of Portugal, 'the Navigator', a succession of captains headed out into the waters to Portugal's west and south. There, they (re)discovered quite a number of islands, settling on most of them: Madeira (1420), the Azores (1433), the Cape Verde Islands (1462) and São Tomé (1470). There's no arguing with the Portuguese national anthem, which in its first line calls these men HERÓIS DO MAR, 'Heroes of the sea'. Of the discoveries just listed, Madeira and the Azores have remained parts of Portugal; in Cape Verde and São Tomé, Portuguese is the official language even today. The Canaries were also visited by the Portuguese, but it was the Spanish who defeated the indigenous population and settled there. They've stayed ever since.

This was how both Iberian countries developed a taste for maritime exploration, settlement and (in the Spanish case) conquest. They also quickly initiated a trade in captured Africans. Buyers were found in the motherlands and on plantations in Madeira and São Tomé.

In the second half of the century, both Portugal and Spain set their sights on finding a sea route to India, which promised to yield huge profits. In 1488, the Portuguese Bartolomeu Dias became the first European to sail around the southern tip of Africa, thereby putting an end to the old discussion as to whether the Atlantic and Indian oceans were connected or not. Europeans, it turned out, could reach India by sea. Columbus knew this, yet tried to reach India by a different route. In 1498 another Portuguese, Vasco da Gama, took advantage of the best available knowledge and became the first European to actually reach India, via the Cape of Good Hope. And when, two years later, one more Portuguese 'hero of the sea', Pedro Álvares Cabral, struck out on a westerly course to

India, he made another momentous, though probably unintended, discovery: he became the first European to land in Brazil.

For the next hundred years, the seas were dominated by Spain and Portugal. The other European powers were not yet able to follow in their wakes. France's energies were spent in domestic religious wars and England had its Reformation and Irish colonisation to keep it occupied, while the Netherlands was busy revolting against Spain, an episode that inadvertently produced the Dutch Republic. Relations between the two Iberian competitors were mostly nonviolent, as they had divided the world between them upfront: Spanish was to have the Americas minus Brazil, while all of Asia was earmarked for Portugal.

The story of how small groups of Spaniards miraculously brought huge Amerindian empires to heel, aided by infectious disease, superior weapons and occasionally good luck, has often been told. But at least as remarkable is the fact that tiny Portugal managed to monopolise trade in the Indian Ocean. Portuguese men-o'-war (the ships, not the jellyfish) fought more than twenty battles against the Ottoman Empire and its Asian allies between 1506 and 1589, and though they didn't win every one, the overall outcome was that Portugal acquired an extremely profitable trade monopoly along the Indian Ocean coast. It built a series of fortified factories or trading posts in India (including in Goa, Daman and Diu, which were to remain in its possession until 1961) and Africa (Mozambique, a colony until 1975).

While India was the initial pearl in their crown, quite early on the Portuguese also began to establish plantations in thinly populated Brazil. The labour needed there was imported from across the Atlantic. Increasing numbers of Africans were captured (mostly by fellow Africans), transported to America under appalling conditions (mostly by Portuguese) and worked like animals on the plantations (by the Portuguese, but also by the Spanish in their own colonies). To facilitate this human trafficking, the Portuguese built fortified factories on the West African coast, in territories including Guinea-Bissau and Angola, which would remain Portuguese colonies until the mid-1970s. Even as the captured Africans suffered unimaginable hardships, they also had to overcome the problem of communication both among one another, as speakers of many different languages, and between themselves and their European exploiters. As a result, the forts, ships and plantations became forges of language creation. We'll get back to the resulting creole languages later on.

In 1580, Portugal came under the Spanish crown, a state of affairs that would last for sixty years, costing the smaller country dearly in both economic and political terms. France, England and the Netherlands managed to secure much of the Indian Ocean trade for themselves in this period. Dutch traders had a particularly strong position for a while. Their United East India Company (or VOC) built and conquered factories and forts, operating in India (1606–1825), the Spice Islands, or Moluccas (1599–1949), on Java (1619–1949), in Malaysia (1641–1795) and Japan (1641–1854). In Taiwan (1624–1662) and Sri Lanka (1640–1796) they controlled substantial territories. Near the southern tip of Africa, the VOC established a re-supply and layover port for ships on their way to and from the Indies. Unplanned by the VOC, substantial numbers of Dutchmen and other Europeans settled in the area, resulting in a colony roughly half the size of today's South Africa. In 1795, Britain captured both the Cape Colony and several Dutch possessions in Asia, but not Java and the Moluccas. These would gradually expand to form the Dutch East Indies (now Indonesia), which from then on was the most important part by far of the country's colonial empire.

On the American continent, too, France, England and the Netherlands got busy in the seventeenth century. In North America, New Netherland (1614–1667), centred on New Amsterdam (New York), was no less serious a colony than New England, Virginia, New France, New Spain and even New Sweden. There was no New Portugal. Meantime, around the Caribbean, a century-long game of Sorry was played by Spain, England, the Netherlands and France (as well as Denmark, Sweden and, believe it or not, the German Baltic duchy of Courland). Most islands were won and lost several times over, the record-keeper being Tobago, which changed hands thirty-three times between six empires (if we consider Courland one of these). The flourishing plantation economies of both South America and the Caribbean islands fired the slave trade, in which the English, French and Dutch also got involved.

224

In Asia, European colonialism now gradually became what it had been in the Americas all along: territorial in nature. Britain beat France in the battle for hegemony in India; the Dutch controlled ever more parts of Java and bridgeheads on other islands. As the hold on the colonies became more direct, increasing numbers of Europeans spent major parts of their careers there. But given the large populations of South and Southeast Asia, the European merchants, sailors, military men, priests and officials never constituted more than a tiny minority. In Brazil, a gold rush attracted hundreds of thousands of Portuguese men, but few women. The numerous marriages between these men and Afro-Brazilian women resulted in a booming Portuguese-speaking population.

The early nineteenth century saw most of South and Central America as well as Mexico gain independence, stripping Spain and Portugal of the lion's share of their overseas territories. (It didn't stop the Portuguese for long from migrating to Brazil: after 1880, another 1.4 million sailed across.) Near the end of the century, Spain would also lose the Philippines, Cuba and some other islands. But the Dutch possessions in the East expanded to nearly the whole of what is now Indonesia, while Britain consolidated its South Asian colonies into one vast, near-contiguous domain stretching from today's Pakistan to Singapore and northern Borneo. France rebounded from its losses and built a new overseas empire that encompassed all of today's Vietnam, Laos and Cambodia, and later established another substantial colony in North Africa, where hundreds of thousands of French settled.

During the so-called Scramble for Africa, between 1880 and 1913, nearly the entire continent was divvied up between the traditional colonial powers, minus the Netherlands but plus three newcomers, Belgium, Germany and Italy. Portugal expanded two of its traditional coastal possessions deep inland, Mozambique and Angola, and by the 1970s, up to a million Portuguese were living in Angola and Mozambique.

Then in the decades after the Second World War, nearly all overseas territories gained independence. The Netherlands found it difficult to acquiesce in the loss of Indonesia, which was nonetheless formalised in 1949, and today only six Caribbean islands maintain a political link with the Netherlands. Portugal, governed by dictators between 1926 and 1974, clung on to its overseas territories even longer. Its South Asian possessions were captured militarily and annexed by India in 1961. But its African colonies only became independent in 1974 and 1975, when three-quarters of the Portuguese settlers left the young countries, many heading back for Portugal.

Language shifts in the colonies

One would expect five centuries of domination, mass killings, pandemics, migration and human trafficking to have turned the distribution and spread of the world's languages upside down. And indeed they did, in at least four ways.

In some regions, a European language is now generally spoken. Madeira, the Azores, the Falklands and a few other small places were uninhabited until Europeans settled there. But these are exceptions. Much more often, indigenous populations became minorities or marginalised majorities in their own lands as a result of massive immigration from Europe, with military support. Typically, many of the indigenous people died because of infectious diseases, ruthless exploitation or outright genocide. This scenario has played out with particular frequency in the Americas, so that European languages are now dominant in both continents. (Australia later saw a similar sequence of events.) Or to be more precise, the dominant language spoken in any one country tends to be that of the *first* power that permanently established its supremacy, such as English in the US and Portuguese in Brazil. Even huge numbers of later immigrants, such as Italians, Germans and Eastern Europeans, would adopt whatever language they found spoken in their new country.

A second change was the emergence, especially in the Caribbean area, of entirely new languages, born from contact between speakers of one European and several African languages. The vocabularies of these 'Atlantic creoles' have originated largely from some European language – Portuguese, French and English being the most frequent sources – but their grammars have clearly African features. In Haiti, Curaçao and Aruba, as well as in Suriname, nearly the entire populations speak a creole language (called Haitian, Papiamento and Sranan respectively), and the first two of these three have acquired an official status, alongside French and Dutch respectively. Haitian, with over ten million speakers in Haiti and many more among migrants elsewhere, may well be the most widespread of all American languages that originated on this continent – which technically makes it an indigenous language, though it's unusual to categorise it in this way.

Creole languages also emerged elsewhere in the world, some among enslaved Africans, others among ethnically mixed groups. Most of them are now nearly or entirely extinct, but in the Indian Ocean islands of Mauritius and Réunion they are alive and well. The creoles of Papua New Guinea and the Seychelles, called Tok Pisin and Seselwa, respectively, have even acquired official status, once more alongside European languages. Creoles are also widespread

Creole in Cape Verde: a sign in Portuguese prohibits the entry and presence of minors, while underneath, beer is advertised in local Creole.

in some West Africa countries, including Nigeria. A special case is South Africa's Afrikaans, more about which later.

Thirdly, there are numerous countries where a European language is – to use a term from chapter 12 – the Very Important Language or VIL, playing most formal roles in society, but where other, usually indigenous languages dominate in daily life. This situation is typical for Africa except its Arabic north. Most of the continent didn't attract great numbers of European settlers, and as a result their languages never spread much beyond administration and education. Since independence in the 1950, 1960s and 1970s, most new states have maintained both the colonial borders and languages, in an effort to prevent conflict. As a result, European languages represent a compromise between linguistic minorities. The same situation is not unknown outside Africa: in India and the Philippines, English plays this intermediary role, in Suriname, Dutch does, and in East Timor, Portuguese. Thanks to the increase in education, the knowledge of European languages is on the rise, especially in cities, which tend to be more ethnically mixed than the countryside. The places where this trend is strongest include Portuguese-speaking Angola and Mozambique and Dutch-speaking Suriname.

And finally, there are countries where yesterday's colonial languages today play second fiddle, or are conspicuous only by their absence. This is common in Asia, a continent where, except in Russia and some former Soviet republics, relatively few Europeans settled for good. Yet even here, colonialism has often transformed the linguistic landscape by centralising government and causing one indigenous language to become official and widespread. In Vietnam, French is a negligible factor, but Vietnamese is now universal; the Philippines has done away with Spanish, but Tagalog has spread to all the islands; and in Indonesia, where only historians and lawyers now learn Dutch so as to gain access to old documents, Malay has boomed. The position of English in former British colonies is more robust, but that's mainly due to its status as the language of the world economy. In Myanmar, which spent more than a century under British rule but afterwards didn't integrate much into the world economy for decades, English today is merely a subject in school. Speaking it is not a widespread skill.

A special case is the Maghreb, consisting of Algeria, Morocco and Tunisia, where French and Arabic are locked in a struggle for dominance. The relative strong position of French here compared to Indochina can be explained by the many hundreds of thousands of settlers who lived here for nearly a century. By the time they – or rather their descendants – returned to France, which was around independence (1956–1962), the local elites had become thoroughly Gallicised.

The two tiny tongues of 1500

Five centuries ago, the Portuguese and Dutch languages were spoken by limited numbers in small countries. Portugal and the Dutch Republic went on to establish colonial empires. In the process, the Portuguese language spread enormously and keeps spreading today, whereas Dutch hardly did nor does. How come?

The answer in a nutshell is this: far more speakers of Portuguese than of Dutch were at the right places at the right times. With hindsight, the best opportunities for long-term language spread were the early colonisation of the Americas (minus the Caribbean) and, much later, the Scramble for Africa. And those are exactly the places where Portugal, but not the Netherlands, concentrated much of its colonial effort, sending sailors for exploration, soldiers for occupation, merchants for exploitation and great numbers of settlers for occupation and population shift.

In the early sixteenth century, the Portuguese founded their Brazilian colony, which they defended successfully against interlopers and then populated in a massive transfer of population: in the late eighteenth century, nearly one in three Portuguese migrated to Brazil, and the period between 1880 and 1960 saw another massive emigration, similarly fuelled by the old country's poverty. In Africa, the Portuguese stubbornly retained their slave forts along the coast even as they were no longer profitable. This enabled them to participate in the Scramble for Africa in the late nineteenth century, then settle the new territories.

Not so the Netherlands. It rushed to colonise and settle the Americas all right, but it soon lost its North American possessions to the British and the South American ones to the Portuguese. Being prosperous in the seventeenth and eighteenth centuries, it didn't produce large waves of emigrants to its colonies. Like Portugal, it had slave forts in Africa, but when they became unprofitable, it sold them to Britain. When soon afterwards Europe's Scramble for Africa began, the Netherlands was left out. Belgium (the historical southern Netherlands) did grab substantial spoils, but it did so in French. When large numbers of Dutch speakers emigrated in the nineteenth and twentieth centuries, their main destinations were (former) British colonies, where they were among the first to not only learn English but also give up their heritage language.

The Netherlands did have a strong colonial presence in Asia and the Caribbean, including Suriname. But these were the very parts of the world where European languages didn't stand much of a chance: the Asian populations were so huge that European newcomers were a drop in the ocean, while in much of the Caribbean, creole languages were paramount.

South Africa is a unique case. No other Dutch overseas possession ever attracted as many settlers as the Cape Colony, and the Dutch language was spoken there for a long time. However, it soon underwent significant changes under the impact of numerous European and African second-language speakers. After the colony was seized by Britain, 'Cape Dutch' no longer felt the standardising influence of European Dutch, gradually drifting away in terms of grammar, pronunciation and vocabulary. It took until 1925 formally to be given the new name of Afrikaans, justifying the development of its own standard. At 7 million native speakers and 10 million second-language speakers, it's now in the same order of magnitude as the Dutch tongue it has descended from.

The giant and the little country

And so it was that Portuguese came to rank seventh among the world's most widely spoken languages, whereas Dutch remained merely medium-sized even within Europe. And so it was, too, that Portugal, the source of a mighty tongue, became largely irrelevant to it. Most foreign students of Portuguese prefer the

World Cup 2018: the three best footballers on the planet played out their destinies in Russia. Two of them spoke Portuguese, the other Spanish. None of them, however, progressed beyond the quarter finals.

Brazilian variety: it is spoken by over 80 per cent of the *Lusofonia* (the Portuguese-speaking world), and in a country that is far more economically significant and culturally vibrant. Portugal is home to a mere 5 per cent of Portuguese speakers, and is just no match for the giant it has created.

Among the Portuguese there is a widespread sentiment that, as the inventors of the language, they're surely more entitled than their trans-Atlantic cousins to be the judges of what is proper and correct usage. The Brazilian variety has an impoverished grammar, or so many Portuguese people feel. They dislike the Brazilians' indifference to the TU-VOCÊ distinction (for informal and formal

231

'you', like French TU and VOUS). They dislike the way the Brazilians move pronouns to positions where no pronouns ever ought to move, or omit some of them altogether. Some Portuguese even dislike that the Brazilians have done away with their pet archaism, a conditional mood with a pronoun placed smack bang in the middle of the word: in COMÊ-LO-IA (would eat it), COMERIA means 'would eat', with the object pronoun LO spliced in (erasing the r).

If the Portuguese are unhappy about their linguistic dethronement, the Brazilians are hardly aware of any such acrimony. They seem to look upon Portugal in much the same way that many people look upon their ageing parents: after the turmoil of adolescence and the economic struggles of early adulthood, a new, more distant fondness has set in. The Brazilians' nickname for their European parent-nation sums up their attitude to a nicety: Portugal, to them, is A TERRINHA, 'the little country'.

6

Bengali

বাংলা

bangla

275 million speakers

250 million native speakers, nearly all in Bangladesh (155 million) and India (95 million). Over 20 million second-language speakers, mostly in Bangladesh. Over a million migrant speakers in Pakistan, Saudi Arabia and the UAE; substantial groups in other Gulf states, the UK and US.

Bengali

SELF-DESIGNATION বাংলা (bangla), বাংলা ভাষা (bangla bhasha); also called Bangla, Bengal, Bengalese (outdated).

FAMILY Indo-Aryan branch of the Indo-European family. Indo-Aryan languages are spoken in much of South Asia.

SCRIPT Bengali has its own script, which is also used by some smaller languages in the region. See main text.

GRAMMAR Nouns and pronouns do not have gender. Pronouns distinguish animate and inanimate as well as several levels of status. Adjectives are not inflected. While verbs have extensive conjugations for aspect and tense, they do not distinguish between singular and plural (yet the pronouns do).

SOUNDS Twenty-nine consonant sounds; seven vowel sounds, each with its nasal counterpart. Words tend to end in a vowel.

LOANWORDS Sanskrit, Persian, English.

EXPORTS *Jute*, *ganja* (for 'marijuana').

LAUREATE Rabindranath Tagore, who wrote in Bengali and English, in 1913 became the first non-European to win the Nobel Prize for literature, seventeeen years before Sinclair Lewis became the first American.

6: **Bengali**

World leaders in abugidas

In nearly all regions of the world, one script dominates. In Africa, the Americas, Oceania and most of Europe, the great majority of languages are written in the Roman alphabet. In large parts of Eastern Europe and Central Asia, Cyrillic is practically the only show in town. In a belt stretching from North Africa in the west to Pakistan in the east, you're likely to see the Arabic script wherever you turn. And while the characters of Chinese origin are prevalent in a mere handful of countries, they are nonetheless used by about one sixth of all human beings.

There is one region, however, that couldn't be more different from these: South and Southeast Asia. An observant backpacker travelling slowly and sinuously all the way from the Punjab in Western India to Bali in Indonesia can come across not one or two, but dozens of writing systems, and even the least attentive traveller couldn't fail to notice that there are several. Within this region, no country is more diverse than India, and within India, no state more so than West Bengal. (Since 1947, the former province of Bengal has been divided into West Bengal, a state of India, and East Bengal, which first joined Pakistan and in 1971 became independent as Bangladesh. In both parts, Bengali is the majority language, with English widely used in business and administration.)

The scriptural riches to be found in West Bengal do not immediately jump out at the visitor. Indeed, you could be forgiven for thinking that the West Bengalis use just two scripts. Of course, even that's not very common elsewhere (except in cities with migrant communities), but nor does it constitute an exciting multiplicity.

Of these two scripts, one would be the Roman alphabet, because English is one of West Bengal's official languages. It is widely used in speech and writing by those with a certain level of education, so

Multi-script India – Bengali (top), Hindi and English greet arrivals to Murshidabad in West Bengal.

all sorts of signs, posters, inscriptions and publications, both official and commercial, feature at least some English text.

Pride of place, however, goes to a competing script that, before I embarked on writing this book, I might carelessly have referred to as 'the Indian alphabet'. It bears some slight resemblance to our own script in that it runs from left to right and it has spaces between words, unlike Arabic and Chinese respectively. However, the differences are more conspicuous: not only is it entirely impregnable to the novice – unlike Greek and Cyrillic – but all the letters look like they're hanging from a top stroke. Calling it 'the Indian alphabet', however, would be a blunder, because no such thing exists. What one sees most in Bengal, West and East, is the Bengali script, used to write the Bengali language. And whenever non-English public texts in West Bengal are *not* in the Bengali script, they're usually written in Devanagari, India's most widespread writing system. Devanagari – the stress is on *na* – is used for Hindi, one of India's two official languages. In West Bengal, it can be found in such official and 'national' places as town halls, railway stations and airports, typically underneath the same text in Bengali. In a few districts of West Bengal, the Nepali language has co-official status, and it so happens that it too is written in Devanagari.

Unless you can read at least one of them, it's easy to confuse Bengali and Devanagari, just as an outsider could easily confuse the Latin and Cyrillic alphabets: they're similar in their overall appearance. But take a closer look and you see that they are rather different in their particulars. In the case of these two Indian scripts, only a few letters are practically identical, such as (I'll be giving the Bengali examples first) ন and न, or থ and थ. The rest are vaguely similar at best and quite distinctive in most cases. By way of example, have a look at this word, written in two different scripts: ভারত and भारत. Both are transliterated as *bhaarat*, both mean 'India', but visually they have little in common except the top line and their length. Since Devanagari and Bengali are the most widespread of all Indian scripts, it's only natural for outsiders to think of the top stroke as typical of all Indian scripts, or even 'the' Indian script. But in fact, few of the country's other scripts share this feature.*

If Roman, Bengali and Devanagari can be found written and printed throughout West Bengal, then why my enthusiasm over the state's diversity in this area? For one thing, the Arabic script is used by the 2 per cent or so of the population who write Urdu. But most of the answer lies in what we might call 'scriptural enclaves': linguistic minority communities with idiosyncratic writing systems. Thanks

---

* Historically speaking, the stroke is something of an outgrowth. North Indian scribes of old, writing with a reed pen on banana or palm leaves, liked to add the occasional little hook to their strokes, not unlike the serifs of many Roman fonts such as Gentium (in which this book has been set). Even as these hooks gradually came to be regarded as integral parts of the letters, they expanded and merged into today's continuous line. In South India, the use of the stylus led to a different style. Writing angular hooks would rip the leaves, and as a result, curvier letter shapes arose. Scripts have changed since, of course, but the contrast has left clear traces to this day.

to them, West Bengal is 'by far the richest in the country when it comes to scripts. As many as nine different scripts exist here and efforts are on to develop several others.' So said Ganesh N. Devy, director of the People's Linguistic Survey of India (PLSI) in a 2013 interview with *The Times of India*. Adding the Roman alphabet and the Chisaya script, which was only recently designed and published, we get the following list.

SCRIPT	LANGUAGE	LANGUAGE FAMILY	SPEAKERS WORLDWIDE
Bengali	Bengali	Indo-Aryan (IE*)	> 100m
Devanagari	Hindi	Indo-Aryan (IE)	> 100m
	Nepali	Indo-Aryan (IE)	> 10m
Roman	English	Germanic (IE)	> 10m
Perso-Arabic	Urdu	Indo-Aryan (IE)	> 100m
Sadri Thepa	Sadri	Indo-Aryan (IE)	> 1m
Ol Chiki	Santali	Munda (AA**)	> 1mn
Barang Kshiti	Ho	Munda (AA)	> 1m
Tolong Siki	Kurukh	Dravidian	> 1m
Limbu	Limbu	Sino-Tibetan	> 100,000
Chisaya	Kurmali	Indo-Aryan (IE)	> 100,000
Lepcha	Lepcha	Sino-Tibetan	> 10,000

Some of these languages are also written in one of the more widespread scripts.
* IE: Indo-European. ** AA: Austro-Asiatic, the family that includes Vietnamese.

Saved from *kakhagagha* and *aaaiii*

All the above writing systems could be called alphabets, but only in a loose manner. The word *alphabet*, which was used for practically all modern writing systems except Chinese and Japanese until a few decades ago, has acquired a more precise modern definition, and most of the scripts in the above list don't fit the bill.

In a genuine, card-carrying alphabet, every vowel sound and every consonant sound have their own separate character, or sometimes combination of characters. At least, in principle they do. In practice, it often doesn't work exactly like that: history has a way of messing up writing systems. Still, 'a letter for each sound' is the basic idea. The Greeks were the first to come up with it, and since their list of letters began with alpha and beta, this type of writing system came to be called *alphabet*. Roman and Cyrillic are genuine alphabets and so, against all appearances, is Korean.

A few of the world's scripts come very close to being alphabets, except that they discriminate against vowels: these are either omitted or coded for with consonants. They're called *abjads* and in today's world the best-known examples are the Arabic and Hebrew scripts. Just as the word *alphabet* is derived from the first letters of the Greek alphabet, so *abjad* is derived from the first letters of the Arabic abjad, ʾALIF, BĀʾ, JĪM and DĀL.

Like abjads, the Bengali script emphasises consonants, preferring not to use separate characters for vowels. But unlike abjads, it does represent all vowel sounds, only in a different manner than alphabets do: it equips the consonant characters with smaller vowel signs. As a matter of fact, Hebrew and Arabic too have the wherewithal – dots, lines and wriggles – to do this, but they rarely use it; in Bengali, the vowel signs are compulsory. Scripts of this type are called *abugidas*, a name that was derived from the word that an Ethiopian language, Ge'ez, uses for its own script. It's a good thing this word was borrowed from Ethiopia, for if abugidas had been named after the first letters of some Indian script, that would have given us either *kakhagagha* or *aaaiii*. We'll see why, later on.

While we're on the subject, let me also mention the third and final kind of writing system that is almost but not exactly alphabetic: the *syllabary*, two of which we'll meet towards the end of this book. As the name suggests, every single sign of a syllabary represents a syllable. That makes them similar to abugidas, but unlike these, they consist of characters that cannot be dissected into a consonant part and a vowel part. Think of it as the difference between the ± and the $ signs: while it's perfectly clear where the 'plus' and the 'minus' are represented in ±, the $ sign is not composed of a 'dol' and a 'lar' element. The former is reminiscent of the abugida method, the latter of the syllabary.

Bengali as a beauty

As for the Bengali abugida, its basic workings are of an elegance that borders on the boring – at first sight at least. Once you've mastered its thirty-five consonant characters and eleven vowel signs, you just start clicking the vowels on to the consonants. Take the character called *na*, which in its barest form looks like this: ন. When it appears in a word, it's usually pronounced /n/. Next, take the signs া, ু and ে, which stand for the sounds /a/, /u/ and /e/ (as in *bar, book* and *bay*). Tacking the signs on to the character gives us না for /na/, নু for /nu/ and নে for /ne/. Note that in না, the vowel sign is positioned to the right of the consonant, as we would expect in a script read from left to right, but the vowel is placed underneath it in নু and to its left in নে – indeed, some vowel signs are placed *around* the consonant. This corroborates the idea that the vowel signs are not to be considered as separate characters. Each consonant-plus-vowel combination has to be read as a whole, as one compound character. Otherwise, it would be tempting to pronounce নে as /en/ rather than the correct /ne/.

But this apparent consistency starts to crumble on closer inspection, because Bengali has a few intricacies up its sleeve, some useful, others less so. The best of them is the fact that the consonant characters have what you might call an 'inbuilt vowel sound'. When I said just now that ন is pronounced /n/, I hedged the statement with 'usually', and that was because when ন appears not covered with a vowel but in the nude, so to speak, it is actually pronounced /no/ (as in *not* without the t). The greeting NOMOSKAR, for instance, is written as নমস্কার, with the bare ন as its first sign. That's a neat trick. Syllables with /o/ are very frequent in Bengali, so the default option saves a lot of time and ink.

But what to do when the sound you want to write is actually just /n/, not /n/ plus a vowel? There's a solution for that: you add something that looks like a grave accent (as in *learnèd*) to the bottom right of the consonant: ন্. The sign goes under several names, among them the evocative term 'vowel killer'. Killing vowels is an excellent solution to the problem just mentioned, but here we encounter the first failing in the Bengali system: in practice, the sign is often omitted, thereby creating ambiguity.

There are other shortcomings too. The pronunciation of the inbuilt vowel is not as consistent as I made it sound just now. It's usually the regulation /o/ sound, but in quite a few cases it's /ō/ (as in *know*), even though there is a separate vowel sign for this sound. And as we just saw, it may even be silent, namely when the vowel killer is omitted. So whenever you see a consonant such as ন in the nude, there's no way of telling whether it represents /no/, /nō/ or /n/. Ah, and by the way, the Roman transliteration of the Bengali inbuilt vowel is not *o*, as would make sense, but *a*, because that used to be the pronunciation centuries ago.

The great poet Rabindranath Tagore – who wrote in Bengali and English – with fellow Nobel laureate Albert Einstein, 1930.

Next, in another surprise move, Bengali occasionally uses full characters to write vowels instead of vowel signs tacked on to consonant characters. This occurs when a vowel is not preceded by a consonant to carry it, which is to say at the beginning of a word. The designers of the script could have created a silent character to carry any of the vowel signs, which is exactly how some abugidas work (Limbu for one), but not Bengali. Instead, eleven full vowel characters have been created, in addition to the more frequent eleven vowel signs. And while we might hope for, indeed expect, these vowel characters to be similar in shape to the vowel signs, most aren't. The sound /u/, to give one example, looks like উ as a full character, but like ু when it's a vowel sign.

Bengali as a behemoth

The designers of the Bengali abugida could have stopped here, and they probably should have. What we've discussed so far is all that any abugida needs: a complete, perhaps somewhat overequipped, toolkit for writing consonants and vowels, both in pairs and when occurring separately. But I said it before and I'll say it again: history has a way of messing up writing systems. While any language is always changing, writers tend to resent this and try to keep it stable on the page. They don't mind frilly spellings that reflect old pronunciations, underlying grammatical patterns and foreign word origins. They get a kick out of exceptions, complications and subtleties that are beyond the ken of mere mortals. Recall what a member of the French Academy wrote: it's a good thing if a spelling 'distingue les gens de Lettres d'avec les ignorans et les simples femmes'.

Bengali, like French, is a case in point. So what bells, whistles and hidden defects does this particular script have? It has two separate signs for the same /i/-sound (as in *beat*) and another two for /u/ (as in *book*), but none for /e/ (as in *rest*, not as in *bay*) – because, well ... history. For the same reason, the /sh/ sound can be represented by three different characters, two of which moonlight as /s/. (Of course, it's no worse than aspects of English, where the /i/ sound – or to be precise /ī/ – can be spelt as *ee, ea, ei, ie, y, ey, e* or even *i*.)

More troubling even than these inconsistent spellings is the issue of the so-called conjunct signs or ligatures, which fuse several consonant characters into one. Authentically Bengali words rarely if ever have two consonants at the beginning of a syllable, but words borrowed from Sanskrit, Persian or English do. The language regulators could have decided to use vowel killers to write these. Take the word SKRU for 'screw'. They could have ordained that this be spelt with three characters: an *s* equipped with a vowel killer, a *k* with a vowel killer, and an *r* with a *u* sign attached. Instead, they decided that the correct spelling consists of just one character, a monster ligature fusing *s*, *k* and *r*, with a *u* sign tacked on. I can't even reproduce this thing in MS Word, because the software rips it apart into three separate characters plus two vowel killers and a *u* sign, exactly as I suggested.

Now, if these ligatures were a marginal phenomenon, like the French œ, the Dutch capital IJ or the more frequent Danish-Norwegian Æ, anyone could live with them; I would have discreetly ignored them. But there exist no fewer than 285 different ligatures, and while many follow simple rules, quite a few don't. Between them, they bring the sum total of Bengali characters to 331, and that's without counting the vowel signs, some historical characters and a handful of essential diacritics. This means that the ligatures really play havoc on Bengali as a system: it's complexity bordering on chaos. Imagine what schoolchildren have to go through. Imagine the problems that printers and typewriter manufacturers used to face. Bengali should have done as MS Word and I suggested: use vowel killers to take care of consonant clusters. Impossible? Ugly? In Tamil, they do just that, and don't go telling the Tamilians there's something wrong with their language.

The Phoenician connection

While Tamil deals with this cluster issue rather cleverly and while Limbu, as I mentioned earlier, does a more efficient job writing word-initial vowels, the take-home message about India's scripts is that most of them are similar – not visually, but structurally speaking. Of the big ones, only Arabic and Roman do not fit the pattern, and they were introduced from outside rather than being home-grown. With these two exceptions, all of India's major scripts are abugidas, and while each one of them has different character shapes and many have this or that individual foible, they all share many features. For this, there are two historical reasons: they've all sprung from the same common source and their users have a long tradition of writing Sanskrit, the classical language of South Asia.

The common source, the great-grandparent, so to speak, of all later Indian abugidas, is called Brahmi, which is why all the offspring – dozens upon dozens of them – are collectively referred to as 'Brahmic'. The family tree would be huge and full of arcane names, so I've pruned it to the bare essentials, leaving only the four branches that are represented in this book. If we were to study every individual branch of the whole family tree of Brahmic scripts, we would note that the modern scripts have maintained most of the original characters, and it's principally their shapes that have morphed through the centuries. Only occasionally were old characters jettisoned or new ones created from scratch. This implies that most of the modern characters in each Brahmic script are historically linked to their counterparts in the other Brahmic scripts. It's just that all these centuries of gradual divergence have obscured the old links – which is why ভারত no longer looks anything like भारत (that's *bhaarat* for 'India', if you remember).

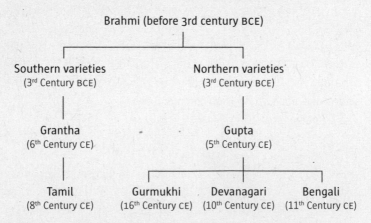

Dates indicate first known occurrence; older scripts may continue to exist alongside newer ones for a long time.

In the severely pruned family tree above, we see Brahmi perched on top, yet this shouldn't be taken as an indication that it had no ancestor. Most experts, especially those outside South Asia, trace Brahmi to the Middle East, though they disagree over the details. The most likely scenario seems to be that Brahmi was an improved successor of a slightly earlier, more westerly abugida called Kharosthi, used in and around today's Pakistan. This in turn was inspired by, but far from a carbon copy of, the Aramaic script. The scenario makes geographical and chronological sense, since the Aramaic script was used at the time by South Asia's powerful westerly neighbour, the Persians. If the Indian scripts are indeed the offshoots of Aramaic, this implies that they and our Latin scripts share a common origin:

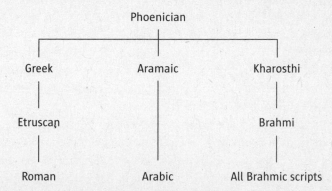

In this family tree, the middle column consists of abjads, the right column of abugidas and the left column of alphabets

How on earth could this one common origin result in systems as dissimilar as the Indian, European and Arabic scripts – in abugidas, alphabets and abjads? The thing is that Phoenician and Aramaic are Semitic languages, just like Arabic and Hebrew, and they all use abjads because they actually prefer them. It sits easily with their structure, in which vowels are not all that important. In a word, Semitic and abjads are a happy marriage.

But when these scripts spread west to Greece and east to South Asia people in those regions soon discovered that an abjad just wouldn't work for their own tongues, which were all Indo-European, not Semitic*. To make writing work, vowels sounds had to be represented. The Greeks chose a simple solution: they took a couple of old Phoenician consonant characters they had no use for and turned them into vowels, thereby creating the first alphabet. Unsophisticated though the idea was, it has worked remarkably well for nearly three thousand years.

The South Asians tackled the problem differently, perhaps more ingeniously. A rich scholarly tradition of linguistic analysis gave them keen insight into phonology. Like the Greeks, they realised that writing their languages without vowels would make the resulting texts unintelligible. And since their syllables were typically of the 'one consonant, one vowel' type, they hit on the novel idea of equipping the consonant characters with vowel signs. Seeing how the /a/ (as in *Iraq*) was more frequent than others, they chose to make it the default vowel (later to be pronounced /o/ in Bengali). Additionally, their phonological acumen enabled them to substitute a more logical order of the characters for the haphazard one that Middle Eastern and European scripts have always had: they clustered consonants that share the same 'point of articulation', the place in the mouth where they're produced; they also made the vowels a separate group. It's this rearrangement of the characters that explains why Bengali's list of consonants begins with *ka, kha, ga, gha*; and that of the vowels begins with short *a*, long *a* (*ā* or *aa*), short *i*, long *i*. As I mentioned a few pages ago, this new order doesn't make for a sonorous coinage like *alphabet*, *abjad* or *abugida*; however, the organising principle behind it makes admirable linguistic sense.

For Greek, an abugida system like this wouldn't have worked as smoothly, because like most members of the Indo-European family (remember Russian's VZGLYAD), it thinks nothing of multiple consonants at the beginning of a syllable – think of Greek names such as Plato, Strabo and Ptolemy (with non-silent p!). When in the second millennium BCE people of Indo-European stock first

---

* It is tempting to put this even more grandly, saying that 'the idea of writing' spread, but that would be incorrect. In both Greece and South Asia, other forms of writing existed before, only to be forgotten when the associated cultures collapsed. Quite a few South Asian experts believe that instead of Phoenician, the Indus Valley script is ancestral to Brahmi. However, they have to explain away a 1,400-year gap in the archive and a curious lack of resemblance.

ກະຊວງຍຸຕິທໍາ

MINISTRE DE LA JUSTICE

The script of Lao, Laos's national language, is one of many in South East Asia that are derived from an old Indian script. Colonial French is still sticking it out, but for how much longer?

reached South Asia, their language, an early form of Sanskrit, was much like that. But mingling with the Dravidian aboriginals of the subcontinent, their language gradually changed. In Dravidian languages, consonant clusters were non-existent, and as a result, the Sanskrit speakers gradually began to avoid them too. When some time around about 500 BCE writing was reintroduced to the subcontinent, the living languages of the day had few or no consonant clusters left. The abugida concept fitted them like a glove.

Writers and their banal pursuits

If it required an extraordinary leap of the imagination to turn the Aramaic abjad into an abugida, yet another aspect of early Indian writing was more exceptional still. Typically, wherever writing takes root, the scribes and their scriptures carry high prestige. There's something supernatural about this skill of catching the ephemeral spoken word and fixing it on some surface from which it can be retrieved and made to sound and echo and echo again. In societies with a low degree of literacy – all societies until not so long ago, that is – capable writers were generally not mere craftsmen, but could climb to lofty positions in the spheres of religion and state. In China, the script was a defining feature of civilisation. In Europe, the Roman alphabet became the signature of Western Christianity (which is why the pagan runes were pushed into disuse). In the Muslim world, the Arabic script attained almost divine status.

Not so in South Asia. The elites stubbornly clung to the oral tradition, which had preserved for centuries not only the ancient Hindu Vedas but also more recent works of Buddhism, philosophy, poetry, drama and even science and technology. The underlying reason for their resistance to writing may have been to protect their position: memorising all those venerable texts was part of what justified their privilege. Or it may have been because they didn't trust the new-fangled medium to be sufficiently durable – a worry that was eventually borne out, as most texts from the era, unless carved in stone, succumbed to South Asia's hot and humid monsoon climate.

Such writing as was done served commerce and other quotidian pursuits. It briefly played a more exalted role when the Buddhist King Ashoka (mid-third century BCE) had his social and moral precepts published on pillars, boulders and cave walls throughout his extensive empire. But on the whole, South Asian elites would drag their feet for over half a millennium before taking to writing in the mid-second century CE.

This was to have two major consequences for the scripts themselves. Firstly, when the oral literature was finally committed to paper (or rather, to dried leaves), an acute spelling problem made itself felt. The abugidas had been tailor-made to suit the vernaculars, but the whole cultural tradition was in Sanskrit, which still had all those Indo-European consonant clusters. Whereas the daughter languages of Sanskrit had KISĀN for 'farmer', TĀRĀ for 'star' and TIN for 'three', (Old) Sanskrit itself had KRSHĀNA, STR and TRI. If the South Asians had begun to write in Sanskrit right from the moment they put pen to leaf, centuries earlier, their scholars might well have decided against an abugida, developing something more akin to an alphabet instead, just like the far-away Greeks. But by this time, the abugida was well ingrained in the Indian literary mind.

Rather than being replaced, the system was merely adapted to Sanskrit by creating those ligatures that today torment schoolchildren, printers, typewriter manufacturers and software developers. They need to learn them not because they read and write the Sanskrit language itself – they don't, any more than the average European reads and writes Latin. But the modern languages have adopted a huge number of Sanskrit words, in much the same way that English and other European languages have borrowed words from classical Greek and Latin: in modern Bengali, KRSHĀNA is once again used for 'farmer', after centuries of absence from the vocabulary. And just as our spelling has kwiksotikally maintained the expendable but classical characters *c*, *q* and *x*, so nearly all Brahmic scripts have maintained the equally superfluous ligatures.

The other consequence of the belated acceptance of writing by the elites is India's present multiplicity of scripts. If they had embraced the new invention as soon as it hit the market and applied it to the ancient holy texts, Brahmi (or even its predecessor) would have become a revered standard throughout the region. But they didn't, and by the time writing was finally used for purposes of religion, scholarship and literature, a tradition of freely designing new script types had already taken hold. After all, writing for a long time was just this thing merchants and humble desk-workers did, and just as human languages are continuously diverging into dialects, so scripts will likewise diversify unless there's a centripetal force to stop them. That unifying role can be fulfilled by a holy book – the Koran, Bible and Tanakh all prove this – but in terms of prestige, the Hindu scriptures never eclipsed the oral tradition. Alternatively, an empire of long standing can have the same effect of preserving the script as it is, but in South Asia this never happened, as for most of its history the region has been either divided or ruled by elites wielding foreign scripts.

In the absence of a holy book and a solid empire, the script is bound to hit the fan, resulting in numerous varieties scattered all over the place. This happened in several parts of Europe in its pre-empire and pre-Bible period: there were not only several Greek and Roman alphabets, but also Etruscan, Oscan, Iberian, Tartessian, Ogham, Runic and others. The same happened in South

লেখন   ১

শুধু তোমার কথায়
দীপ্ত জ্বলের মালিকা,
উক্ত আঁধার নিশীথে
উড়িছে আলোর শিখা॥

My fancies are fireflies
    specks of living light—
        twinkling in the dark.

আমার লিখন ধূলি পথীনের
        ক্ষণিক কালের ফুলে,
চলিতে চলিতে দেখো যারা তার
        চলিতে চলিতে ভুল॥

The same voice murmurs
        in these desultory lines
which is born in wayside pansies
        letting hasty glances pass by.

প্রজাপতি সেটা গুন না সনে,
        নিমেষ গণিয়া যাবে,
সময় তাহার ঢেলাই আছে আছে॥

The butterfly does not count years
        but moments
and therefore has enough time.

Part of a poem handwritten by Tagore in Bengali and English.

Asia, resulting in a whole family of abugidas. And when the Hindu and Buddhist scriptures spread to Southeast Asia, along with a culture that held the oral tradition in high esteem, local writers would soon adapt the script to the needs of their own tongues. The national languages of Burma, Thailand, Laos and Cambodia are written in as many abugidas to this day; many languages of Malaysia, the Philippines, Vietnam (though not Vietnamese) and Indonesia (including Javanese) used to have their own varieties before adopting the Latin alphabet. To the north of South Asia, the Tibetan script is yet another Brahmic offshoot, and even Japanese writing drew some inspiration from India. In the end, all these Brahmic apples rolled away so far from the Brahmi tree that the ancient texts at some point became inaccessible. They wouldn't be deciphered until the nineteenth century, by outsiders.

One language, one script

Has the proliferation of scripts continued to this day? Not quite. For a long time, their number did keep growing. This brought about a widely accepted idea that a real language ought to have a script of its own; not having one involved the risk of being relegated to dialect status. By adopting an existing writing system, a region would signal its linguistic (or sometimes religious) affiliation; by developing a script for itself, it would lay claim to having a fully fledged language of its own, as well as a distinct regional identity. Before we dismiss this as a silly idea, let's realise that language ideology is just another dimension in which cultures may differ, just like kinship systems, food taboos and rites of passage. The 'one language, one script' idea is no sillier (and probably more benign in its consequences) than the 'one language, one country' notion that has held sway in Europe since the rise of nationalism in the late 1700s.

In South Asia, the number of scripts finally began to wane in the nineteenth and early twentieth centuries, mostly to accommodate the spread of the printing press. The Nepali script, for instance, was gradually replaced by Devanagari between 1900 and the 1950s. Nonetheless, in the course of the twentieth century there began a new surge of script creation, which shows no signs yet of abating. Ethnic groups struggling for social and cultural emancipation typically demand official recognition of their languages, and having a writing system of their own is felt to strengthen their case. That is why 'efforts are on to develop several others [i.e. scripts]', as Ganesh N. Devy said in his *Times of India* interview. These efforts are aimed at languages such as Bodo (of the Sino-Tibetan family; over a million speakers) and Rangpuri (Indo-Aryan, well over ten million).

While the speakers of Bodo and Rangpuri are still making do with a script which they feel is not 'theirs', millions of others can and do write their minority languages in their very own letters, as shown in the table earlier in this chapter. While some scripts have taken off more strongly than others, the fact is that they're all being used, both in publications and in people's handwritten notes and letters. Spoken as these languages are by people that are fewer in number and lower on the socio-economic ladder, their scripts are nowhere near as publicly visible as Bengali, Roman, Devanagari and Arabic. But still, these riches are out there, alive and thriving. They are valued by their own communities, whose linguistic identity they symbolise and whose emancipation they aim to serve.

Which is why, if you're considering a script safari outside the world's big multicultural cities, there's no better place to go than West Bengal.

5

Arabic

العربية

al-'arabiyyah

375 million speakers

Around 300 million people have Arabic as their first language, mostly in North Africa and the Middle East (including minorities in Israel, Iran and Turkey). Second-language speakers number around 75 million but Muslims worldwide tend to know at least a little Koranic Arabic.

Arabic

SELF-DESIGNATION العربية (al-'arabiyyah), عربي (arabī)

FAMILY Arabic is the most widely spoken of the Semitic languages, which is a group within the large Afro-Asiatic family. Outside the Arab world, Semitic languages are spoken in Israel, Ethiopia and Eritrea, while the Afro-Asiatic family covers all of North Africa and the Sahara, the Horn of Africa and the region around Lake Chad.

MIGRANTS Substantial minorities live in Western Europe, the Americas, Australia and Indonesia.

SCRIPT Arabic has its own script, which was later adopted by many other languages.

GRAMMAR See main text.

SOUNDS Standard Arabic has three vowels (/a/, /i/ and /u/), each in short and long varieties. Most spoken dialects have two additional long vowels, /ē/ and /ō/. These are used in some modern words in the standard language as well. There are twenty-eight consonants, a remarkable proportion of which are articulated fairly far back in the mouth or in the throat.

LOANWORDS Aramaic (a closely related Semitic language), Persian, French, English.

EXPORTS See the 'Concise Dictionary'.

KORANIC LANGUAGE The modern standard language is more similar to sixth-century Koranic Arabic than to any of the modern varieties, known as 'dialects'. The modern standard is used only in very formal settings, and many Arabs cannot speak it, though they will understand it.

5: **Arabic**

A Concise Dictionary of Our Arabic

In the seventh and eighth centuries, European Christendom got an unexpected new neighbour: Islam. Its rapid expansion, led by Arabs, was followed by its gradual pushback in Spain and Portugal, a series of Crusades, the Ottomans' conquest and loss of the Balkans, British and French colonialism in North Africa and the Middle East, Arab nationalism, and today's distinctly uneasy relationship.

One of the things about this neighbour that Europe has never warmed to is the language. Europe's successive ringleaders have always spoken some Romance or Germanic tongue, with Russian as the only outlier (but still related; see chapter 8). Arabic, in contrast, is something else altogether. It sounds different, in a way that Europeans tend to describe as guttural or dark. It looks different, with a script that most Europeans cannot decipher. And under the bonnet it's pretty different too, though few Europeans have examined its inner workings in any depth.

The combination of religious antagonism, geographic proximity, political enmity and linguistic disparity has caused many Europeans to regard the Arab world as the quintessential Other, speaking the quintessential Otherish. This outsider's perspective couldn't contrast more starkly with the view from within. Arabs think the world of their language. To Arabs who are Muslim – that is to say, the large majority – it's the blessed tongue in which God chose to reveal the Koran to Muhammad. Arabic is, to quote the Arabist and linguist Clive Holes, 'revered by rich, poor, educated, and illiterate alike as the linguistic jewel in the Islamic cultural patrimony ... unsurpassable in beauty, an ethereal ideal of eloquence, perfect symmetry, and succinctness'. And that is without mentioning the script, with its tradition of ornate calligraphy. In a word, Arabs adore their language in a way that makes the French seem moderate in the appreciation of theirs.*

But you can't spend over thirteen centuries separated by a mere Mediterranean or land border without some exchange of people, stuff and ideas. By people, I mean fighters, traders, diplomats and pilgrims; by stuff, I mean inventions, foods and books; and by ideas, I mean Greek philosophy, Indian mathematics, Arabic medicine and much else. A lot of it was so new to the receiving parties that along with the novelties, words to describe them were imported too. As a result, European languages adopted a substantial chunk of vocabulary from Arabic, some of which originally came from Persian, Sanskrit, Aramaic or other Asian languages. Conversely, Arabic took up a fair number of loanwords from Europe. (The language has a reputation for maintaining purity and an aversion to borrowing, but that's not quite the whole truth, as we will see.)

Below, I will try to nibble away at the idea that Arabic is deeply alien and unapproachable. My main gnawing implement will be a *Concise Dictionary* of Arabic words that you and I, knowing English as we do, can relate to, some intuitively, some after a little etymologising (or sometimes a bit more). In my personal language-learning experience, such connections, however tenuous, make memorising words less daunting, and that often makes all the difference. And even if you don't want to study a language in-depth, seeing the historical links brings it psychologically closer.

The entries in my *Concise Dictionary of Our Arabic* are varied in character. Many are the originals of words that we borrowed from Arabic, some of them a long time ago, such as *garble*, others more recently, such as *ayatollah*.

---

* The spelling QUR'AN is a fairly good transliteration of the Arabic, though better still would be QUR'ĀN, with a hamza instead of an apostrophe and, importantly, a macron on the a. However, it's not, in my opinion, the English name of Islam's holy book. KORAN is the English exonym for the book, while QUR'AN or QUR'ĀN is the Arabic endonym; in the same way, AUSTRIA is an exonym for the German-speaking endonym ÖSTERREICH, and LANDAN (لندن) is the Arabic exonym for LONDON. There is a tendency in English to adopt endonyms in the mistaken belief that exonyms are disrespectful. In fact, they're usually just adaptations of foreign names to a language's phonology and spelling. Rather than making the Qur'an more venerable, this faux-thentic spelling makes it look alien. As for pronunciation, speakers of English and other European languages rarely get near the original, regardless of how it is spelt.

A Modern Standard

Before inviting you to plunge into the *Concise Dictionary*, I need to explain a few things about Arabic that are different from most other languages.

First, the term 'Arabic', more or less like 'Chinese', covers a much wider variety than does the term 'English'. Arabic, like English, has many varieties, commonly referred to as 'dialects': one, or sometimes several, for each country where it's spoken. But mutual comprehension between these is much more difficult than in the case of English, especially between speakers from the geographic extremes of the Arab world, say Mauritania, Yemen and Iraq. The Arabic 'dialects' are as diverse as the Romance languages. But these differences all but disappear on the page, because the dialects are rarely written. For this purpose, Modern Standard Arabic is mostly used, which is a modernised version of the Koran's classical Arabic. This is nobody's mother tongue and will be heard spoken only in very formal situations. Unlike Standard English, Modern Standard Arabic changes very little

The Arabic script owes its high prestige to the Koran, which is usually read in Arabic throughout the Islamic world.

if at all, apart from the coinage of new vocabulary, since it is guided more by the Koran than by the spoken languages. All words in our *Concise Dictionary* belong to the classical language or the modern standard and usually both, unless a regional origin is mentioned.

Besides words, the list also contains a number of so-called 'roots'. These are sequences of consonants, usually three (written here with hyphens between them), that cannot as such be used in a sentence, but do have approximate meanings. On the basis of these three consonants, Arabic creates actual words – nouns, adjectives and especially verbs – by inserting vowels between the consonants and by adding prefixes and suffixes. This elaborate system can produce a great number of meaningful forms based on each root, and while their exact meanings are not always predictable, the connection is usually self-explanatory. The conjugation of verbs and the declination of nouns and adjectives follow the same principles: consonants form the skeleton of each word, vowels and additional consonants flesh it out. This root system is typical of (and more or less unique to) Semitic languages.

Another feature of Arabic is the absence of the /p/ sound in its phonological system. When there is a /p/ in words borrowed from other languages, these will be changed into either /b/ or /f/. Several examples can be found in the dictionary.

Finally, a word about spelling. Arabic vowel sounds are easy, since there are only three (/a/, /i/, /u/), which can be short (written as *a, i, u*) or long (*ā, ī, ū*)(though the occassional dialect-derived *ē* and *ō* can be heard in the standard language). Some consonant sounds are much more different from the ones we're used to, and this is reflected in the writing. If you want to know what the consonants sound like, you will easily find the information online. As for the transliteration in the Latin alphabet, note that letters written with a diacritic sign represent different sounds from those written without (*ḍ* versus *d*, *ḵ* versus *k*, *š* versus *s*; and *ḡ*, which doesn't, however, have a *g* for company), but I've treated them as identical when alphabetising the list. Two other Arabic consonants are easily overlooked in transliteration, as they are represented as mere half ringlets. I've followed the tradition of transcribing the *hamza* as ʾ (representing the so-called glottal stop, as heard in *uh-oh*) and *ayin* as ⟨. I've placed them at the very beginning of the list, before A; they also influence the order of entries starting with other letters: e.g. BAꜥL comes before BĀBĀ.

And now, without further ado, may I present:

Babel's Concise Dictionary of Our Arabic

' (hamza)

'AB – father. In the form 'ABŪ it is often part of Arabic men's full names. The word *abbot* is derived from 'ABBĀ, 'my father' in Aramaic.

'AMĪR – commander, prince. This has given us English *emir*. The Arabic compound 'AMĪR AL-BAḤR 'sea commander' has given us *admiral.*

'IKSĪR – elixir. The English word includes a form of the article AL. The Arabic word was borrowed from Greek: XĒRÍON was a desiccative powder for wounds, based on XĒRÓS 'dry'.

'-M-M (*root*) – go, lead the way. This root has produced some remarkable derivatives: 'IMĀM is an Islamic leader. 'UMM is a mother (as in the famous singer 'Umm Kulthum). The 'UMMA is the worldwide Muslim community, while *a* (instead of *the*) 'UMMA is a people, a nation. The Arabic expression 'UMM AL-... (literally 'mother of ...') was borrowed into European languages as 'mother of all ...', meaning the largest of its kind.

ꜥ (ayin)

ꜥARAQ – arrack. The name of the liquor is related to the Arabic root for 'sweat'. The names of the Balkan liquor *rakija* and Turkish *raki* are derivations from ꜥARAQ.

ꜥ-L-Y (*root*) – to go up; high. It has produced the names ꜥALIYY (Ali) and ꜥĀLIYA (Alia, Aleeyah), meaning 'high, exalted', as well as ꜥALĀ' AD-DĪN (*Alladin*); see under DĪN.

ꜥŪD – wood, oud, lute. Our *lute* – both the word and the instrument – derives from the Arabic AL-ꜥŪD.

ꜥULAMĀ' – ulema, the learned ones, the clerics. Based on the root ꜥ - L - M for 'knowing'.

A

AL – the. This a frequent first syllable in loanwords from Arabic, because the article was borrowed along with the noun. It occurs either in its full form (*alchemy, alcohol, alfalfa, algorithm, algebra, alkaline, Allah, Algeria, elixir* and others) or as a mere *a-* due to the regular Arabic merger of AL with some consonants following the article (*adobe, apricot, arroba, arsenal, artichoke, azimuth, hazard,* et cetera).

ALLĀH – God. This is a contraction of the article AL and the old word for 'god, deity', 'ILAH. The word is present in many compound names and other nouns, such as *Abdullah* ('servant of God'), 'IN SHĀ'A LLĀH (*inshallah*) 'God willing', BISMI LLĀH (*bismillah*) 'in the name of God', 'ĀYATU LLĀH (*ayatollah*), 'sign of God', ḤIZBU LLĀH (*Hezbollah*), 'party of God'.

B

BA'L – lord, owner. As Baal, we know this word as the name for several Middle Eastern deities, including Beelzebub.

BĀBĀ – daddy; pope. Ali Baba, of forty thieves fame, means 'Daddy Ali'.

BABAĞĀ' – parrot. The Arabic word has been borrowed by most European languages, including by English as popinjay.

BADAWIYY – bedouin. The European languages have adopted the colloquial plural form BADAWĪN. The Arabic word derives from BADW for 'desert' or 'camp'.

BARIYY – savage. In Andalucian Arabic, BARRI came to refer to the outer, less civilised parts of the city; hence the Spanish meaning of 'neighbourhood' for BARRIO, a word adopted by American English.

BURQA' OR BURQU' – burka. Derived from the verb BARQA'A for 'cover, hide'.

BURTUQĀL – oranges. The word for the fruit comes from the name Portugal. Also see NĀRANJ.

D

DĀR – house. The name Dar-es-Salaam means 'house of peace'.

ḌIMMIYY – dhimmi, non-Muslim in a Muslim state. Literally 'protected person'.

DĪN – faith. Seen in names like Aladdin ('ALĀ' AD-DĪN; also see '-L-Y), which means 'height (or nobility) of the faith'.

F

FALĀFIL – falafel. FALĀFIL is the plural of FILFIL, 'pepper', which was probably borrowed from a South Asian language that was also at the origin of our word pepper. All these words for falafel and pepper may ultimately mean 'round thing'.

FALLĀḤ – fellah, peasant.

FAQĪR – poor man. A specialised meaning is 'religious mendicant' or 'ascetic'.

FATWĀ – fatwa, a formal legal opinion. A person who delivers such opinions is a MUFTIN, 'mufti'. Both are derived from the verb 'AFTĀ, 'to opine'.

FIRDAWS – paradise. Both the Arabic and the English words have travelled a long way from their Iranian origin, which has been reconstructed as PARIDAIĴAH, meaning 'circular boundary wall' or 'space enclosed by such a wall'.

G

ĞARBALA – sift. Through medieval Latin (GARBELLARE) and Anglo-Norman (GARBELER), the Arabic word has produced garble, now 'mutilate, make false', but formerly 'sift, especially spices'.

ĞAZĀL – gazelle.

Ğ-R-B (root) – go down, go away. The west, where the sun goes down, is called AL-ĞARB. This is at the root of the name Algarve, in Portugal, as well as Maghreb (MAĞRIB), the westernmost part of the Islamic world. Trafalgar Square is named after a place in Spain whose Arabic name was ṬARAF AL-ĞARB or 'Western cape'.

ĞŪL – ghoul, demon.

H

ḤAJJ – hajj, pilgrimage. A ḤAJJIYY, English hajji, is someone who has fulfilled this Islamic duty (see under -IYY).

ḤALĀL – halal, permitted, especially under Muslim customs.

ḤALĀWA – halva, a confection made of sesame seed paste. Derived from the adjective ḤULW or ḤALW, 'sweet'.

ḤAMMĀM – bath(house). In English, the Turkish form *hamam*, with one *m*, is used for a Turkish bath. The Arabic form with double *m* is the original; it's derived from the root Ḥ-M-M for 'heating'.

ḤARĪSA – harissa, a spice mix. A culinary term from Tunisian Arabic, from a verb meaning 'to crush'.

ḤAŠĪŠ – grass, dried herbs; also hashish. Traditionally the word *assassin* has been linked to ḤAŠŠĀŠĪN, 'hashish users'; alternatively, it may come from ʾASĀSIYYŪN, meaning 'fundamentalists'.

Ḥ-B-B (*root*) – related to love and seeds. The name ḤABĪB (*Habib*) means 'beloved'. ABŪ ḤIBĀB ('baobab') means 'father of seeds'.

ḤIJĀB – hijab, headscarf. From a root denoting concealment.

Ḥ-K-M (*root*) – wisdom, judging, ruling. The South Asian *hakims* who practice traditional medicine owe their name to this Arabic word. *Hakim* ('wise, ruler') and *Abdul Hakim* ('servant of the all-wise [God]) are given names.

Ḥ-M-D (*root*) – praise, thank. The names MUḤAMMAD (*Muhammad*) and MAḤMŪD (*Mahmud*) both mean 'praised'. ḤAMĪD ('praiseworthy') and ḤĀMID ('praiser'), both reduced to *Hamid* in English, contain the same root.

Ḥ-R-M (*root*) – forbidden. Three well-known words are derived from this root: *harem* (borrowed via Turkish), the part of the house forbidden to all males except close relatives; *haram*, the opposite of *halal*; and *Boko Haram*, the West African terrorist organisation that objects to *boko*, a Hausa word for 'fake', used to refer to 'Westernisation' or 'Western education'.

Ḥ-S-N (*root*) – goodness. The given names ḤASAN (*Hassan*: 'good-looking, manly, strong') and its diminutive ḤUSAYN (which has numerous English spellings) have evolved from this root.

ḤUMMUṢ – hummus; chickpeas. *Hummus* and Hebrew KHÚMUS are loanwords from Arabic. The full Arabic name is ḤUMMUṢ BI-ṬAḤĪNA, 'chickpeas with tahini' (see ṬAḤĪNA)

ḤŪRIYYA – houri. A tricky term, this. The Koran mentions the houris several times as fair women with large eyes, but the story about sventy-two virgins is of later, and hearsay, origin. The English word 'whore' is unrelated.

I

IḰTĀRA – choose. The 'choicest' wool would be MUḰAYYAR, which via Italian and French gave English *mocayre*, later changed to *mohair*. The chosen leader of a village is the *muḵtār*.

INTIFĀḌA – shaking off, uprising. From the root N-F-Ḍ, which means 'shake'.

-IYY – suffix forming adjectives and nouns, indicating a relationship to what is mentioned in the headword. One frequent use is in nationalities, such as YAMANIYY (Yemeni) and ʿIRĀQIYY (Iraqi).

J

JAMAL – camel. A word from Arabic or some other Semitic language that has reached English through Greek, Latin and French. Said to be derived from the root J-M-L for 'beauty', whence also the given names *Jamila* (JAMĪLA) and *Jamal* (*jamāl*), but the connection is unlikely.

JARRA – earthen jug. Our workaday word *jar* has a surprising but solidly validated Arabic lineage, with French acting as the link.

J-B-R (*root*) – (to restore) strength. AL-JABR for 'the setting of bones' has, through a title of an influential book, given us *algebra*. (The book was written by a Persian scholar named AL-KHWĀRIZMĪ, whose Latinised name ALGORITMI has given us the word *algorithm*.) The name Gabriel (Arabic: JIBR(Ā²)ĪL) means 'God is my strength'.

J-H-D (*root*) – to struggle, labour. One derivation is JIHĀD for 'effort, struggle', including, but not limited to, 'holy war'. People involved in a struggle are MUJĀHIDĪN.

JUBBA – outer garment, jubbah, jibba. It has given French its standard word for 'skirt', JUPE, which is used in English for a specific kind of skirt or jacket. It may also be, through some roundabout maritime conection, at the root of the word *jumper* for 'sweater'.

J-Z-R (*root*) – to cut off. TV station Al Jazeera and the country Algeria both derive their names from AL-JAZĪRA, 'the island'.

K

KAʿBA – Kaaba, cube. The Kaaba or 'cube' in Mecca is the holiest place of Islam and one of the destinations of the HAJJ (pilgrimage).

KABĀB – kebab. Related to a root for 'roasting'. The English form was influenced by Turkish KEBAP.

KĀFIR – non-believer. The original meaning was 'concealer', namely of the truth. Whether Jews and Christians, the other ²AHL AL-KITĀB or 'people of the book', are included or not is a matter of some debate.

K-B-R (*root*) – to be big or great. It has gained notoriety due to the phrase ALLAHU AKBAR 'God is supreme' which traditionally was a simple expression of gratitude, not unlike 'thank God'.

KĪMIYĀ² – chemistry. It is at the root of both our words *chemistry* and *alchemy* (with the article AL). The Arabs borrowed it from Greek KHUMEÍA.

K̲-L-F (*root*) – change, transition. The *caliph* (K̲ALĪFA) is the 'successor', the leader of the faithful in Muhammad's stead.

K-T-B (*root*) – write. One of the best-known Arabic and indeed Semitic roots, though none of the derivations is all that frequent in English. The ²AHL AL-KITĀB are the 'people of the book' (see KĀFIR). A *maktab* in English refers to a traditional Islamic school, where children mostly learn to read the Koran; in Arabic, the meaning has moved on to 'office'. The word MAKTŪB, meaning 'written, fated' as an adjective and 'destiny' as a noun, is regularly quoted in English as *maktub* to express acceptance of fate.

KUḤL – antimony; kohl. A dark powder, used as eye make-up. The word may also be at the root of *alcohol*, but this is contentious.

ḲURŠŪF – artichoke. The Spanish kept the article AL and changed the whole word into ALCA(R)CHOFA, Medieval Italians turned it into ARCICIOFFO, the North Italian Lombards preferred to say ARTICIÒC and this badly mangled name reached English.

L

LAYMŪN – lemon. From Persian *limu*, which in turn may have borrowed it from a language related to Malay.

LĪLAK – lilac. Originally from Sanskrit NĪLĀ for 'dark blue'. From this origin, the word has travelled through Persian, Arabic and French to English.

M

M – prefix for 'place'. A MASJID is a 'place of prostration'; European languages have metamorphosed the word to *mosque* (*Moschee*, *mezquita*, etc.).

MADĪNA – town, city. In English, *medina* refers to the older part of a North African town. Since the Arabs traditionally didn't have towns, the word was borrowed from Aramaic.

MADRASA – school. The Arabic word, unlike the English loanword *madrasah*, refers to any kind of school, not just the religious kind. It's based on the root D-R-S for 'study'.

MAḴZAN – storehouse, place for storage. The plural MAḴĀZIN has, through Italian and French, produced the word *magazine*, originally meaning a military storehouse, later a 'storehouse' of information, and thus a 'journal'.

MASĪḤ – anointed. The Arabic cognate of Hebrew MĀŠÎAḤ, which has given us *messiah*. Christianity is in Arabic called MASĪḤIYYAH, 'Messianism'.

MASSA – feel, touch. French Oriental travellers added a French ending to the Arabic word, giving the world MASSAGE.

MIQRAM; MIQRAMA – bedspread; cloth. Through Turkish, this has resulted in a French word that is now widespread, *macramé*: a knotting technique for producing decorative textile, said to be of Arab origin.

M-L-K – rule, possess. Hence MALIK(A): king, queen. The word *mameluke* for '(European) slave' comes from Arabic MAMLŪK. Several Muslims rulers of slave origin called their empire or dynasty *Mamluk*.

MU- – participle prefix, either active (as in 'doing') or passive (as in 'done'). Active: a *mujahideen* is a fighter, a *Muslim* is an Islamic believer, a *mufti* delivers formal opinions or *fatwas*. Passive: the first names *Mustafa* and *Mukhtar* both mean 'the chosen one', and MUḤAMMAD is 'the praised one'.

N

NĀʾIB – deputy. The plural NUWWĀB was borrowed into Persian, then Hindustani as NAVĀB, where it came to refer to an Indian ruler within the Mughal empire, rendered as *nawab* or *nabob* in English.

NĀRANJ – bitter orange. This wandering word probably started out in a Dravidian language, passed through Sanskrit, Persian, Arabic and Spanish before losing its initial *n* in French, where UNE NORANGE ('an orange') was reinterpreted as UNE ORANGE.

NAẒĪR – The first part of the geometrical term NAẒĪR AS-SAMT 'the counterpart to the zenith' (see under SAMT) produced the Medieval Latin NADIR, which English adopted.

Q

QĀ῾IDA – foundation, (military) base. The name of the terror organisation translates as The Base. In the plural, QAWĀ῾ID, the word means 'grammar'.

QĀḌIN – judge. As *qadi*, the word is used in English for a civil judge in an Islamic context. The Spanish ALCALDE (mayor) has the same origin.

QAHWA – coffee. The Arabic word reached English through Turkish, Italian and Dutch.

QALIY – ashes. Based on the verb QALĀ for 'bake, fry'. With the article AL, this has given us *alkali*. The 'ashes' were those of a plant rich in an alkaline substance.

QAṢR – castle. An *alcazar* /al-KA-sar/ is a Moorish castle in Spain, directly derived from AL-QAṢR. QAṢR was borrowed from Latin, where CASTRUM means 'castle'. Through French, the same word has given us CASTLE and CHÂTEAU.

QĪRĀṬ – carat. The English word was borrowed, via French and Italian, from the Arabic, which in turn took it from Greece, where it meant 'carob seed'.

QĪṬĀRA – guitar. It's not quite clear how this word travelled from

one language to the other. All forms can be traced back to Greek (KITHÁRĒ), which seems to have borrowed it from some unknown local language. The string instruments *zither* and *cittern* have the same origin.

QIṬṬ – cat, tomcat. Many languages in Europe, the Middle East and North Africa have similar words for 'cat'. As felines were first domesticated in Egypt, the likely origin is a language spoken in that region.

QUBBA – dome. With the article AL, it has produced *alcove* for 'a small recessed area set off from a larger room'. The Dome of the Rock on the Temple Mount in Jerusalem is called QUBBAT AL-SAKHRAH. Arabic borrowed the word QUBBA from Persian.

QURʾĀN – recitation; Koran.

QUṬN – cotton. The Arabic word has reached English through Italian and French.

R

R-ʾ-S (*root*) – to be at the head. The word raʾīs for 'head, chief' has given English *reis* or *rais* for 'leader' or 'captain' in Middle Eastern contexts. The explorer Piri Reis may be the most famous.

RĀḤA – leisure, ample space, palm of the hand. A (tennis, badminton) *racket/racquet* is a device for amplifying the palm of the hand.

RAMAḌĀN – Ramadan. Month of fasting.

RIBĀṬ – tie, bond, frontier post, and later small monastery. The word *ribat* is sometimes used in English for a military frontier post in the Arab world. A MURĀBIṬ is someone dwelling in a RIBĀṬ, a soldier or a hermit, which has given us *marabout* for 'Muslim holy man or mystic'.

RIZMA – bundle, package. Via Spanish RESMA and Old French RAIME, the word has resulted in *ream*, a bundle or package of paper.

S

SĀFARA – to travel. The English word *safari* stems from Swahili SAFARI, which is of Arabic origin.

ṢĀḤIB – companion. Via Persian it reached Hindustani, where it became a term of respect for European males. The first syllable of the female form, *memsahib,* derives from English *ma'am.*

SĀḤIL – coast. The singular has given us the name *Sahel*, the 'coast' or fringe of the Sahara desert. The plural SAWĀḤIL is the origin of the name Swahili Coast, the coastal areas of Kenya, Tanzania and Northern Mozambique, where the Swahili language originated.

ṢAḤRĀ' – desert, Sahara. The English name stems from the Arabic plural, ṢAḤĀRĀ.

SALAF – predecessor(s), ancestor(s). Salafism is a movement that takes early Islam as its ideal.

SAMT – path. Medieval Latin corrupted it to CENIT, which has given us ZENITH.

ŠARĪ'A – path; sharia. The latter meaning is a specific, metaphoric case of the former.

ŠARĪF – noble. A *sharif* or *shareef* is a person of noble ancestry.

ŠĀŠ – muslin, white cloth. This is where the word *sash* comes from.

ŠAYḴ – sheik. The name is related to a word for 'ageing, growing old', like the English words *alderman* (compare *old* and *elder*)

and *senator* (compare *senior* and *senile*).

ṢIFR – zero. The original meaning of ṢIFR was 'empty'. The Arabs used it to translate Sanskrit ŚŪNYA, which also first meant 'empty' and was then extended to the concept of 'zero' (via ZEPHIRUM in Latin). ṢIFR also begat CYFRE in Old French, which became CIPHER (or CYPHER) in English.

SIKKA – coin. Italian borrowed it as ZECCA and turned it into the diminutive ZECCHINO which was adopted by French and then English as *seguin.*

S-L-M (*root*) – to be safe, at peace; to submit. This has been a very productive root of words and names well known in the West. Words based on it include SALĀM for 'peace' (as in DAR-ES-SALAAM, 'house of peace' and the greeting AS-SALĀMU ʿALAYKUM, 'peace be upon you'), 'ISLĀM for 'Islam, submission (to God)' and MUSLIM for 'person who submits (to God)'.

Š-R-B – drink. The word ŠARĀB (a drink) has left several traces in English: *syrup, sorbet, sherbet.*

Š-R-Q (*root*) – to rise (sun); East. ŠARQIYY for 'eastern wind' led, through a dialectal form SHORUQ, to the Italian word SCIROCCO, the sirocco desert wind. ŠARQIYY is also the likely origin of Greek SARAKENOS, which became *Saracens.*

ṢŪF – wool. The adjective ṢŪFIYY means both 'woollen' and 'Sufi'; the Sufis would wear wool instead of silk.

ṢUFFA – stone bench, sofa. The word travelled from Aramaic to Arabic and thence to French and English.

SUKKAR – sugar. Yet another word that has come to us along a path well travelled: from Sanskrit (where ŚÁRKARĀ for 'grit' or 'gravel' was applied to the sweet stuff) through Persian to Arabic, and hence via Italian, Medieval Latin and French to English. Spanish and Portuguese have maintained the Arabic article: AZÚCAR, AÇÚCAR.

SŪQ – market. Rendered in English as *souq* or *souk*.

T

ṬAḤĪNA – tahini, sesame paste. Derived from the root Ṭ-Ḥ-N for 'to grind'.

TĀJ – crown. Best known from TĀJ MAHAL, a Hindustani name meaning 'crown of palaces'. MAHAL also derives from the Arabic: MAḤALL means 'place' or 'residence'.

ṬĀLIB – seeker, student. *Taliban* is the plural, not in Arabic but in Pashto, one of Afghanistan's two major languages.

TAMR HINDIYY – tamarind. The Arabic name literally means 'Indian date'.

ṬARAḤA – throw. The 'place where something is thrown' is MAṬRAḤ in Arabic, which, through Old French, became *mattress*. 'That which is thrown away' is ṬARḤA, which through Italian (TARA) and French became *tare*, the empty weight of a container, as in the formula 'gross weight = net weight + tare weight'.

ṬŪB – brick. With the article AL, assimilated to the initial consonant of the noun, this has produced the Spanish word ADOBE for 'sun-dried brick'. This has become part of English vocabulary. In California, there is an Adobe Creek, after which a well-known software company was named. Arabic borrowed the word from Coptic, the previous language of Egypt.

ṬŪFĀN – storm. A regional word that also exists in Persian and Hindustani, borrowed by English as *typhoon*. Its ultimate origin may be Chinese.

W

WĀDIN – valley, riverbed. The form WĀDĪ can be recognised in many Spanish river names, such as *Guadalquivir*. In English, a *wadi* is a dry riverbed occasionally filled by flash floods.

WAZĪR – helper, minister. Through Turkish VEZIR and probably one of the Romance languages, this became English *vizier* for a high-ranking Ottoman official.

Y

YĀSAMĪN – jasmine. Via French *jasmin* from Arabic, which borrowed it from Persian.

Z

ZAʿFARĀN – saffron. The Arabic word, possibly of Persian origin, has reached English through Medieval Latin and French.

ZAHR – flower, di(c)e. The English word *hazard*, whose first meaning was 'game of chance', has come via French from Spanish AZAR (now 'chance, misfortune', but originally also 'game of chance'), which in turn is derived from an Arabic noun with its article: AZ-ZAHR. The semantic connection is that the lucky side of the dice had a flower on it.

ZARĀFA – giraffe. English borrowed the word from French, which had it from Arabic.

Different letters, different litters

So much for vocabulary. How about the other major aspects of language: the sounds, the grammar and the script?

We saw in the previous chapter that the Arabic abjad and the Latin alphabet share a common origin. But that's not much use when it comes to learning to read and write Arabic. The best that can be said is that the script has a manageable number of different characters, more or less on a par with Latin and Cyrillic. That makes Arabic easier than the Brahmic scripts and much easier than Chinese and Japanese. Also, unlike in Chinese and Vietnamese, it's usually clear where words begin and end.

Phonologically speaking, all varieties of Arabic are rather different from European languages. But then again, it has no tone, no complicated consonant clusters and few vowels. It's not exactly easy to pronounce Arabic correctly, whether the standard language or any of the 'dialects', but neither is it exceptionally difficult.

The grammar is, again, different in many ways from English and its ilk. But though unrelated to the other European languages (except Maltese), Arabic still shares with many of them at least two features that are far from universal. Firstly, it has a definite article – AL. And secondly, it has a gender system which is ultimately based on the biological sexes. In other words, all nouns fall into a category labelled either masculine or feminine, rather than, say, human, animal, vegetal and mineral. Such a sex-based gender-system is frequent in both the Indo-European family and the Afro-Asiatic family, including the Semitic languages. Elsewhere, however, gender systems have some other base or are absent altogether.

Also, let's not forget that our own Germanic group shares the most salient grammatical characteristic of the Semitic languages. Arabic forms many words on the basis of roots by inserting different vowels (as well as tacking on consonants), and so does English: we could postulate an English root K-N-W which then produces words such as know, knew, known, knowledge and unbeknownst; or a root S-NG to produce sing, sang, sung, unsung, song, singer, et cetera. Granted, this is rather stretching the point, because the English (and Germanic) system is much less systematic and extensive. On the other hand, since this type of word formation is uncommon worldwide, the resemblance is striking. Indeed, a few linguists have daringly argued that there must have been a strong prehistoric influence of Semitic peoples (the seafaring Phoenicians would be good candidates) on the Germanic languages.

Anyway, in spite of all the mutual borrowing and slight similarities, there's no getting around the fact that Arabic (Semitic, Afro-Asiatic) is very different from English (Germanic, Indo-European). So much so that when linguists attempt to group the major language families into even larger superfamilies – an endeavour fraught with difficulties and therefore avoided by most – they do not usually place Indo-European and Afro-Asiatic close together.

When, in the seventh and eighth centuries, Islam came to live next door to European Christendom, the new neighbours' cultures were in some ways not quite as different as both of them liked to think. Since their religions originated in the Middle East, they shared many ancient stories, most of their prophets and the unusual belief in a single supreme deity. And the languages? Even there, similarities can be found and contact, as our *Concise Dictionary* has shown, has led to mutual influence. Arabic is far from an alien.

4

Hindi-Urdu

hindi

urdu

550 million speakers

It's estimated that 325 million are native Hindi-Urdu speakers and 225 second-language speakers, though much higher numbers result if related languages are counted as dialects. Hindi is spoken in large parts of North and Central India; Urdu is spoken in Pakistan, mostly as a second language, and by Muslims in North and Central India. Millions of Indians and Pakistanis live in the UK, the US and the Arabian Peninsula, but Hindi-Urdu is not always their main language.

Hindi-Urdu

SELF-DESIGNATION Either हिन्दी (Hindi) or اردو (Urdu).

ALSO CALLED Hindustani; historically also Hindavi or Delhavi.

FAMILY Hindi-Urdu belongs to the Indo-Aryan (Indic) branch of the Indo-European family.

SCRIPT The choice of writing system has become one of the defining differences between Hindi and Urdu, the former typically using Devanagari, the latter a Perso-Arabic alphabet.

GRAMMAR Nouns have two genders, two numbers (singular and plural) and commonly two cases (rarely, three). Adjectives agree with nouns in gender and number, but in a very limited manner. Pronouns do not specify gender, but do distinguish two degrees of distance (like *this* and *that*) and two and sometimes three levels of politeness. The verbal system, like that of English, has a substantial number of tenses and aspects but few different forms.

SOUNDS Hindi-Urdu has three short and seven long vowel sounds and no fewer than thirty-five consonants, including a group of eight that were borrowed from the Dravidian language group (which includes Tamil). In loanwords from Arabic or Persian, some additional consonants may occur. Stress is usually on the penultimate syllable.

LOANWORDS Persian and Arabic (especially Urdu); Sanskrit (Hindi); English (both).

EXPORTS *avatar, bandana, bangle, cheetah, chintz, chutney, coolie, cot, cushy, dinghy, dungaree, guru, juggernaut, jungle, loot, pajamas, pundit, purdah, Raj, shampoo, shawl, tank, thug, tom-tom, veranda, yoga* and *yogi*.

ROMANS ONLINE The Roman alphabet is used surprisingly often for both Hindi and Urdu: in film titles, in some advertisements, in Bible translations, and online. Internet use in particular may allow more Indians and Pakistanis to realise that their languages are much less different than official discourse would have it.

4: Hindi-Urdu

Always something breaking us in two

Aren't I cheating when I treat Hindi and Urdu as one, rather than two, of the world's twenty largest languages? They're undoubtedly twins, no argument there, but twins are individuals and should be counted separately. And it's a fact that their names can't be used interchangeably. No longer, anyway. Don't tell a Pakistani they speak Hindi – no sir, it's Urdu! Don't tell an Indian they speak Urdu – the horror of it! Unless, that is, you happen to be among Urdu-speaking Indian Muslims (of whom there are tens of millions, a sizeable minority even by Indian standards), in which case they'll be pleased. But horrified or happy, most Indians and Pakistanis will maintain that Hindi and Urdu are different in important ways.

But the claim is debatable, and much debated. Not among the general populace, who will take any fiery orator's word for it, and not among the orators, who will take any third-rate linguist's word for it. But debate there is, and for good reasons.

One reason to question the separateness of Hindi and Urdu is that alongside their different names there's another that they share: Hindustani. You don't hear it much anymore on the subcontinent, but it used to be common until the mid-twentieth century and it's still the prevalent term among heritage speakers elsewhere, for instance in Fiji and Suriname. Largely outdated though it may be, it would be greatly useful, as it describes a living reality in a way that's less confusing than this double-barrelled 'Hindi-Urdu'. Bollywood films are as popular in Pakistan as in India, because the dialogues are in a language easily understood by many people in both countries. Conversely, self-proclaimed Hindi speakers can fully and effortlessly appreciate songs said to be in Urdu. In spite of their own strong views on the matter, it's generally impossible to tell whether the chatter of ordinary people in India is in Hindi or Urdu.

On balance, therefore, I think it's reasonable to discuss them as one. In my book, people who can freely communicate with each other speak the same language. The divide running through Hindustani is recent, artificial and regretted by more than a few. It's a rift rather than a break and, left alone, it would gradually heal. Left alone, however, is what it has little hope of being. Not while the rhetoric of nationalism and identity politics so easily wins elections on both sides of the border.

Numerous books have been written about the Indo-Pakistani Partition of 1947, and quite a few about the linguistic intricacies of Hindustani, Hindi and Urdu. Most of them could fairly be titled: Why the Other Side Is To Blame, this Other Side being either the Muslim, the Mughal, the Pakistani or the Hindu, the Brahmin, the Indian. There's an additional scapegoat common to both sides, namely the British, but while the Brits provide a welcome relief from the reciprocal finger-pointing, they make for poor antagonists, since they no longer argue back.

Fortunately, some writers and thinkers do not treat the issues in such a facile way, and this chapter draws heavily on two of them. The eminent Pakistani academic Tariq Rahman in his book *From Hindi To Urdu* critically examines Urdu from its first mention around 1780 to its U-turn about a century later, when it went from being just another name for 'Hindi' to meaning 'the opposite of Hindi, the language that is most definitely not Hindi' – from synonym to antonym. No blame game for Rahman, but scholarly accuracy and detachment. The other source, titled *Hindi Nationalism*, is of a different nature. Its author, the Indian publicist and university teacher Alok Rai, is more outspoken, more overtly polemical and, truth be told, more fun. He eloquently criticises the 'Hindiwallahs', the advocates of a 'pure' Hindi who patrol the artificial linguistic border that they themselves have drawn. Rai calls the official languages of India and Pakistan 'Hindi' and 'Urdu', never omitting the inverted commas, because he strongly feels that these are travesties of the people's real *bhasha* ('language, tongue, speech'). As far as he's concerned, this real language could be termed Hindi or Urdu or Hindi-Urdu or

The border between India and Pakistan has its absurdities – as does its linguistic equivalent.

Urdu-Hindi, without inverted commas (though he seems to dislike the term Hindustani).

In Rahman's book he approvingly quotes Rai, and if the two were to meet I'm sure they would have discussion without any hostility – though perhaps with considerable passion, especially on Rai's side, if the heated tone of his book is anything to go by. It's safe to say that India and Pakistan would both be better off with a number of Rahmans and Rais in high places.

The story of Hirdu

So what's the real story of South Asia's biggest language – the story of 'Hirdu', as one exasperated linguist has called it? Nothing special until modern times, frankly. Its early ancestor was an Indo-European language, labelled Proto-Indo-Aryan, whose speakers seem to have reached north Pakistan and north India sometime during the second millennium BCE, spreading further south and east for many centuries thereafter. This statement about the far past comes with the usual caveats and disclaimers, because alternative interpretations exist. One theory, held by several scholars in South Asia but few elsewhere, holds that the Indus Valley, rather than the Ukrainian steppe or Asian Turkey, was the birthplace of the Indo-European family as a whole. But that's the same damn nationalism piping up again. Let's ignore it.

As in Europe, where several groups of Indo-European languages spread and then diverged, influenced by the older local tongues, so in South Asia: Indo-Aryan came to dominate a growing area, while at the same time diversifying due to contact with aboriginal languages. In some places, these older languages survive to this day. Remember the Dravidian family, spoken in the south, with Tamil as a prominent member?

In an attempt to come to grips with an otherwise intractable tangle of old tongues, linguists have named the ones spoken from 1500 until 300 BCE 'Old Indo-Aryan'. That sounds arcane, but the most important member of the group is one we've met more than once in this book: Sanskrit – the name, as befits a superstar, means 'perfect' or 'refined'. Its career, and especially that of the variety labelled classical Sanskrit, is strongly reminiscent of classical Latin's: both languages were deliberately standardised versions of the vernaculars, were mostly used in writing and had a cultural impact that spread far beyond their areas of origin and continues right down to modern times.

On to the next stage: the 'Middle Indo-Aryan' group of languages, spoken from 300 BCE to 1500 CE. These are called Prakrits, meaning 'natural', for they were the people's lingos of their day. Meanwhile, Sanskrit remained the written language of choice, again like Latin in the West. In other respects too, India's linguistic situation around 1000 CE was much like Europe's. It can be summarised with one of those concepts that linguists would dearly love to be household terms, but aren't: dialect continuum. Let me explain. A continuum – whether of wavelengths, personality traits or any other phenomenon – is a range characterised by gradual variation. So a dialect continuum is a range of dialects or languages, spoken across a substantial geographical area, with the ones close together being pretty similar, and the ones farther apart being less so. In practical terms, this means that travellers setting out from home can talk to people easily for a few hours or even days, but the further they walk, the harder this gets, without there ever being a steep drop in mutual understanding. Great Britain used to present a dialect continuum, and to a certain degree it still does: hiking from Southampton to Aberdeen, we'll hear the dialects slowly changing, and even the Scottish border is no sharp linguistic boundary between English and Scots. Welsh and Scottish Gaelic, however, would not be part of the continuum.

This was the situation in South Asia a thousand years ago, except that it had no 'umbrella' language the way that we have Standard English. But, given that most people did not travel in those days, the situation hardly ever caused any communication problems. That's how it used to work in most of the world at the time, including the Germanic, Romance and Slavic zones of Europe and the Indo-Aryan parts of South Asia. In today's North India, which was the heartland of that extensive zone, there were five closely related Prakrits that can be considered forerunners of Hindustani.

These and most other Prakrits were spoken by the masses and their rulers alike. In the westernmost part, however, west of the Indus River, things were different: while the people spoke Prakrits, their rulers spoke Persian. This situation was a taste of things to come.

1206 and all that

Starting in the eleventh century, growing numbers of invaders, merchants, mendicants and holy men came into India from Persia, and from 1206 onward the political scene was dominated by Muslim dynasties. First, the Delhi Sultanate became the most powerful state of South Asia; later, it was succeeded by the Mughal Empire. The rulers of these states were of Central Asian origin, but had in previous centuries been culturally and linguistically Persianised (as we saw in chapter 15). The Delhi Sultanate was ruled by mostly Turkic dynasties. They introduced the Persian habit of referring to the languages of South Asia as 'Hindi', which simply means 'spoken in the land of the Indus river' – in other words, Indian. The Mughal emperors were of mixed stock, part Turkic, part Mongol (*Mughal* is derived from *Mongol*), but they too spoke Persian. Both empires at their greatest extent reached far south, but neither ever encompassed the whole subcontinent.

What happened to the region's languages? That would make a nice question in an exam for linguistics undergraduates: 'Suppose there is a large area with a dialect continuum, which is then dominated for several centuries by a comparatively small ruling class of foreign extraction, who speak a language that is not closely related. What do you expect to happen to the local dialects and to the rulers' language?' The answer might be something like: 'The local dialects (the substratum) will be influenced by the elite language (the superstratum), but in the longer run, the ruling class will first become bilingual and ultimately give up their old language altogether.' The student need not have thought of India; the question describes equally well what happened in northern Gaul after the Germanic Franks came to dominate it in the late fifth century; what happened in Normandy after the Vikings acquired it in the early tenth century; and what happened in England after these Vikings-turned-Normans conquered it in 1066 – not to mention many similar cases.

How did this play out in South Asia? First of all, throughout the Sultanate and Mughal periods, the local tongues borrowed loads of Persian words, many of which were of Arabic origin, with a few Turkic elements thrown in. It is often claimed that this happened mainly in the military camp or *urdu* (a Persian word of Turkic origin), but that is incorrect. No matter how much a ruling elite tries to keep itself to itself, it can't help interacting with the lower classes. Language contact occurred not only in the military camps, but also, probably to a greater extent, in shops and markets, palaces and mosques, taverns and brothels. Through this contact, people would learn and adopt new words. That's how Hindi-Urdu or Hindustani ended up with a lot of Persian vocabulary, such as JAVĀN for 'young',

PARDA for 'curtain' and DARIĀ for 'river' or 'sea', and a good deal of Arabic too, such as KITĀB for 'book', JAHĀZ for 'ship' and DUNIYĀ for 'world'. Today's speakers do not regard these words as 'foreign' or 'borrowed' any more than we think of *river, curtain, simple* and *very* as French. (They are derived from RIVIÈRE, COURTINE, SIMPLE and VERAI, which in modern French is VRAI.)

And what about the second part of the student's answer, the one about the elite? Did they become bilingual? Not during the Delhi Sultanate, it seems. But the Mughal court did fairly soon, in the sixteenth century, when the men began to marry Indian noblewomen. For the next two centuries, Persian would slowly lose ground in favour of Hindustani, known at the time as Hindi.

Early Urdu and Hindi, in hindsight

In the seventeenth century, the linguistic situation in South Asia was still fairly unremarkable. No-one at the time could have foreseen the Hindi-Urdu rift. The Middle Indo-Aryan languages had diverged into several New Indo-Aryan languages: Bengali, Punjabi and others, as well as a central group consisting of regional tongues often lumped together as Hindi. Without exception, they were packed with Persian and Arabic words. While classical Sanskrit was still in use for liturgical purposes, the vernaculars were now routinely written, in a variety of scripts (see chapter 6). Muslim authors used the Perso-Arabic script, a variety of the Arabic alphabet; they would be familiar with this through the Koran and state documents. Hindi was written in various indigenous scripts, depending on caste: the Brahmin priests and teachers preferred Nagari; the Kayastha scribes and administrators used Kaithi, which was the more widespread of the two.

Only with hindsight can we trace the stirrings of Urdu to this time. While the Muslim elite's grasp of the Persian language became more and more tenuous, their poets began to intersperse Hindi with highfalutin Persian loans, but without eschewing the ordinary vernacular words. This is not unlike the craze for Latinate terms in literary English (*illecebrous, obtestate, adminiculation*) around 1600. In the eighteenth century, however, the Mughal poets took things further: many ordinary Hindi words became taboo, resulting in a highly Persianate literary style. Around 1780, this language was for the first time called 'Urdu', a shortened form of the phrase ZABAN-E-URDU-E-MUALLA, meaning 'language of the exalted city' (not 'military camp'), in reference to the capital of Delhi. This Urdu had a function like that of the Ottoman Turkish of chapter 17: it was a refined elite language, a badge of social distinction, not of religious identity. It served as – to quote an Indian scholar – 'the class dialect of a nervous aristocracy' that saw its position of power and privilege going to pieces with the ascendancy of the British East India Company. Indeed, the values surrounding the new language were perplexingly elitist: according to one of its codifiers, correctness was defined by the usage of just a few aristocratic Delhi families.

Even as a Persianised Urdu was budding among the Muslim elites, some learned Brahmins were striving to 'purify' their Hindi, cleansing Persian and Arabic loans from it and introducing long-forgotten Sanskrit words instead. However, these were the ivory-tower efforts of a small unworldly minority. Their doings appear much more significant now than they did at the time.

The eighteenth-century poet Mir Taqi Mir, regarded as one of the pioneers who gave shape to the Urdu language.

278

Missionaries and scholars

British traders had been present in India since the early 1600s, cap in hand at first, throwing their weight about later. But in the early 1800s the Brits began to have a linguistic impact on Hindustani (or Hindoostanee, Hindoostaneeh, Hindoost'hanee, Hindostani, Hindoustany, Hindostany or Hindustany – it took a while for the spelling to settle).

Two separate groups were involved. The first of these, the missionaries, started publishing school books to convert young illiterate Hindus and Muslims into literate Christians. As the British colonial administration would do later, they decided that Hindustani should do for the whole of North and Central India – Punjabi, Bengali and other languages be damned. They set out to hammer and chisel the Hindustani dialect continuum into a written standard for their textbooks. Or rather, two written standards, as Hindu and Muslim pupils were to get different versions. This was not an attempt to divide these groups – remember that the big idea was to unite them in a new faith. Rather, it was a pragmatic response to the fact that in the spiritual domain, Hindus and Muslims did indeed use very different terminology: the former Sanskrit, the latter Arabic and Persian. Scripts were another reason: for Muslims, it was unthinkable to read about religious matters in anything other than an Arabic alphabet, while for Hindus, this was the realm of the Nagari script (later called 'Devanagari', the deva part meaning 'heavenly, divine'). Today, this early two-language policy is much appreciated both by fervent Hindus supporting Sanskritised Hindi and by zealous Muslims defending Persianised Urdu – even though the Christian missionaries' express aim was to 'save' their pupils from Hinduism and Islam.

The other (partly) British group with a linguistic impact were the scholars of Fort William College in Calcutta, an institution set up by the East India Company to teach company officers Hindustani. This tended to be the Urdu variety (spelled Oordoo at the time, which better reflects pronunciation), as the Indian elite was still predominantly Muslim. However, some of the Fort William linguists, together with the Indian staff under their supervision, set out to 'purify' the language. In this effort, some chose to be guided by the living language of 'the best people' of the day, but others tried to turn back history by replacing many loanwords with purisms, often fabricated from Sanskrit. To replace JAHĀZ ('ship'), a word of Arabic origin, they created PŌT, based on Sanskrit PŌTA. DUNIYĀ ('world'), an Arabic loan used in many languages, was to make way for alternatives such as SANSĀR, based on Sanskrit SAMSĀRA. Apparently, the purists didn't realise that to nineteenth-century Indians Sanskrit was no less foreign than Persian and Arabic – and the purisms much more so than the old words that they sought to purge. Other 'foreign' words were too deeply entrenched for even the most determined of Sanskritisers to have a go at, among them JAVĀN for 'young' and PARDA for 'curtain', both of Persian origin.

It would be preposterous to suggest that the Fort William crowd were plotting for linguistic partition. If their work, along with that of the missionaries, was the thin end of the wedge, it was gleefully driven into the language by other, later forces. And many of the Fort William linguists explicitly argued in favour of one common Hindustani. But there's no denying that their work strongly contributed to, as Rai puts it, 'the idea of two-ness, of linguistic duality' between a Persianised Urdu for Muslims and a Sanskritised Hindi for Hindus. But only to this *idea*, for in practice, nearly all people of each creed spoke neither of these extreme varieties. The speech of the millions remained the same jumble (or continuum) of Hindustani dialects as before: Indo-Aryan by origin, inadvertently Persianised by history.

The fight between 'evil' and 'barbarism'

The two-ness became more relevant in the 1830s, when the British gradually substituted Hindustani for Persian as the language of administration. The reason for the shift was simple: it seemed sensible for the population at large to be able to understand the language of judges and other officials. The Perso-Arabic script was maintained, however: Hindustani had a long tradition of being written in it, so why replace it?

From the late 1850s on, the expansion of formal education created a need for new textbooks. Religious men of both persuasions were

This British recruitment poster from the First World War reads: 'Who will take this uniform, money and gun?' The language is Urdu, which at the time was the more commonly written variety of Hindustani. More than a million Indian troops served in the war, and 2.5 million in the Second World War.

charged with writing them. For stylistic guidance, they didn't look to the living vernacular so much as to their separate literary heritages. Like the missionary textbooks some decades earlier, but on a larger scale, the new materials did much to widen the breach between Muslim and Hindu pupils. Even so, this only affected a small minority, given that decades later, illiteracy still stood at a whopping 97 per cent. But by now, the language issue had become a point of contention.

The later decades of the nineteenth century saw full-fledged Muslim-Hindu conflict. The region went through a process of modernisation, with the introduction of railways, a postal system, censuses and an increasingly professional civil service. As a result, there were economic spoils to be divvied up. The traditional Muslim elite felt naturally entitled to these, but at the same time saw its position threatened by an aspiring Hindu elite. Both began to garner support from the masses, thus creating solidarity of a type that had never before existed: based not on region or class, but on religion. All over the country, neighbours could suddenly find themselves in opposing camps.

Language was drawn into this conflict right away. Urdu had a head start, favoured by centuries of Muslim rule and the official status of the Perso-Arabic script. For decades, the Hindu elites fought for the recognition of the Nagari script and, by implication, the Hindi variety of the language. The tone of the debate was like some of today's internet forums. A prominent Hindu official wrote that the Perso-Arabic script 'thrusts a Semitic element into the bosoms of Hindus and alienates them from their Aryan speech ... Cursed be the day which saw the Muhammadans cross the Indus; all the evils which we find amongst us we are indebted for to our "beloved brethren" the Muhammadans.' Not to be outdone, a furious Muslim newspaper editor commented thus on the British recognition for Nagari in a province where the fight had been particularly long: 'The question of Urdu versus Nagari ... was a contest between refinement and culture on the one hand, and prejudice and barbarism on the other ... history will have to tell a vandal chapter as to how a British administrator by one stroke of his pen dealt a death blow to the cause of culture and refinement.' The name-calling would go on and on, with the Hindus decried as low-born yokels and the Muslims as tyrants plunging Indian culture into a dark age. The flowering of Hindu literary culture during the Mughal Empire was conveniently ignored, as it suited neither side's agenda.

In this caustic atmosphere, the independence movement unsurprisingly failed to unite the two religious communities, in spite of some people's best efforts. Politically and linguistically, the situation escalated, culminating in the political Partition of 1947 and the official linguistic partition soon thereafter. Pakistan made Urdu its state language on 2 February 1948. India's choice of Sanskritised Hindi was less of a foregone conclusion. Mahatma Gandhi, murdered on 30 January 1948, was all for Hindustani, written in either Devanagari or the Persian alphabet – this was actually part of what enraged his murderer. Even so, the Sanskritisers managed to defeat the supporters of Hindustani in the Constituent Assembly in September 1949. 'Pure Sanskrit words are used in the same form everywhere', their leader said. 'Therefore only that language can be acceptable all over India which is rich in pure Sanskrit words' – Sanskritised Hindi, that is.

But while guards and guns can make people respect new borders, they will not change how they talk. The lower classes in both countries still speak Hindustani, not the standardised Hindi or Urdu. Outside the 'Hindi Belt' of north central India, the middle classes in both countries pick up the language mainly through Bollywood films – which are in Hindustani. And the elite? In India and Pakistan, they prefer the international glamour and usefulness of English. The middle class, being what it is, has already begun to follow their lead and increasingly aims for English too. In India, the official, Sanskritised Hindi is declining in relevance – indeed, Rai claims that this type of 'Hindi'

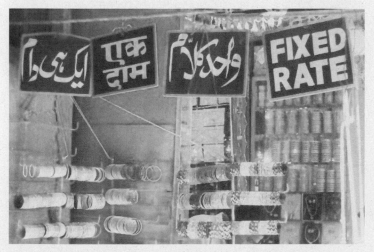

No bargaining here –whether in Urdu, Hindi, Arabic or English!

(as ever he uses inverted commas) is 'sulking in a provincial corner, begging for scraps'. In Pakistan (halved in 1971, when Bangladesh broke away), most people can speak some form of Urdu as a second language, but few care much for it, let alone for its 'purity'.

Retroactively separated

Today, the official language ideologies of India and Pakistan are as identical as can be expected of mirror images. Hindi linguists portray Hindi as 'the eldest daughter' of Sanskrit, a statement that – insofar as it can be translated into something meaningful – no serious historical linguist can support. As mentioned before, some go as far as to claim that the Indo-European protolanguage had its roots in South Asia. In Pakistan, students are indoctrinated from a young age with the idea that Urdu was born as a mixed language in the Mughal military camps. This is a fiction that reflects Pakistan's militaristic culture more than any historical reality. In apparent contradiction, and just as nonsensically, some Pakistani linguists like to assert that the common ancestor of Hindi and Urdu originated not in North India, but in Pakistan.

Like the country and the language, their historical literature too has been partitioned. Anything written in the Perso-Arabic script, even before the seventeenth century, is now anachronistically considered to be part of Urdu literature; books in Nagari are automatically seen as Hindi. Never mind that their authors wrote in the same language; never mind that they lived in the same regions; never mind that they read each other's work: Urdu and Hindi must be separate, so they are retroactively separated. This is falsification of history at its most glaring.

So am I cheating when I treat Hindi and Urdu as one, rather than two, of the world's twenty largest languages? A little, perhaps. But the real cheats are elsewhere.

3

Spanish

ESPAÑOL

575 million speakers

With 425 million native speakers and some 150 million second-language speakers, Spanish is the majority and (main) official language in twenty countries: one in Europe, two Caribbean islands, seven in North and Central America, nine in South America and one in Africa. Spanish has become the second language of the United States, with nearly 40 million Americans speaking it as their primary language at home, and co-official status in the US territory of Puerto Rico. In Europe, there are substantial Spanish-speaking minorities in France and Switzerland.

Spanish

SELF-DESIGNATION Español or castellano (not be confused with Catalan, spoken in the northeast of Spain).

FAMILY Spanish is a member of the Romance branch of the Indo-European family.

SCRIPT The Latin alphabet with three diacritics: acute accent (á), tilde (ñ) and diaeresis (ü); the ñ is considered a separate letter. Spanish spelling is fairly regular; stress is consistently indicated by the spelling though often omitted in informal writing.

GRAMMAR Quite similar to the other Romance languages (except Romanian): complex verbal conjugation, two genders in nouns and adjectives, no case system.

SOUNDS Spanish has just five vowel sounds and, depending on the dialect, up to twenty consonant sounds.

LOANWORDS Spanish borrowed thousands of Arabic words during the Middle Ages, when Muslims ruled much of the Iberian Peninsula. French, Italian and English are among the other main sources. A small number of words can be traced to the Germanic occupation of the fifth to eighth centuries.

EXPORTS *Cork* is a very early borrowing from Spanish – it goes back to 1300. Hundreds more would follow, such as *armada*, *maize*, *mosquito*, *guitar*, *aficionado*, *potato*, *chocolate* and *barbecue*. The US has endless place names of Spanish origin, from Los Angeles, CA to Fernandina Beach, FL.

ESTADOS UNIDOS Spanish was the first European language spoken by settlers in today's United States – in Florida, where permanent settlement began in the 1560s, after failed attempts in the 1520s. The first European language spoken in North America was Old Norse, by Vikings in Newfoundland around 1000 CE.

3: **Spanish**

¿Ser or estar? That's the question

From an English-speaker's perspective, Spanish is probably the easiest of the Babel languages to master. It isn't exactly *easy*, mind you. There are still long lists of words to be learnt, a lot of grammar to be grasped and a whole new accent to be acquired.

My own *conquista* of Spanish took me years of effort and practice, and while it was a comparatively successful campaign, I have not yet quelled the last pockets of resistance. One of these hides deep in the Subjunctive Jungle (*la Selva del Subjuntivo*), a red zone which I nominally control, but where all sorts of sentences shelter booby-traps and landmines that frequently explode in my face. Being large and central, the Spanish Subjunctive Jungle can't be treated as a no-go area, but treading carefully and keeping to the marked paths is advisable. English has conserved only tiny patches of its subjunctive jungle ('if I *were* you', 'we demanded that he *be* silent'), which is as nothing compared to the thicket of today's Spanish.

But the subjunctive is an old bugbear for Spanish learners. In this chapter, instead, I will look into two other notorious regions: the orange zones of *to be* and *to have*.

Six *is*'s and one *was*

Let's start with a brief story: *There is a supermarket. A supermarket is a shop. John is at the supermarket. He is buying eggs. This supermarket is big. The supermarket is open. The supermarket was built last year.*

Not a gripping narrative, but what it rather neatly illustrates is the versatility of the English verb *to be*, represented in this story by six *is*'s and one *was*. If we are finickety – and that's exactly what we're going to be here – these seven brief sentences represent no fewer than seven variations of *to be*. (And even these don't exhaust the verb's potential.) Let's take them in turns.

There is a supermarket: here, *is* means 'exists', 'is present'.

A supermarket is a shop: it 'can be defined as' a shop; it 'falls into the category of' shops.

John is at the supermarket: he 'finds himself' or 'is situated' there.

He is buying chocolate: here the verb *to be* helps to form the continuous or progressive aspect of the main verb, *to buy*. It's therefore called an auxiliary verb, after the Latin word for 'help', AUXILIUM.

The supermarket is big: it 'has the permanent quality of being' big.

The supermarket is open: it 'has the momentary quality of being' open.

The supermarket was built last year: it 'got' built; unnamed people built it. Here again, *to be* is an auxiliary, but this time for the passive voice.

None of these sentences will seem remarkable to you. (Or, they will not seem *to be* remarkable – an alternative that illustrates how English can sometimes omit *to be* with no loss of sense.) After all, we're looking at an extremely frequent verb: if we include all of its many forms, from *were* to *being* and from *'m* to *'re*, it's the second most frequent word in the English language, after *the*.

This situation is far from universal among the world's languages, and Spanish is one of many that deal differently with this business of being. In Spanish, the seven different roles of *to be* that we just identified would be spread across four 'solutions' (to use a marketing term). Two of these solutions do not even involve anything like a verb *to be*.

The first sentence, 'There is a supermarket', translates as HAY UN SUPERMERCADO; the closest literal translation would be 'it has a supermarket'. If you're familiar with French or German, you'll be reminded of how these languages express 'there is': IL Y A UN SUPERMARCHÉ (literally 'It there has a supermarket') or ES GIBT EINEN SUPERMARKT ('It gives a supermarket'). In all these cases, the supermarket is the object of the verb, unlike in English, where it is ... what? The answer depends on your grammar book, but an object it certainly isn't. Nowadays, however, many Spanish speakers do not perceive the noun after HAY as its object and instead treat it as if it were its subject. As a result, they often put the verb in the plural when talking about more than one thing, especially in the past tense: HABÍAN MUCHOS SUPERMERCADOS, rather than the prescribed singular HABÍA, for 'There were many supermarkets'. It's one of those things that are frowned upon by many but used by even more, much like, in English, saying *less people* instead of *fewer people*.

Spanish has its own Academy. Each of the forty-six members occupies a seat designated with an upper case or lower case letter. Here's the most Spanish of all letters: ñ.

For the last of the seven sample sentences, the one with the passive, Spanish has two options. One exactly mirrors the English construction (EL SUPERMERCADO FUE CONSTRUIDO, where FUE means 'was'), but it's not very common. Much more frequently, another construction will use itself. Yes, strange as it sounds in English, that's exactly how it's said ('how it says itself') in Spanish: with a reflexive pronoun – EL SUPERMERCADO SE CONSTRUYÓ. Spanish speakers are as alive as anyone else to the fact that it takes real people to erect the walls and close the roof and do the plumbing and so forth, but that doesn't stop them saying that the thing 'built itself'.

Perhaps it bears mentioning that in Spanish, these reflexive pronouns are more modest than their English counterparts. English reflexive pronouns are bisyllabic mouthfuls – *myself, themselves* – that come across as somewhat, well, self-important. Not so in Spanish, where they're merely one syllable long (as they used to be in older English before the *self* bit was tacked on). Their use as a more common alternative to the passive sounds less conspicuous than a literal translation into English might make it seem.

Temporarily married, champions forever

That leaves us with five other sentence types where Spanish does indeed use its word for the verb *to be* – or rather its *words*, for it has two: SER and ESTAR. And the annoying thing is that although native speakers of course unerringly know which one to choose, the rules are so complex that second-language speakers are unlikely to ever master the art completely.

The easiest bit of the puzzle is when you translate a continuous tense, as in 'he's buying eggs'. Spanish and some other Romance languages have the same kind of construction and routinely use it. The Spanish verb we want here is ESTAR: JUAN ESTÁ COMPRANDO HUEVOS (John is buying eggs). Its twin SER just doesn't make sense in this context, ever.

That leaves us with four other meanings: 'has the momentary quality of being', 'is situated', 'can be defined as' and 'has the permanent quality of being'. And this is where Spanish can drive you to tears.

Teachers will tell you that the division of labour works as follows: ESTAR is in charge of the first two meanings and SER of the last two. That gives us the following correct sentences:

a) The supermarket is open: EL SUPERMERCADO ESTÁ ABIERTO. It will close later today, so 'open' is a momentary quality and ESTAR is used, here in the form ESTÁ.

b) John is at the supermarket: JUAN ESTÁ EN EL SUPERMERCADO. He finds himself there; it's where he's situated. Hence ESTAR.

c) A supermarket is a shop: UN SUPERMERCADO ES UNA TIENDA. ES is a form of SER and SER is used because a supermarket is inherently a shop.

d) The supermarket is big: EL SUPERMERCADO ES GRANDE. The supermarket can't help being big – it's what it's like, it's in its nature, it has this permanent quality (until, with a little help from the builders, it 'makes itself' smaller). Therefore: SER.

So far, so feasible. And true enough, most sentences obey these rules: *Mary is happy* (type a) and *she is at the office* (type b) both get a form of ESTAR, but in *Mary is my sister* (c) and *she is intelligent* (d), we find SER. Fair enough, since happiness is notoriously fleeting and time at the office mercifully finite, while intelligence and family are forever, sort of.

But then the weirdness starts. Given that *the kitchen is* (ESTAR) *inside the house*, one would expect a party to be (ESTAR) inside the house as well. But alas, there's a sub-rule for events 'being' or 'taking place' somewhere, and it requires SER instead.

Equally puzzling is the choice of verbs in the realm of marriage. Spanish manages to have *John is* (SER) *Mary's husband*, where the verb suggests permanence, alongside *John is* (ESTAR) *married to Mary*, which makes it sound as if divorce lawyers are never far away. The reason is that SER is compulsory in combination with nouns – not only 'to be his brother' and 'to be her husband', but even with such transient glories as 'to be prime minister' or 'to be the champion'. More surprising still, when John is said to be

ABURRIDO, he is 'boring' if SER is used, but 'bored' in the company of ESTAR.

There's more. If SER refers to permanence and ESTAR to temporariness, one would expect that today is (ESTAR) Monday and it is (ESTAR) twenty past ten. Not so: in both cases, SER is the verb of choice.

But my favourite is this, an existentially bewildering surprise hidden at the heart of Spanish: after you've died, you are (ESTÁS) dead. Not irrevocably dead, it sounds like, but only – what? Waiting

Bilingual America. The US already has more than fifty million Spanish speakers and by 2050 the Cervantes Institute estimates that it will have more Spanish speakers than any other country in the world.

for the final judgement, perhaps? There is a strong statistical correlation between speaking Spanish and being a Catholic, so that sounds plausible. However, the real reason for the choice of ESTAR over SER is grammatical. The word for 'dead', MUERTO, is technically speaking a past participle of the verb MORIR 'to die', denoting the result of that verb: think of it as 'having died'. And irreversible though death may be, the law of the land, or rather of the language, demands ESTAR in such cases. Grammar trumps nature.

This vodka – good

This whole SER versus ESTAR business is not only baffling for the student of Spanish, it also comes as a surprise for those who, like myself, spent their youth studying Latin rather than doing healthy outdoor sports. In many ways, Latin is a more complex linguistic edifice than its daughter languages, but on this particular issue it's simpler: it has just one verb for 'to be', ESSE, which covers all four meanings that we've just discussed. Its modern Spanish daughter is SER, and that is all the language would have needed. But its evil twin ESTAR is an equally legitimate offspring of Latin, tracing its origin to the verb STARE, 'to stand'.*

How can a word for 'to stand' end up meaning 'to be'? Easily. Think of English idioms like *I stand corrected, we stand in awe* and *as it now stands*, where *to stand* has more to do with a state of being than with an upright posture. If such expressions are used more and more frequently (*she stands accused, he stands convicted ...*), *to stand* can gradually replace *to be* not only in constructions that are closely parallel, but in ones that are less similar. Would it really be so strange to have *I stand perplexed* or *I stand invited*? Ultimately, the difference between *to be* and *to stand* may dwindle to a mere technicality, in which case it will become part of the grammar. This is a process known as grammaticalisation, and while it hasn't occurred with *to stand* in English, it has with STARE in several

---

* To be exact, SER is the hybrid offspring of two Latin verbs: ESSE, later ESSERE, 'to be'; and SEDERE, which means, and is an etymologic cognate of, 'to sit'. The infinitive SER and some other forms come from SEDERE, whereas ES, FUI and many others come from ESSERE.

Romance languages. Portuguese and Catalan use SER and ESTAR in much the same way as Spanish (though not exactly); in Italian, the rules for ESSERE and STARE are different, but grammaticalisation has taken place there as well.*

Getting the hang of SER and ESTAR may be hard for us, but distinctions somewhat like this are not rare. In several languages, distinguishing between two or more forms of being is the norm rather than the exception. Returning to our four meanings of 'to be' (a – temporary quality; b – location; c – definition and d – permanent quality), we see that languages may cluster them in different ways. Swahili, for instance has one form for b and another for a, c and d. Tamil has one for b and c, another for a and yet another for d. Vietnamese group a and d, with separate forms for b and for c. In a word, there's no telling.

Some languages introduce other niceties still. Japanese, for example, has created the complication of using two different verbs in meaning b, one for lifeless things, another for living beings. Which, if you think about it, is perhaps no more peculiar than using different pronouns for things (*it*) and living beings (*he* and *she*). What's more, as we saw in chapter 13, Japanese also encourages women to omit the verb 'to be' in certain constructions where men are expected to use it.

Russian is like English in that it expresses all four meanings of 'to be' in the same way. Yet it is rather unlike English in *how* it employs them. Russian does have the word BYT' (a relative of *be*; the present tense YEST' IS related to *is*), but much more often than not it's omitted in the present tense. In speech, it will leave no trace; in writing, it can be replaced with a dash.

Many languages leave out the verb in at least some sentence types where we would use *to be*. But this non-use of 'to be' is generally unproblematic. Vietnamese does many things that drive me up the wall, but usages such as NHÀ CAO (literally 'house tall') for 'the house is tall' is not one of them. After all, *to be*'s standing is somewhat precarious even in English. With verbs like *to seem*, we may or may not add *to be* – it seems (to be) optional. And is there

---

* French has merged the two verbs into one: ÊTRE and forms like ÉTAIT come from ESTAR, while SUIS, EST, FUT, SERA and all other forms come from ESSE.

really a difference between 'the sooner you do it, the better' and 'the sooner you do it, the better it will be'? The thing is, 'to be' is so frequent and so light in meaning that if a language feels like getting rid of any verb, 'to be' will be the people's choice.

Hangover for sale

The second most common verb in English, after *to be*, is *to have*. And while it immediately puts us in mind of possession, its range of meanings is, again, wider than that: you *have a hangover* (you 'possess' – well, kind of), because you *have drunk* too much (you 'did', and you still feel it), so too bad you *have to work* now (you 'must').

Spanish has two different verbs here, TENER and HABER, plus one special form, HAY. That may seem complicated, but compared to the SER and ESTAR maze, it's child's play, for several reasons.

First of all, the casting of the two verbs and the special form is crystal clear. TENER has two roles: possession and, in combination with QUE, obligation. To 'have a hangover' is TENER (UNA) RESACA, while TENER QUE TRABAJAR means 'to have to work'. HABER also has two roles, one demanding, the other cushy. Like the English 'to have',* it forms the perfect tense of all verbs that have one: HABER TOMADO (DEMASIADO) is 'to have drunk (too much)'. With the preposition DE, it can indicate obligation: HABER DE TRABAJAR means 'to have to work', but this is much rarer in modern Spanish than the formula with TENER QUE. Finally, there is this special form HAY, which in etymological terms is a compound of HA (a form of HABER) and a trace of AHÍ, meaning 'there'. Combined with QUE, it expresses an impersonal necessity: HAY QUE PENSARLO BIEN means something like 'we should' or 'one must think this through carefully' (much like IL FAUT in French). We met HAY before, because without QUE it means 'there is' or 'there are'. I should add that the conjugation of both TENER and HABER is highly irregular, and of course there

---

* It seems obvious that *have* and HABER are cognates, but they aren't. The English *have* is cognate with the Spanish verb CABER, 'to fit, to enter'. The Spanish HABER, like French AVOIR and Italian AVERE, derives from an old Indo-European root that has left no traces in English, other than Latinate borrowings such as *habit* and *prohibit*.

is, as ever, the red zone of the Subjunctive Jungle. But choosing the right verb is a breeze.

As for grammar, English and Spanish are almost uncannily similar in their use of *have* and HABER or TENER as an auxiliary verb, both to express obligation and to form the perfect tense. Using a verb meaning 'to have' to express obligation is fairly uncommon across languages; using it as the sole auxiliary to form the perfect tense is far from universal in Germanic and Romance languages, and decidedly uncommon elsewhere.

But even in their basic roles as indicators of possession, their similarity is more striking than may strike *us*. In both English and Spanish, possessive sentences with *have* or HABER display the same construction: a possessor possesses a possession. What – you may ask – could be more natural, logically speaking? Well, statistically speaking, only a minority of languages worldwide do likewise (among them Portuguese, French and German but also Persian). I'll call the English way of doing this type 1, and it is found in about 25 per cent of all languages.

Type 2 (another 25 per cent) is based on simultaneity, which is difficult to render in English. 'The possessor is with the possession' may come closest. This type is very common among African languages, including Swahili.

Type 3 (20 per cent) can be translated as '(regarding) the possessor, there exists the possession'. This type is frequently found in Southeast Asian and Chinese languages. It displays strong surface similarity with the English type 1: possessor first, then a verb and finally the possession. Indeed, when I was learning Vietnamese, I initially memorised the word CÓ as meaning 'to have'. However, that didn't work for many other uses of the same word. Thinking of it as 'to be (the case), to exist' helped to bring all these meanings together. This is true for all the languages in this group: the operational verb does *not* mean 'have', but something akin to 'exist'. Therefore, what we would consider the object (the possession) is really the subject, and what we could consider the subject (the possessor) has a function called topic, which is often conveyed in English as 'regarding' or 'as for'. So while the Vietnamese TÔI CÓ MỘT CHIẾC ĐIỆN THOẠI MỚI is correctly translated as 'I have a new telephone', it literally says, 'as for me, there exists a new telephone'.

Type 4 (20 per cent) expresses possession as 'the possession is at/ on/with the possessor'. We find this in Babel languages as far apart or unrelated as Tamil, Hindi-Urdu, Japanese, Arabic, Korean and Russian, as well as Finnish, Hungarian and the Celtic tongues.

Type 5 (10 per cent), the smallest of them all, has 'the possessor's possession exists'. In *Babel*, it's represented by Turkish and Bengali.

So these are the five ways in which the languages of the world may express 'to have' – except that often they don't. In both English and Spanish, we have this habit of pretending that 'having a car', 'having a mother', 'having a hangover', 'having a party' and 'having some time to spend' are all instances of one and the same phenomenon. But try selling or buying these 'possessions' and you'll notice the

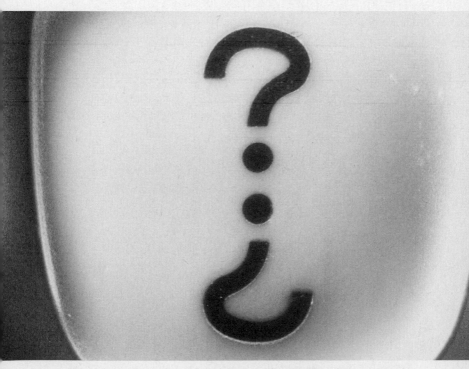

The Spanish question mark announces itself at the beginning and end of a sentence. ¿And, indeed, why not?

practical, moral and commercial differences. Other languages are less obsessively possessive. They prefer to say things like 'the head splits me', 'we're partying' and 'there is time I can spend' rather than use sentences with 'have'.

Many languages differentiate between so-called alienable and inalienable things, requiring two different verbs or other devices to talk about them. The cut-off point between the two can differ from one language to the other. In Japanese, for instance, one can use a verb, MOTSU, for things that you really own, such as a fishing net or money. It's a type 1 usage, literally meaning 'to hold', 'to carry'. The other option is a type 4 construction: 'the possession is at the possessor'. While this *can* refer to concrete things in one's possession, it's the only option when talking about relatives, complaints, medical conditions, time and other things one cannot take to market. Tamil also makes this distinction, but in a different way from Japanese. Someone who has money can be a rich, moneyed person, in which case Tamil would say that the money is 'to the person'. But if he or she just happens to have some money right now, the cash is 'on the person'. Two different case suffixes distinguish 'permanently having' from 'having at the moment'. Of course, money is never really inalienable, but if you permanently own lots of it, it's much less ephemeral than if you merely happen to have some ready cash in your pocket.

Are such distinctions unfamiliar? Certainly. Illogical? Not so much. Hard to learn? You bet. Which is one reason why, from an English-speaker's perspective, Spanish is so much easier to master. *¡Que tenga un buen día!*

2

Mandarin

普通話

PŬTŌNGHUÀ

1.3 billion speakers

Mandarin has some 900 million native speakers, more than any other language, and 400 million second-language speakers. China, Taiwan, Singapore and Malaysia are the major Mandarin-speaking countries. Most migrants of Chinese extraction used to speak Chinese languages other than Mandarin. Today, Chinese emigrants will often speak Mandarin.

Mandarin

SELF-DESIGNATION 普通話 (PǓTŌNGHUÀ, used in mainland China; literally 'common speech'), 國語 (GUÓYǓ, in Taiwan; 'national language'), 華語 (HUÁYǓ, elsewhere in Asia; 'Chinese language'). Also called Standard Chinese, (Modern) Standard Mandarin; (loosely) Chinese.

FAMILY Mandarin is one of the Chinese languages, often called 'Chinese dialects'. This group belongs to the Sino-Tibetan family, of which it is the largest by a very wide margin.

SCRIPT Mandarin has a unique character script. See main text.

GRAMMAR Mandarin has hardly any inflection, which means that words have only one form: for singular and plural, for present, past and future, for subject and object. Nouns do not have a gender, but they fall into classes, each of which requires a specific classifier in some grammatical contexts, for instance after a numeral. This is often compared to the English word 'cattle', which cannot be counted directly ('one cattle, two cattles'), but only by adding the classifier-like word 'head': two head of cattle.

SOUNDS Mandarin is probably the most famous of the tonal languages (see chapter 14). Mandarin syllables are remarkably simple in structure: they usually start with a consonant, followed by one or two vowels; the final consonant, if there is one, is /n/ or /ng/. In writing, there is also a final *r*, but this is never pronounced as a consonant.

LOANWORDS Sanskrit (religious terms), Japanese (scientific and economic terminology) and English.

EXPORTS *Chow*, *feng shui*, *gung-ho*, *kowtow*, *pinyin*, *tai chi*, *tao* (or *dao*) and *yin-yang*. Loan translations include *brain-washing* (from XǏNǍO), *paper tiger* (ZHǏ LǍOHǓ), *long march* (CHÁNG ZHĒNG) and *scorched earth* (JIĀOTǓ). Culinary terms such as *chop suey*, *kumquat, lapsang souchong* and *bok choy* tend to have originated in Cantonese; *ginseng* comes from yet another Southern Chinese language.

CONFUCIUS Since 2004, China has actively promoted the study of Mandarin through its Confucius Institutes. As of late 2017, there were 516 branches in 142 countries. According to the Institute, more than 7 million students took language courses over the past thirteen years. Also, outside these institutes, the study of the language has seen a considerable rise in popularity since the early 2000s.

2: **Mandarin**

The mythical Chinese script

If Spanish is the easiest of the Babel languages for English speakers to learn, Mandarin and Japanese are probably the hardest. It takes persistence to master the Chinese tones, while the linguistic intricacies of Japanese-style politeness are unlikely to become second nature in a hurry. Yet, they would perhaps not be among the world's most difficult languages if it weren't for the immense complication of their writing systems.* No other system in the modern world requires schoolchildren and second-language learners to memorise a greater number of symbols than the Chinese character script. It's no exaggeration to compare it to a Great Wall around the language – not impregnable, to be sure, but formidable nonetheless. Japanese, though using a smaller number of characters, has found ingenious ways to create additional complexity, a feat which we'll admire in a separate chapter.

Nowadays, Westerners will come across Chinese writing in restaurants and news stands, online, on packaging material, and increasingly on necks, arms, ankles, backs and other parts of the human anatomy. Tattoo accidents have been known to happen, resulting in people's skin proudly proclaiming 'mad diarrhoea' or 'coffin dude', while other supposed characters are meaningless or back to front. Fortunately for them, five out of six people on the planet can't tell the difference.

While we can hardly be expected to know hundreds or even thousands of Chinese characters (learning them would take years), it's certainly possible to know a bit *about* them. But somehow, even after centuries of contact, Western ideas about Chinese writing

---

*. Or perhaps they would. Certainly Mandarin, if sinologist David Moser is to be believed. Do yourself a favour and read his very funny article 'Why Chinese Is So Damn Hard': http://bit.ly/MoserMandarin.

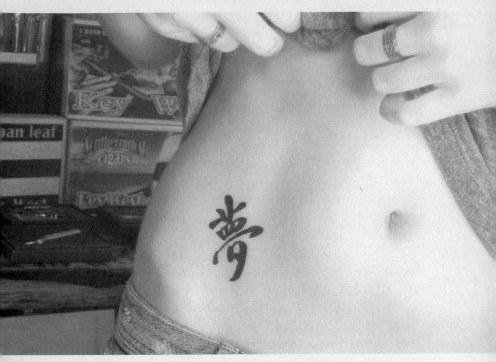

It's all too easy to get your Chinese (or Japanese) tattoo wrong. But this one is good to keep: the character means 'dream' or 'ambition'.

are still beset by misconceptions. 'There is probably no subject on earth concerning which more misinformation is purveyed and more misunderstandings circulated than Chinese characters or sinograms,' said J. Marshall Unger, a professor of Japanese who wrote a book about them. What makes it hard to dispel the misconceptions is that they generally contain a kernel of truth. I'll mention these kernels first, and then chip off the crusts of inaccuracies.

1. Chinese writing goes from top to bottom

What's true. Traditionally, Chinese text was indeed written in columns from top to bottom and ordered from right to left. If there was no space for columns, for instance on certain signboards, the text would be written right to left. In Taiwan, Hong Kong and overseas Chinese communities today, the vertical, right-to-left writing style is not uncommon in newspapers and books. Books that are laid out in this way have their binding on the right, as Arabic and Hebrew books do.

On the spines of books, titles are written top to bottom, with each character in its normal upright orientation. This is different from the practice in English and other European languages, where most titles are rotated 90 degrees: mostly clockwise in the case of English, Dutch and the Scandinavian languages, but more often anticlockwise in French and Spanish – while the Germans can't seem to make up their minds.

But then there's this. Most Chinese text these days is written and printed from left to right on horizontal lines. In mainland China, it's rare to find anything else; everywhere else, this orientation is increasingly the norm.

2. Chinese characters are basically pictures

What's true. Some Chinese characters *are* stylised pictures of objects or fairly intuitive visualisations of ideas. It doesn't take much imagination to work out that 人 (RÉN), which means 'person', depicts the legs of a person, or that there is a relation between 二 (ÈR) and its meaning, 'two'. Even though it's not immediately evident, it's easy to believe that 木 (MÙ) began life as an attempt to draw a tree, which is indeed what it represents. Other characters are harder to trace to their roots, such as the one for SHUǏ ('water'): 水. There's good historical evidence that it originated as a winding river flanked by four drops or whirls.

Other characters are not single pictograms or ideograms, but compounds of two or more. Well-known examples include the double-tree character for 'grove', 林 (LÍN), and the triple-tree one for 'forest', 森 (SĒN).* Another much-quoted specimen from this category is 休 (XIŪ) for 'shade' or 'rest': to the left of the tree, we

---

* SĒN is one of many Chinese characters that can be said to have a meaning without being – in the modern language anyway – an independent word. Some examples of this same phenomenon can be found in English: the *were* in *werewolf* means 'man', the *ly* in *quickly* is derived from a word meaning 'body' and *ceive* in *receive* and other verbs can be said to mean, or have meant, 'seize'. For those who like their linguistics well-spiced with jargon, the name for these bits is 'bound morphemes'.

see 亻(which is a squeezed variety of the 人 character for 'person' that we saw above). The idea then would be 'person resting in the shade under a tree' – so neat and appealing an explanation that many experts consider it a just-so story.

A good deal of fun is to be had from the few pictographic characters that exist. According to experts, the character for 'egg' 卵 (LUǍN) displays a pair of what are called 'eggs' in Arabic, Russian, Spanish, German and other languages – but 'nuts' in English, and not the ones growing from trees. Equally unsafe for work, the character 母 (MǓ) has reduced the concept of 'mother' or 'female' to a mere set of Cubist-style breasts, with the nipples in full view. Or, turning from the puerile to the mathematical, let's wonder why the character for eight, 八 (BĀ) looks the way it does. Etymologists agree that this sign originally meant 'to divide'. Some claim that 八 also acquired the meaning 'eight' because this number is so easily divided – three times even, since 8 equals 2 to the 3rd power. Isn't that a rather lovely explanation? However, the dominant party-pooping school of thought holds that the Chinese words for 'to divide' and 'eight' were at some point in history homophones – they sounded the same, that is.

A character consisting of two pictograms is 兄 (XIŌNG) for 'older brother'. The square shape is a frequently found component meaning 'mouth', while the two legs carrying it are a variant of a character for 'child'. So 兄 represents a child with a (big) mouth. Apparently, older brothers are defined as the siblings who order their juniors about.

But then there's this. The overwhelming majority – 98 per cent or so – of Chinese characters are not pictograms or ideograms like these. However hard and long you look at them, you will never work out their meaning on the basis of any resemblance to things in real life. Or if you can, you only have your own creativity to thank, because it's not how they came about.

3. Chinese characters have existed for 3500 years

What's true. The oldest preserved Chinese inscriptions date from about 1500 BCE, and Chinese writing has developed without interruption since. So it's correct to claim that writing in China has been around for 3,500 years, and even longer: the oldest finds, far from being the tentative and irregular scribblings of an inventor, show the confident hand of a writer using a mature system.

But then there's this. Modern Chinese readers can't make head or tail of these oldest texts, because – with rare exceptions such as 二 for 'two' – the earliest characters are nothing like today's. The differences are so vast that after finding these earliest inscriptions, it took scholars a while to figure out that they represented Chinese writing at all.

But wait – if Chinese writing has this long and uninterrupted tradition, doesn't that in itself justify the claim that the characters have indeed been around for thirty-five centuries? Well, that is one way of looking at it. But in that case, it follows that our Latin script has been around for even longer: at least thirty-eight centuries, or even 53. That's because our alphabet has descended, in another uninterrupted tradition, from the first alphabet, designed in the Near East (in either Egypt or Canaan) around 1800 BCE. This first alphabet was largely made up of Egyptian hieroglyphs – of the small subset that represented single sounds, to be exact. And with hieroglyphs dating back to about 3300 BCE, this places the Latin script in a fifty-three-centuries-old tradition.

Admittedly, there is one difference: whereas in China both the script and the language have undergone a gradual development, in 'our' case, this is true only for the writing system. On its way from Egypt through the Near East, Greece and Rome to this book, the Western writing tradition hopped from one language to the next, indeed from one language family to the next, several times.

4. There are 50,000 Chinese characters

What's true. The figure of 50,000 is probably based on three famous dictionaries from the years 1076, 1716 and 1915, each of which contained between 47,000 and 54,000 individual characters. The publication with the largest number of characters so far has even more: the 2004 *Dictionary of Chinese Variant Form*, published in Taiwan, contains a whopping 106,230.

But then there's this. Many of the characters in these dictionaries are only in local use or refer to highly specialised meanings, relevant only to, say, junk builders or reed-pipe players. Other characters are unusual varieties of more common ones or are deeply archaic. Including these in the count is like claiming that *plough* and *plow* are two different English words and that *thilke* is a word because it existed in Chaucer's day (it's related to *ilk* and meant 'that' or 'those'). Of the characters listed in the huge 2004 dictionary, at most one in eight is relevant today. And even this doesn't mean that an educated Chinese person knows over 13,000 characters – a mere quarter of that number is nothing to be ashamed of. Font designers, however, will have to make sure that all of them can be written.

5. Characters tell us nothing about pronunciation

What's true. Characters are not reliable, systematic guides to pronunciation. Indeed, a beginning student of Mandarin will just have to learn the correct pronunciation by rote, one character at a time.

But then there's this. Most characters do hint at their pronunciation. Not all of them do, it's true, and these phonetic clues are not as reliable as one could wish for, but at least it's something.

The favourite textbook illustration of how this works is 媽. The crucial thing to know is that, like most other characters, it consists of two elements. Part of it, the leftmost third in this case, is taken up by something that looks like a narrow version of the character 女 (NǙ) for 'woman'. That is indeed exactly what it is derived from, but it's crucial to realise that if something's *derived* from a character it no longer *is* a character. A character has two characteristics (pun not intended): on paper, it more or less fills a rectangle, while in speech, it gets pronounced. The latter may seem a platitude, but it's actually at the heart of the matter: while 女 is pronounced, its narrower version (the left-hand part of 媽) is not. As for the right-hand two-thirds of the character, it is taken up by a slim 馬 (MǍ, meaning 'horse').

Learning to read and write characters is a matter of repetition, repetition and more repetition. In practice, it is increasingly done by keyboard.

Now, if you're unaccustomed to Chinese writing, you may well suspect that媽 means 'female horse', in other words 'mare'. But that's not how the system works. The right way to tackle these sorts of compound characters, or form-sound characters as the Chinese call them, is by finding a word that *sounds* like one of its components and has a *meaning* related to that of the other. In this particular case, the 'woman' element gives the semantic clue and the MǍ element helps with phonetic information: the character under consideration means 'mother' and is pronounced /mā/ – that is, in the same way as 馬 (MǍ), though with a different tone. Of course, Chinese readers do not solve this puzzle every time they come across the 媽 character; they memorised it in childhood and now they just *know*. But at least there is a puzzle to be solved, which helps Chinese children and foreign students to memorise the character. (Incidentally, these compound characters also make short shrift of the common misconception that 'most characters tell us nothing about their meaning'.)

This method falls flat, of course, with characters that are not compounds, such as 馬 (MǍ). They 'sit silent and imposing on the page', to quote linguist David Moser, and their pronunciation 'can only be remembered through countless hours of repetitive practice'. The same is true for their meaning, unless the character gives some visual hint. This particular one actually does, because 馬 has evolved from the representation of a horse. The four legs are still visible, and the stroke in the lower right corner was once a tail.

If this sounds easy – and I rather fear it didn't – here are some problems with the two-hint system. One is that it can be unclear which part gives which clue. The semantic component within the compound character may be on the left (as the 'woman' element in 媽) or on the right (as in 奻), at the bottom (婪), or the top (no example found – no woman on top, it seems), and one element may even surround the other (威). Fortunately, the number of semantic clues is limited: most of them, including the one for 'woman', are on a list of just over 200.* So unless a character contains two of these – a complication that is by no means rare – the semantic clue can be identified.

Another problem is that there's considerable variation in the degree of similarity between the pronunciation of the character and that of its phonetic clue. Occasionally, it's perfect: the phonetic clue and the actual pronunciation are identical. More often, it's pretty good, in that the consonant(s) and vowel(s) are identical, but the tone is not. This is the case of 媽 (MĀ), whose phonetic clue has an Ǎ, not an Ā. But often the resemblance leaves a lot to be desired. A good example is 聞. At the bottom we see a micro version of 耳, which means 'ear' (it originated as the picture of an ear), and is remarkably similar to the English *ear*, namely ĚR. It is the semantic element of 聞, which used to mean 'hear', though confusingly, its meaning has shifted to 'smell'. The rest of the character is clearly visible above the ear: 門 (for 'gate'). As a full character of its own

---

* Technically, this list of somewhere between 201 and 214 items contains *radicals*. A radical is not exactly the same thing as a semantic component, but for present purposes, it's a good-enough approximation.

it would be pronounced /mén/. Here it's just a phonetic clue, but quite a poor one, for the compound character is pronounced /wén/. At some point in history, the two characters were pronounced more similarly, perhaps something like /muən/ and /miuən/ respectively. Unfortunately, they drifted apart, leaving us with a very imperfect phonetic clue.

This is far from being the worst case. The pronunciation of other words has changed so dramatically that the original similarity can no longer be ascertained. Some people believe this is the true story behind 休 (xiū; 'shade' or 'rest') that I mentioned above: not a person resting in the shade of a tree, but a sound similarity that we can no longer reconstruct. Not that it makes the just-so story less charming, nor less useful as a mnemonic device.

6. Characters are words

What's true. Practically all characters have meanings, unlike some English syllables, say *der*, that convey nothing whatsoever until they're part of a word (*wonder, derby,* et cetera). Many characters *can* be used as words in Mandarin, or (as described in the footnote on p.303) as parts of compounds; others are no longer commonly used as such in the modern language, but are or were in regional or historical varieties of Chinese.

But then there's this. A large majority of Mandarin words are compounds, consisting of two or more characters. Some 88 per cent of the words in today's language consist of more than one character. In running text, the rate is lower because a limited number of short words – pronouns, prepositions and other so-called function words – are very frequent. But among nouns, verbs and adjectives, single-character words are very much a minority.

Take the word for 'oak', 橡樹 (xiàngshù). The first character can be used as a word in itself, meaning 'oak' or 'acorn'; the second one means 'tree' or 'plant'. Usually, however, the combination rather than just the first part is used. That is because xiàng has numerous other meanings, which are as diverse as 'statue', '(in the) direction (of)', 'elephant' and 'neck'. However, these are all represented by different characters, so on paper it would suffice just to write 橡, because it can only mean 'oak' (or 'acorn', but that would typically be called XIÀNGZǏ, 'son/young/egg of the oak'). In other words, XIÀNG is a homophone with several meanings, so in speech, clarification is needed – hence the added SHÙ for 'tree'. In writing, this would not be necessary, as 橡 'oak' contains all the information required. But modern Mandarin writing follows the spoken language, so today the word for 'oak' is written as two characters. Until the early twentieth century, however, the 樹 'tree' character would have been omitted, because the written language was based on classical Chinese, not on contemporary speech.

(By the way, please note that compound characters and compound words are very different things. Under 5, we saw that 媽 for 'mother' is a compound *character*, composed of a semantic and a phonetic element, but it is not a compound *word*, consisting as it does of just one syllable: MĀ. Here, under 6, we encountered a compound *word*, 橡樹 (XIÀNGSHÙ) for 'oak'. It consists of two full characters, both of which are fully pronounced. As it happens, both characters of this compound word are also compound characters, but that is a mere coincidence.)

7. All Chinese languages are written the same way

What's true. Until 1956, speakers of all Chinese languages used (nearly) the same characters, usually with the same meanings. As a result, two Chinese people who were both monolingual in two different Chinese languages (say, the Beijing dialect of Mandarin and the Cantonese dialect of Yue) would understand most of each other's writing even though they would not understand each other's speech. Even within Mandarin, dialects can be so different that people may have trouble recognising some particular word; writing it down will solve the problem. That's why Mandarin-language films are subtitled in Mandarin: if native speakers of, say, Cantonese do not catch a spoken Mandarin word, they will still usually be able to read it.

All of this is *largely* still the case today – with the added facilitating factor that everybody has learnt Mandarin at school so that even those who can't really speak it will still be literate in it. The situation can be compared to what occurs when English speakers with broad and very different accents, say Appalachian and Scouse, run into a comprehension roadblock: writing down what they're saying will clear up the problem. However, Mandarin and Cantonese are much more different from each other than any two varieties of English.

But then there's this. There are some grammatical differences between Chinese languages (word order and the use of certain particles) which show up in writing. Also, some Chinese languages, especially Cantonese, have developed special characters for words not used

認識了一個蠻不錯的男生
I met a pretty great guy.

Mandarin (and English) subtitles are standard on Chinese films. This is a Taiwanese rom-com called *My Egg Boy* featuring a chef and his dog.

in Mandarin. On the other hand, most Chinese languages are rarely written at all.

More importantly, the People's Republic in 1956 simplified thousands of characters, while in Hong Kong and Taiwan the traditional characters have been retained. Many simplified characters are so different from their traditional shapes that somebody literate in one cannot easily recognise the other.

On balance, however, there's more truth to this commonly held idea about Chinese writing than to most of the other ones listed in this chapter.

8. Chinese characters are great for punning

What's true. Mandarin is the ideal language for wordplay, because it's rich in God's gift to the punster: homophones.

But then there's this. The great opportunities for wordplay arise not thanks to the characters, but in spite of them. On paper, most of the Mandarin homophones are easily distinguished. A pun like the one about the duck who orders a beer and tells the bartender 'to put it on my bill' would never work in written Mandarin. Two words might sound identical, like *bill* for 'beak' and *bill* for 'cheque', but they would be represented by different characters.

On the other hand, in Mandarin you can occasionally use an incorrect character that is homophonous with the intended meaning, and still get the message across. That would be like writing *The Gnu Whirled* instead of *The New World* – computers will be stumped, but most human readers won't, or not for long anyway. Punning opens up great possibilities to circumvent the Great Firewall (as the People's Republic's massive online censorship apparatus is known), which largely relies on computer intelligence to suppress all sorts of utterances; not just political protests, but also simple profanity. The most famous example is CǍONÍMǍ, 'grass mud horse', which was, until the censors got wise, an alternative way of saying CÀO NǏ MĀ – 'do your Mom', in bowdlerised translation. Grass Mud Horse has now even become the title of an online 'glossary of memes, nicknames and neologisms created by Chinese netizens and encountered in online political discussions'.

9. Mandarin would be better if it ditched characters

What's true. There's no denying that learning to read and write characters is much more time-consuming than learning an alphabet, not only for second-language learners, but also for native speakers of Mandarin.

But then there's this. Even if switching to the Latin alphabet could be proved to be a highly beneficial move, it still wouldn't happen. And that's not because Chinese culture is particularly conservative, or some such Orientalist cliché. Rather, it's because *all* cultures are conservative when it comes to writing. Even small spelling reforms stir up strong emotions. Big reforms happen only in revolutionary times – think of Turkey under Atatürk. But it didn't happen in China under Mao (though he toyed with the idea), and it's not going to happen until the next revolution – maybe not even then.

Might the Chinese be right to stick to their 'awful writing system', as the US *Chronicle of Higher Education* put it? The obvious alternative would be pinyin, the Latin transcription system that was developed in Mao's day, and which has achieved wide currency, both among students of Mandarin (mostly to find out how characters are pronounced) and among native speakers (mostly to input characters on to telephones and computers). But while pinyin painstakingly indicates the tone of each syllable, as in the famous quadruplets MĀ, MÁ, MǍ and MÀ, it does not differentiate between Mandarin's many homophones, that is to say, all those items that sound perfectly identical, including the tone. As a result, pinyin would produce many more misunderstandings than the character script.

Or so the reasoning goes. But wait, not so fast: pinyin has something that the character script sorely lacks, namely spaces. What we call homophones in Mandarin are mostly *syllables* that sound the same, not *words*. In character script, it's not immediately obvious whether a character is a word in itself or a part of a longer word. In pinyin, on the other hand, no such ambiguity exists. Earlier on, we saw that

XIÀNG could mean 'oak', 'statue, '(in the) direction (of)', 'elephant' and 'neck'. But in fact, Mandarin speakers often do not say XIÀNG for any of these concepts. Just like they frequently say XIÀNGSHÙ for 'oak', they will frequently use DÀXIÀNG or 'big elephant' for 'elephant', JǏNGXIÀNG or 'neck-neck' for 'neck', DIĀOXIÀNG for 'statue', where the DIĀO part means 'to engrave', and FĀNGXIÀNG for 'direction', where FĀNG means 'place' or once more 'direction'.

In pinyinised Mandarin, these words are instantly recognisable as words, whereas in character script they could simply be two words that happen to be sitting next to each other. As a result, pinyin leaves far less scope for ambiguity than might seem at first sight. According to Chinese linguists, quoted by the sinologist William Hannas, no more than around one per cent of Chinese words are homophones. They found seventy monosyllabic words whose different meanings, 164 in all, were likely to create real confusion, as well as thirty-nine problematic polysyllables with eighty-two meanings. Given that pinyin is a highly regular spelling system, words that are doppelgangers in speech (homophones) will also be doppelgangers in writing (homographs).

However, the problem can easily be solved. European languages have homophones too: in English, think of *there, their* and *they're, rode, road* and *rowed, here* and *hear*. Mandarin homophones could easily be distinguished in writing by adding a silent letter, like the silent letter that distinguishes *morning* from *mourning*. Granted, this prop would make it somewhat harder for children to learn pinyin. Compared to memorising characters, however, it would still be as easy as breaking a Ming vase.

But probably this additional prop wouldn't even be necessary. Vietnamese, too, has many homophones. Unlike pinyin, Vietnamese doesn't mark word boundaries, since syllables are usually written separately. Even so, the Vietnamese seem fine with their script.

10. Now you know everything about characters

Not at all true, I'm afraid. Characters are so different from all other writing systems that they raise more questions than I can answer in this chapter. How do you place words written in characters in

Once mastered, there's no limit to the creative use of Mandarin: Lego is a bit of a challenge, but baristas will find infinite new outlets for their art.

some kind of order (I'm avoiding the word 'alphabetical' here), for instance in a dictionary? (It involves counting strokes.) How do you differentiate between two homophonic characters in speech, without writing them down? (By mentioning a familiar word in which it appears, a bit like saying, '*weigh* as in *heavyweight*, not as in *highway*'.) Is it possible to describe a character without writing it down? (The strokes have names, but it's usually more practical to refer to the two component parts that most characters consist of, as discussed under 5, above.) How is Chinese rendered in Braille? (By writing pinyin in Braille.) Et cetera.

Also, there are plenty of other myths around, including the following: 'Every character represents one syllable.' (There are hundreds of exceptions, though the Chinese government doesn't accept most of them.) 'New characters are no longer being created.' (They are, both officially and ad hoc.) And then there's this one: 'Japanese too is written in Chinese characters'.

Is it? That deserves a chapter in its own right.

2b

Japanese (revisited)

A writing system lacking in system

If London's King's Cross station can have a platform 9¾ (and no longer just in fiction), surely a book can have a chapter 2b? My reason for inserting one here is because, before moving on to the world's most widely spoken language, I'd like to revisit a smaller giant, Japanese. One of the things that make the language exceptional is a system that, if not magical or fictitious, is certainly extravagant and harder to learn than any spell, curse or charm. I am talking here about Japanese writing. The reason I didn't discuss it in chapter 13 is that it's based on the Chinese character script, which in itself is quite a challenge, as we've just seen.

'Based on the Chinese character script' should not be interpreted as 'nearly identical to it', for Japanese writing has many more tangles, snarls, coils and knots than Chinese – so much so that it's widely considered the most complex writing system currently in use. So let's walk straight into the seemingly impenetrable wall of Japanese writing to see if we can magically get to the other side.

Kanji and how to pronounce them

The earliest texts in Japanese were written entirely in the Chinese character script, which was introduced to Japan in the fifth or sixth century by Korean scholars. Unlike the Vietnamese and the Koreans, who no longer use the characters, the Japanese never replaced them, but instead added plug-ins. No writing system based on Chinese characters is going to be simple. But since Japanese and Mandarin are fundamentally different in both structure and basic vocabulary, the character script was not particularly suitable for Japanese to begin with. As a result, its adoption for writing Japanese had profound complications.

So what happened when the Japanese decided to use Chinese characters – or KANJI ('Han letters'), as they call them?* For one thing, the clues to their pronunciation were lost. As we saw in the previous chapter, most characters consist of a semantic and a phonetic component, giving the reader clues to their meaning and pronunciation. The semantic part holds good in Japanese too, but the phonetic one doesn't. After all, these characters are now pressed into service to represent Japanese, not Chinese, words, and there's no reason why words sounding similar in one language should also do so in another. To return to the classical example: if the character for 'mother' visually refers to 'horse', that's because the words sound similar in Mandarin, but in English they don't – nor in Japanese. Therefore, children and foreign students have an even harder time in Japanese memorising the relationship between the visual shape and the correct pronunciation than they do in Chinese. In an effort to make writing easier, several post-war governments have published lists of 'regular-use characters', thereby standardising the script and limiting the total number. Even so, there are currently as many as 2,136. In practice, at least another thousand are still in use.

So does the student of Japanese have to learn the correct pronunciation of 2,136 characters? If only. Many of the characters have more than one 'reading' – that is, more than one meaning with a pronunciation of its own. Usually, one of these is authentically Japanese. For instance, 手 can be pronounced as /te/, giving us the Japanese word for 'hand'. This is the native Japanese reading. But in the compound 着手 (literally 'touch hand', meaning 'start'), the second character is pronounced /shu/ rather than /te/. This is based on a Chinese pronunciation of many centuries ago, when the word was borrowed. The first half of the word, 着, is sounded as

---

* Throughout this chapter, I will use the words 'character' and 'kanji' interchangeably. I do not use the word 'character' for other elements of Japanese writing.

/chaku/, based on a long-outdated Chinese pronunciation, /chak/. But again, this character can also represent a native Japanese word, as exemplified by the compound 着物 ('kimono', literally 'a thing to put on'), where it's pronounced as /ki/.

How a 'chakubutsu' is almost a kimono

Two entirely different pronunciations per character, one native, the other imported. Pretty bad, huh? But it gets worse. Some characters have not one native reading but two, and a few have even more. More importantly, many were borrowed two or three times over, in different periods and from different regions of China, resulting in as many different pronunciations. Not all of the 2,136 'regular-use' characters can be pronounced in many ways, but a great number of them have two readings that are in everyday use and one or two more that occur in specialised jargons only, for instance in Buddhist religious writings. The character 泳, which means 'swim', has a native pronunciation rendered in Latin script as OYO, but a Chinese-derived pronunciation EI. It appears in 'to swim' (泳ぐ, OYOGU) and in 'swimming style' (泳法 EIHŌ). It's rather as if English were to spell the words 'swimming' and 'natation' the same way. Some characters go one better by amassing a lot of readings. The record is held by the notorious 生, which has dozens, including nine in indigenous Japanese words alone and many more in borrowings from the Chinese, with a panoply of meanings ranging from 'give birth' to 'raw silk' and 'student'.

What all this means is that reading Japanese involves a continual decision-making process: pronunciation depends on context. The characters of the word 'kimono', 着物, could also be sounded as /chakubutsu/, but that doesn't convey any meaning; the reader has to pronounce it as /kimono/, which of course does. The English language too has a few dozen words where the correct pronunciation must be deduced from context. These so-called homographs include *sewer* (rhyming with either *lower* or *viewer*), *sow* (rhyming with either *cow* or *low*), the well-known *read* (rhyming with either *lead* or *lead* – sorry, make that *bead* and *bed*) and, in honour of this chapter's protagonist, *sake* (rhyming with *make* or *Iraqi*). But in English, your average text has very few such potential pitfalls; in Japanese, there are alternative readings for the majority of characters.

Or am I making this sound harder than it really is? After all, if 手 is pronounced as /te/ whenever it's a separate word but as /shu/ in the compound 着手 /shuchaku/, the reader is best advised to focus on whole words rather than on separate signs. That's more or less what we do in English as well: we don't know how to pronounce the letters CHA until we have seen the word they're part of, be it CHARACTER, CHAPTER, CHAMPAGNE, CHAOS, CHAFE, CHAISE, CHA-CHA, CHALK or GOTCHA (or even CHANUKKA or CHALYBEATE). True enough – except that Japanese doesn't mark word boundaries, as English and most other languages do: there are no spaces. This means that two characters that sit right next to each other may or may not belong to the same word. Any skilled Japanese reader can nonetheless tell which ones do and which ones don't, but it requires paying close attention to context. Reading Japanese is like reading English sentences with lots of SEWERS, READS, SOWS and SAKES in it.

Keeping the endings happy

While the 2,000-plus characters are the hardest part to master, the intricacies don't end there. In Chinese, words have no grammatical endings, so there are no characters to write them. Japanese on the other hand has lots of endings, and writers noticed very early on that ignoring them would make their texts nearly unintelligible. What to do?

Their first stab at a solution was by using characters that *sounded* like the endings, regardless of their meaning. To better understand what this was like in practice, imagine we were to do the same thing in English. Our language has some grammatical endings too, such as *-ing*, so if we had by some accident of history adopted kanji writing, we'd have felt the same need as the Japanese. So how would we write our words ending in *-ing*, say *buying*? 'Buy' would be 買, because that's what this character means. (The Mandarin pronunciation is /mǎi/, but no matter.) The *-ing* bit is slightly problematic, as there is no character pronounced /ing/. But borrowing a foreign script always involves a degree of compromise, so we'll just make do with one that is pronounced /ying/: 妖 (and never mind what it means in Mandarin). Hence, 買妖 would be the correct spelling for 'buying'.

Back in Japan, this early solution had two inconveniences. Firstly, it left undetermined whether a character represented its usual meaning or was merely used for the sake of its sound value. Being accustomed to a lot of ambiguity, Japanese writers and readers might not have minded this so much if it hadn't been for the second inconvenience: the drudgery of having to add elaborate characters over and over again to render mere endings. In our fictitious example, the 妖 or /ying/ character comprises nine strokes, and many others are much more labour-intensive.

Quite soon then, the writers hit upon the idea of *simplifying* the characters with a grammatical function, so that they became different from the real kanji. This solved both problems in one stroke – figuratively speaking, that is, for while the resulting signs were far simpler than the originals, most of them still required several strokes.

Today, these simplified signs are collectively known as *kana*.[*] And while their forms and uses have changed over time, they have remained a major component of Japanese writing, second only to kanji. From a strictly practical perspective, kana is all that Japanese would need, because every word and sentence of the spoken language[†] can be written in kana, without the use of any Chinese characters. Between 1945 and 1965, the Japanese government and its Language Council planned on abolishing the characters altogether. But the cultural perspective is very different from the strictly practical, and literary authors managed to sway the council's position, and thus the government's. Today, a writer relying entirely on kana would to Japanese eyes be a Philistine. That

---

[*] *Kana* may refer to either a single sign (a 'letter', as it were) or to the complete set to which each sign belongs (the 'alphabet', so to speak).

[†] In *written* Japanese, there are many Chinese borrowings that can only be distinguished in writing: their pronunciation is identical, but their kanji spelling is different. This means that, when read aloud, they may well confuse the listener, unless the context gives sufficient clues. It could be argued – I would – that sentences puzzling the listener usually represent bad writing. In that light, kanji that merely serve to differentiate between meanings of otherwise identical words may do more harm than good to the Japanese language.

has not always been the case: while characters have traditionally held higher prestige, there was a time, before 1700, when kana-only texts identified the writer not as uncultured, but as a highly cultured … woman. (The linguistic gender divide that we saw in chapter 13 also included the written language back then.) Known today as HIRAGANA, it is one of two different kana that are currently in use.

A different script for every occasion

Hold on – *two* different kana? But didn't I say just now that kana is all Japanese would need for every single word in the language? I did. And yet, there they are: HIRAGANA and KATAKANA, literally meaning 'smooth kana' and 'partial kana' respectively. They look mostly quite different, but they represent the very same sounds. Each one of the forty-six hiragana signs has one katakana counterpart, and vice versa. The differences, like those between lower case and upper case in our alphabet, are not in pronunciation, but in appearance and function.

As for appearance, hiragana is called 'smooth' for a reason. Its shapes are not angular, but curvy. They make Japanese writing visually distinctive: つ, の or お (representing /tsu/, /no/ and /o/ respectively) could never be (printed) Chinese. Katakana signs do not exist in Chinese either, but this is less obvious to the outsider's eye: ツ, ノ and オ are katakana for, again, /tsu/, /no/ and /o/. The reason they're called 'partial' is that they are parts – fragments – of the characters they were derived from. The オ, for instance, is derived from the left half of 於. Hiragana originated in a similar way, but based on cursively written rather than printed characters.

In function, the two sets of kana are also clearly distinct. Hiragana plays the vital role we discussed before: it spells out the grammatical endings. (It also somewhat remedies the lack of spaces between words, as endings indicate word boundaries.) In addition, hiragana also replaces characters when for some reason they are not a practical option: because the writer doesn't know the right character or because the readers (such as children) may not recognise it. Hiragana are also used to write words for which no character exists. Finally, hiragana is sometimes placed right next to kanji, as a reading aid – a practice called FURIGANA ('assigning kana') or YOMIGANA ('reading kana') that underlines how dispensable the characters are.

The function of katakana, on the other hand, is to mark and make accessible what we might call 'difficult and strange words': those of foreign (but not Chinese) origin, either borrowed or merely quoted; technical and scientific terms including names of species and minerals; and onomatopoeias such as *boom* and *swoosh*. Katakana can also lend emphasis to a word. To summarise the difference, we might say that hiragana is a grammar and pronunciation aid, whereas katakana functionally overlaps with our italic type.

Japanese keyboards are fiendishly clever: you can type in hiragana or Roman letters and they'll convert the words into whatever you want: katakana, hiragana or even kanji – though in the last case, you'll usually be asked to choose between several homophones.

Elegant and not so elegant acrobatics

The beauty of the kana system is that each sign represents one syllable.* But in modern Japanese, over a hundred different syllables exist, while the number of kana in either set is forty-six plus some additional signs. This mismatch has been resolved with orthographic acrobatics, not all of it elegant.

Little diacritical marks get to do most of the work, especially one that consists of two short strokes in the upper-right corner of the sign (DAKUTEN, colloquially known as 'dots'). It softens the consonant, or to put it more technically, it 'adds voice'. Thus, か is pronounced /ka/ (hard, voiceless), but add the dots, like so: が, and what you get is /ga/. There is also a sign called HANDAKUTEN or 'circle' which changes consonants in a different way.

Worse than these Japanese diacritics, at least to my foreign eye, is that the 'one kana, one syllable' regularity seemingly breaks down in syllables where a /y/ appears between consonant and vowel, such as /kya/. This is written as きゃ, which clearly consists of two elements. But a skilled Japanese reader sees only one kana here: the sign on the right is smaller than the one on the left, and therefore it's considered part of the larger one. In other words, the couple form a *digraph*, much like English *ch*. A digraph is made up of two signs, but represents a single sound, and in several languages, including Japanese but not English, they are therefore treated as one and inseparable.

Irashunal, shaw

More than 2,000 kanji, most of them with more than one pronunciation; two sets of kana, comprising more than 100 basic and compound signs each, which sometimes get placed alongside

---

* Which make it, technically speaking, a syllabary, as we saw in chapter 6 about Indic scripts. Though *very* technically speaking, it isn't, because a single sign does not represent one syllable, but one *mora*, which is a linguistic unit of time. Most Japanese syllables coincide with one mora each, but those that end in a consonant or that have a long vowel (written with a macron in Latin script: ā, ō) are twice as long, so *Nippon* consists of two syllables of two moras each, as does the name *Tōkyō*. The Japanese drew their inspiration for kana from a system in which each sign did represent one syllable, namely the Brahmi script used for Sanskrit, the language of Buddhist texts from India.

kanji – surely, this would be enough to earn Japanese the title of 'world's most complicated script'. But we're not quite there yet.

To most of us, Japanese texts are an unintelligible sea of dark kanji waves with lighter kana crests. But every once in a while, we see something familiar. Numbers, for one thing. And more surprisingly, Roman letters. Japanese journalists, bloggers, emailers and other writers don't think anything of including the occasional word in RŌMAJI, as they call our alphabet. After all, their readers have mastered so many signs with so many pronunciations that they don't mind such a trifling little addendum as our twenty-six letters.

Most of the words written in Latin letters are acronyms, either of an international nature, such as km, CD or SMS, or Japanese creations based on English, such as OB and OG for 'alumnus' and 'alumna' (from 'old boy' and 'old girl') and OL for 'office lady', a female service worker in an office.

And there's another complicating factor: Japanese can be written either vertically, in which case the columns will be arranged from right to left, or horizontally, with lines going from left to right. This means that some Japanese books open to the left, as in European languages, others to the right, as in Arabic and Hebrew.

I could ask once more why this complex writing system hasn't been rationalised, but the answer would be the same as in the previous chapter: the idea of tinkering with the written language, be it the rules of spelling or the choice of script, brings out a conservative reflex in most of us, which only in times of great social turmoil is likely to be overcome. Several organisations in the later part of the nineteenth and the first half of the twentieth centuries campaigned for either kana or the Roman alphabet, but all to no avail. In the late 1940s, research produced clear evidence that Roman-script textbooks did not harm primary-school students' performance, and might even enhance it. As this outcome was the opposite from what the researchers had expected and hoped for, the results were immediately hushed up. Irrational? Sure. But language, as we've seen, is also about national identity and culture.

1

English

1.5 billion speakers

375 million native speakers in the United Kingdom and some of its former territories, particularly the US, Canada, Australia, Ireland, New Zealand, South Africa and some Caribbean islands. Over a billion second-language speakers, principally in other former possessions (South Asia, Africa) and Europe, but elsewhere, too. Substantial numbers of English-speaking migrants can be found in all but the most unwelcoming countries.

English

DESIGNATIONS In the other nineteen Babel languages, English is called as follows (the order is that of the chapters): ANH, YŎNGŎ, ĀŃKILAM, İNGİLİZCE, INGGRIS, ENGELISI, AŃGREZĪ, EIGO, KIINGEREZA, ENGLISCH, ANGLAIS, INGG(E)RIS, ANGLIYSKIY, INGLÊS, INGREJI, ʾINGILĪZIYY, AŃGREZĪ, INGLÉS and YĪNGYŬ.

FAMILY English is a Germanic language heavily influenced by Romance, and as such a member of the Indo-European family.

SCRIPT Latin alphabet, practically without diacritic signs. The spelling is infamous for its idiosyncratic and whimsical relation to pronunciation.

GRAMMAR English is remarkable for an Indo-European language in having scanty inflection and the merest traces of gender.

SOUNDS English has an uncommonly high number of different vowel sounds (over twenty, including diphthongs). Its set of consonants, at about twenty-four, is fairly average in size.

LOANWORDS English has borrowed massively from French, Latin and classical Greek, with more moderate numbers flowing in from Spanish, Italian, Dutch, German, Arabic, Hebrew, Persian and Sanskrit.

ON ITS OWN An unusual thing about English is that, due especially to its massive borrowing, no other language is similar enough to make it easy for English speakers to pick it up. For speakers of Portuguese, learning Spanish is a piece of QUEQUE, and my Vietnamese teacher assured me that she found Chinese not terribly difficult. Being a native English speaker has a raft of advantages ... but it does have this one major drawback. Most English speakers are severely monolingual.

1: English

A special lingua franca?

As we've seen throughout this book, lingua francas have been with us for millennia, and in many parts of the world. But no language has ever been such a runaway success as English is today. Reliable figures are once more non-existent, but it seems that roughly one in four people on the planet might speak English – albeit not necessarily very well.

And that number keeps growing: today, Chinese schoolchildren begin to learn English before they have even mastered the art of writing Mandarin. One in five books published worldwide is in English. Over 80 per cent of scholarly articles are written in English. Nearly all international blockbuster films and hit songs are in English. And about half of the homepages of the most-visited sites on the Internet are in English. The official language of non-military aviation is English, the lingua franca of Antarctica is English and the only language ever spoken on the moon was English. In a way, English is the end of Babel – or rather, it's the end of Babel as a problem. Linguistic diversity is still high – towering, if you like – but it's no longer an impregnable wall to communication with strangers. English is the gateway.

It's time for another conversation. And being a second-language speaker myself, let me welcome again the native English speaker we met in Persia.

Thank you – it's good to be back. When we talked about Persian, you explained how it thrived for centuries over a vast area. What are the qualities that have made my own language so dominant?

What makes you think it's a question of qualities?

Its success, of course. If it didn't have some excellent qualities, it wouldn't be so successful, would it?

'Why not? Genghis Khan, bubonic plague and the *News of the World* were all extremely successful in their day. Oil wells have given the Arabian Gulf a huge share of the world's wealth. Many things can thrive if the conditions are just right. English had to wait for centuries before political, economic and cultural developments made it go viral. In the late 1400s, it was spoken by just three million or so people – in England – and by hardly anybody elsewhere. Nobody at the time felt that there was anything intrinsic to English that destined it to become a global lingua franca. The country and its language were pretty marginal. Only in the early seventeenth century did England and English begin to show political and economic promise.

You're talking about British merchants arriving in India? I mean, they laid the foundations for the British Empire that would spread English across the globe, didn't they?

Up to a point. The British Empire was huge, indeed the biggest empire ever, and it sent out roots and shoots for English across the world. But for most of its existence, what came closest to being the world language was French. English only began to make its challenge after the First World War – right after what's sometimes called 'the British Century'. In fact, English didn't begin to look like a world language until after the Second World War, when the American Century began. And its unquestionable hegemony is even more recent: it was achieved with the end of the Cold War, when Russian stopped being a competitor.

Russian, a competitor? You must be kidding.

I'm not. In the democratic and capitalist world, sure, Russian was marginal, but in communist countries it was much more widely spoken – and in the 1970s, there were lots of those. China paid virtually no attention to English either. Even in Latin America, the US backyard, English didn't have much of a presence at the time.

Of course, I'm not saying that Britain played no role at all in the expansion of the language – it did, especially in North America

Par avion: when postal services became global in the nineteenth century, French was still the language of choice.

and the Commonwealth. But elsewhere, the language arrived from America, carried by multinational companies, consumer products, TV shows, films and music. English has spread in much the same way as lingua francas always spread: it has followed the power, the money and the good things in life. It just so happens that thanks to modern technology, it is now possible for one language to have a strong presence in most of the world.

And to be spoken by one in four people.
Yes, perhaps. That would work out at 1.9 billion people. It's possible: 375 million native speakers and a good billion and a half of second-language speakers. Those figures ring true, if we include people whose English is pretty hard to understand and those who are nervous or reluctant to speak it.

I still think the rise of English must be to do with its particular qualities, especially the straightforward grammar. You said yourself that Persian became a lingua franca for builders from all over the empire because it had simple grammar.

Not quite. What I said was that Persian became a lingua franca among those builders, and then, as a result, its grammar was simplified. It lost most of its 'morphological complexity' – its endings and genders, to put it simply. And the same thing happened to English, back when the Vikings settled in England and married local women. Those linguistically mixed households, like the linguistically mixed Persian building sites, produced a simplified language. And the fact that English has few endings and no genders makes it easier to master.

No political borders for English – even North Korea promotes its film festival in the global lingua franca.

330

Which is why it became a world language. Like I said.
You're jumping to conclusions. The simplification took place a
thousand years ago, and the language has developed massive new
complexities since, on top of the ones it maintained in the first place.
As a non-native speaker, I can assure you that English grammar is
weirder and harder than you think. Especially the verbal tenses. The
difference between present continuous and simple present – that
is to say, *she's deciding* versus *she decides* – for example. And then
there are the endless subtleties of 'was going to do' and 'would do'
and 'have been meaning to do' and 'was going to have it done' and
'would have been going to do'...

I'm not sure that we say 'would have been going to do'.
If you're not sure, how can I ever be? And there's much more. The
strong verbs, changing their vowels and sometimes their consonants
too. The articles – definite, indefinite or none at all – which are
much more intricate than they appear at first sight. There's the
troubling realm of prepositions, as in *looking at someone* versus
looking on someone as or *looking to someone for*. There's the vast and
forbidding field of phrasal verbs such as *getting by on* something
and *getting along with* someone and *getting on for* so many o'clock.

**But these prepositions are not grammar, are they, not endings?
They're part of the English vocabulary, which is a different thing.
And it's huge, I agree. It's one of the glories of the language!**

Some of those examples are in the grey area where grammar and
vocabulary meet, granted. But the big vocabulary of the English
language is a problem in its own right. It's the crowning glory
to your mind, I'm sure, but a horror story for us non-natives. An
international lingua franca should be efficient, not extravagant.
Economical, not wasteful. Frugal, not prodigal. Parsimonious, not
profligate. Sparing, not ...

**All right, you've made your point. Too many words, is what
you're saying. But look at it this way: we have a mix of Germanic
and Romance words, like *get* and *obtain*, or *street* and *avenue*.
That makes it the ideal lingua franca – easy to learn not just for**

Germans and Scandinavians but also for the French and Spanish and so on.

Have you ever asked a Spanish-speaker if they find English easy? My strong impression is that they don't. They find the phrasal verbs and the prepositions impossible, they can't wrap their tongues around all the different vowel sounds of English ... Look, I'm not trying to say that English is *unsuitable* as a world language. My point is that it's not particularly suitable. It has some things going for it, such as the lack of endings and gender, but it also has a lot going against it: difficult pronunciation, the messy spelling, an overabundance of vocabulary and a pretty outlandish grammar.

But what of its virtues? It's versatile and adaptable. It readily creates new words, and absorbs words from other languages, and it is known for its egalitarian directness – unlike, say, French, with its tu–vous distinction.

That's a bunch of unfounded clichés, I'm sorry to say, bandied about by people who know little of linguistics. All languages create new words, as and when they are needed. English borrows freely from other languages, true, but there's nothing good or bad about that – borrowing is just one more way of expanding the vocabulary according to need. And in what other ways is it flexible? As an outsider, I often run into trouble with rational word orders that are forbidden by its grammar. For instance, 'Her I like best to kiss' is in many languages an excellent way of indicating who one prefers to kiss above all others, but in English it makes you sound like Master Yoda in *Star Wars*.

As for egalitarian instincts – sure, I'll grant you that English doesn't bother with personal distinctions in its grammar, as most European languages do in a minor way and some East Asian languages in a major way. But there's nothing direct or democratic about the English language per se. Any real-life interaction in English requires a knowledge of linguistic etiquette. In many languages, you can simply ask people what they want, but in English, you have to ask what 'they would like' or 'would prefer', what 'you can get them', whether 'you may help them' or some such convoluted formula. Ordering a pint by saying 'I want a beer' is no less rude than saying

English has limitless 'common mistakes'. This Indonesian site, *Learn English with Demi*, does a fine job of explaining them.

tu to a French waiter. And that's to say nothing of the handfuls of *please* and *thank you* with which so many exchanges have to be sprinkled. I'm not saying it's a bad thing – in fact it rather suits me – but nor is it easy.

Still, at least English isn't a tonal language, like Chinese. That's an advantage, surely?

I'm with you on that one. That is hard to master, so not having it is a good thing for a global language. But English pronunciation is hard in other ways. It's taken me years and years to distinguish, in both speaking and hearing, between *had* and *head*, between *poor* and *pour*, between *coughs* and *cuffs* or between *leaf* and *leave*.

You're playing devil's advocate, right?

No ... not really. When I was learning Vietnamese, I had to learn tone, and I found it hard but doable. The same is true for the subtleties of

English pronunciation: even now, when stressed, I can sometimes mispronounce *leave* as /leaf/, *any* as /annie/ and so on. That's after forty years of practice. Really, just because so many people learn English as a second language doesn't mean it comes easy! It's hard work and it never ends.

Blimey. And here was I thinking we had given the world the ideal lingua franca. Are we English speakers entirely misguided?

No need to be too harsh on yourself. How you feel about English is part of a larger pattern. Let a language, any language, become widespread and dominant, and before you know it, people start fawning over it: how it's so great, so rich, so musical, et cetera, et cetera. In point of fact, every major language has started from unpromising beginnings: Arabic among desert tribespeople, Persian and Sanskrit among steppe horsemen, Mandarin among rice farmers, French among Roman soldiers and defeated Gauls – and yet, a few centuries later, these languages were venerated as the all-time pinnacles of linguistic achievement. Arabic and Tamil were considered divine, Latin and Greek uniquely suitable for literature, Russian was thought to be the language of the classless proletarian nirvana, French to be uniquely logical.

And now it's the turn of English, which is said to be easy, singable, direct, clear, flexible and much else besides. It may well be easier than Russian, more singable than German and more direct than Javanese, but it's probably less easy than Esperanto and most creole languages, less singable than Italian and less direct than ... I don't know, that's not a linguistic feature in the first place. The Dutch can be shockingly direct, or so we're told, but we share our language with the Flemish, and they aren't.

The world's economic centre of gravity is now shifting from the US to Asia. So, once that happens, will English remain the world language?

I'm sure English will maintain its current status for another generation or so at the very least, if only because hundreds of millions of children all over the world are acquiring it right now. But what will happen thereafter? It's not a foregone conclusion that those children's children will learn it too. If in twenty or thirty years' time they feel that kids can spend their time more profitably, the study of English will begin to decline. These things happen. My grandfather wrote my dad letters in French because he considered the language both useful and chic. Which was true in the early 1900s, when he was a boy, but no longer in the 1950s, when he wrote them. Similar shifts have occurred throughout history.

Which is why ambitious parents make their children study Mandarin these days. Are they right?

They're unquestionably right in believing that Mandarin is useful today and will be more useful tomorrow. It's been a safe bet for a long time that China will be the next big power, so speaking its language is a skill worth having. But if you mean 'will Mandarin become the global lingua franca?', that's a very different matter. It's a view that is often expressed – by people who argue that economic dominance will lead to political dominance, which in turn will lead to linguistic dominance – but it's not one you'll find shared by many linguists.

Why so? Isn't it all about dominance?

Not entirely. Noted linguists such as David Crystal and John McWhorter believe that the old political and economic mechanism that has always driven some languages to become lingua francas will not work this time. One reason is that Mandarin is just too damn difficult. Not just for us, but for most people outside East Asia, and in a way even for them, because of the inefficient script.

Any other reasons?

Yes: critical mass. In the past, even the most successful lingua francas were spoken either in certain regions – for instance Aramaic in the Middle East or Latin in the Western Roman Empire – or by global elites, particularly French as the language of global diplomacy in the eighteenth and nineteenth centuries. Their prevalence rested on the power of their speakers. When the Arabs conquered the Middle East, Arabic took over and Aramaic declined, surviving only as a mother tongue. When France lost influence after Napoleon, diplomats gradually substituted English for French, albeit with a century's time lag. However, English today is spread across the globe – a worldwide web of speakers, close-knit in many Western and Commonwealth countries, more loosely elsewhere. And languages are like other communications devices: the more people that have access to them, the more useful they become. I suspect we have passed a threshold beyond which no other language stands a chance of becoming the new lingua franca.

So English has won?
For the time being, yes.

Come again? You just said no other language can hope to defeat it.
I did. But there are a couple of possible scenarios in which the triumph of English is less than final. Remember what happened to Latin in Western Europe?

It morphed into the Romance languages?
Indeed, it became French and Spanish and Portuguese and others. But that's just half the story. The other half is that a slightly streamlined version of Latin remained a lingua franca for another thousand years, albeit among religious and intellectual elites. The future of English may be similar. On the one hand, it may develop into regional varieties that end up as separate and mutually unintelligible languages, influenced by local languages such as Hindi-Urdu, Swahili or Korean. Current varieties known as Hinglish in India, Uglish in Uganda, Konglish in Korea, and so on, may be harbingers of things to come. On the other hand, as native speakers of English represent an ever smaller per centage, the international lingua franca may find its complexities reduced. Many opaque idioms, such as 'to nail one's colours to the mast' or 'not to put too fine a point on it', will no longer be considered part of the language: of native English, yes, but not of the international lingua franca. I wouldn't be surprised if, at some point, certain grammatical exceptions fall by the wayside: the past tense of *swim* may well become *swimmed*, the plural of *sheep* may become *sheeps*. These may sound like atrocities to you ...

This Indian cartoon surfaced on a Montenegrin website – but it could have been understood anywhere in the world.

Atrocities? Downright bizarre, I'd say.

But such changes happen all the time! The past tense of *shape* used to be *shope*, *help* had *holp*, *laugh* had *low*. And the same with plurals: *shoes* were *shoon*, *eyes* were *eyen*, Americans prefer *cannons* for what used to be *cannon*, et cetera. Admittedly, sometimes we get changes in the opposite direction, such as *dived* becoming *dove* and *sneaked* becoming *snuck*. But in a lingua franca, it will always be irregular forms being made to behave, never the other way around. And the process may continue. Perhaps the difference between 'she saw' and 'she has seen' will gradually disappear as few people appreciate the distinction – who knows. And I strongly suspect that it will become perfectly acceptable to pronounce *red* as /ret/ and *three* as /sree/. And once this international English has diverged sufficiently from native English, perhaps the spelling well be slightly simplified too, taking the b's out of *debt*, *dumb* and *doubt* and spelling *tomb* as *toom*, so it will no longer seem to rhyme with *bomb*, but with *doom*.

The horror of it. I'm hoping your other scenario is more palatable?
It's the technological fix: instant machine interpretation.

Ha, the Babel fish! The universal translator of *The Hitchhiker's Guide to the Galaxy*!
Exactly. Or rather its silicon counterpart: the Babel chip. You speak Malay to me, or Portuguese or Punjabi, and in my earphone I hear whatever language I've chosen. The only thing is, we can't be entirely sure if it will ever work as smoothly as science fiction and the boffins at Google have led us to expect. Machine translation is getting better and better for some languages, but it's still pretty atrocious for others. And that's on the basis of written text. If the input is natural speech, perhaps with a regional accent and in a

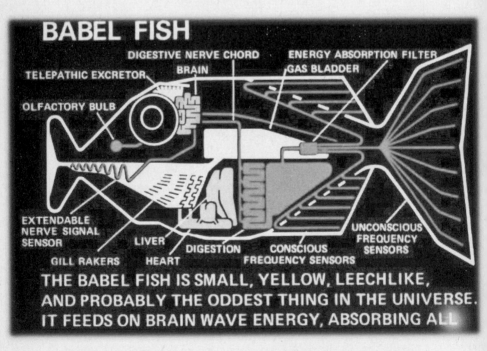

Douglas Adams's Babel fish – once 'probably the oddest thing in the universe' but slowly evolving into the answer to life, the universe and everything.

noisy environment, more often than not today's software will be stumped.

Surely it'll be perfected within a few years?
Maybe. Machine translation has proved to be somewhat trickier than anticipated, but the big tech companies do seem to be making big strides. And if the Babel chip becomes a reality, English will implode as a lingua franca, as fewer people will bother to learn any language beyond their mother tongue.

Then communicating with speakers of a foreign language would be like being in a dubbed film?
Except you would still hear the original at the same time. Or rather, just before, because I expect there would be a little time lag.

So artificial intelligence may come to the rescue. Or Mandarin will take over. Or English will prevail till the end of times. Or it'll degenerate into a bland 'Globish' plus all sorts of regional varieties. Which would you put your money on?
In the medium term, I'd back English to continue its dominance, while undergoing a variety of regional changes, with the Babel chip playing an increasingly important part. In the long run, I expect artificial intelligence will take over – linguistically, and no doubt in many other ways.

Then English will have had its day?
Not necessarily. Native-style English may remain the standard for a global elite of politicians, diplomats, intellectuals and the business aristocracy. Meanwhile, the local Englishes of Asian and African countries will become increasingly regional in flavour. But the rise of Globish may be prevented by the Babel chip.

Thank heavens for the wonders of technology.
Unreliable wonders, though. I doubt that machine interpretation will be perfected any time soon. But give it another decade or so and it may be good enough to convince many people that learning English is not essential – and it will almost certainly reinforce the

belief of many native English speakers that they needn't learn anything other than English.

And is that a good thing?
It's a great loss for both sides! Then as now, most native English speakers will miss out on the joys of bilingualism – the mental agility, better understanding of other cultures and the endless surprises of a second language. But those who depend on their Babel chip to understand English will lose out, too. It's an infuriating language to learn, even if you're Dutch, but once mastered it's an awesome thing. You can read fine literature from many parts of the world and experience many of the best films first-hand. I may struggle with Shakespeare's Elizabethan language, but give me a Wodehouse novel and I'm a happy man when, having just railed with the best against the excesses of English vocabulary, I'll come upon a passage like this: *Intoxicated? The word did not express it by a mile. He was oiled, boiled, fried, plastered, whiffled, sozzled and blotto.*

Try putting that in your Babel fish.

End notes

SOURCES AND FURTHER READING

ACKNOWLEDGEMENTS

PHOTO CREDITS

INDEX

Sources and further reading

General

If the info boxes pique your curiosity, try:

Languagesgulper.com An eclectic website that describes dozens of languages in detail.

Bernard Comrie (ed.), *The World's Major Languages* (1990). Essays on thirty-six languages, including eighteen of the Babel Twenty.

Asya Pereltsvaig, *Languages of the World* (2012).

Chapter 20: Vietnamese

To study this language, I've used many resources, and had some admirable teachers: Phạm Bảo Thanh Huyền (at Huyen IELTS in Hải Phòng, through *italki.com*) and Đặng Thanh Loan (or Saphire Dang; through Vietnamese Teaching Group, Hanoi).

My most useful books were Đỗ Thế Dũng and Lê Thanh Thủy's Assimil's *Vietnamesisch ohne Mühe* (German edition, 2015; there's also a French-language edition, but unfortunately none in English) and Dana Healy's *Teach Yourself Vietnamese* (2003). Gabriel Wyner's *Fluent Forever* (2014) and Alex Rawlings' *How to Speak Any Language Fluently* (2017) are a good preparation for any language-learning endeavour.

Make sure to browse any dictionary before you buy it. I like my set of *Từ điển hiện đại* (published by Nhà Xuất Bản Thời Đại) but it's in German rather than English.

The *Anki* app is a very effective tool for learning vocabulary. Ever since I discovered it, shortly after returning from Vietnam, I've been hooked on it. It's free for all platforms except iOS.

And whatever language you learn, *Forvo.com* is invaluable: a website where you can listen to native speakers pronouncing words and phrases in hundreds of languages, including Vietnamese.

Chapter 19: Korean

I've drawn on many sources, including *Sound Symbolism in Korean* by Young-mee Yu Cho (1977) and a chapter of *Korean Language In Culture and Society* by Ho-min Sohn (ed.) (2006). A good general article on sound symbolism is 'Advances in the cross-linguistic study of ideophones' by Mark Dingemanse in *Language and Linguistics Compass* (2012, pp. 654–672).

Chapter 18: Tamil

My main source was *Passions of the Tongue* by Sumathi Ramaswamy (1997).

Chapter 17: Turkish

The second half of the chapter draws on *The Turkish Language Reform* by Geoffrey Lewis (1999), an entertaining read, highly recommended.

Chapter 16: Javanese

Benedict Anderson's book *Language and Power* (1990), about Indonesia's political culture, has informed much of this chapter. The article by Soepomo Poedjosoedarmo is titled 'Javanese Speech Levels' (*bit.ly/Soepomolevels*).

Chapter 15: Persian

Nicholas Ostler's *The Last Lingua Franca* (2010) has a useful chapter on the history of Persian. With typical flair, John McWhorter discusses some crucial elements of Persian's history in a few pages of his *What Language Is* (2011).

Chapter 14: Punjabi

Several scholarly articles by Andrea Bowden and the duo of Jasmeen Kanwal and Amanda Ritchart informed this chapter. The handbook on tone mentioned is by Moira Yip; its title is simply *Tone* (2002).

Chapter 13: Japanese

Long-winded and beset by jargon it may be, but *Gender, Language And Ideology* by Momoko Nakamura (2014) is an exhaustive and critical discussion of the issue. I liked Yoko Hasegawa's general introduction to the language, titled simply *Japanese: A Linguistic Introduction* (2014), in which chapter 28 is about women's language.

Chapter 12: Swahili

Jonas entered the outside world in 'Multilingualism and second language acquisition in the northern Mandara Mountains', by Leslie C. Moore (PDF: *http://bit.ly/JonasfromJilve*), which was published in *Africa Meets Europe: Language Contact in West Africa* (2014) by George Echu and Samuel Gyasi Obeng (eds.). Among other useful publications I consulted, I'd like to credit the gloomily-titled *Language Decline and Death in Africa* by Herman Batibo (2005) and *Language Attitudes in Sub-Saharan Africa* by Efurosibina Adegbija (1994).

Chapter 11: German

Tyler Schnoebelen's article can be read via *bit.ly/weirdtongues*. Michael Cysouw's can be found under *http://bit.ly/CysouwRARA*; it was published in book form in *Expecting the Unexpected* by Horst Simon and Heike Wiese (2011).

Chapter 10: French

Henriette Walther has written several highly readable books including *Le français dans tous les sens* (1988, many editions since). Less accessible – but exhaustive – is *Histoire sociale des langues de France* by Georg Kremnitz, Fañch (!) Broudic and Carmen Alen Garabato (2013). In English, there is *The Story of French* by Jean-Benoît Nadeau and Julie Barlow (2006).

Chapter 9: Malay

I am indebted to *The Indonesian Language* by James Sneddon (2003) and the Indonesia chapter by Andrew Simpson in *Language and National Identity in Asia* (2007), edited by Simpson.

Chapter 8: Russian

Bernard Comrie's 'The Indo-European Linguistic Family: Genetic and Typological Perspectives' was valuable; it is included in the book *The Indo-European Languages* by Anna Giacalone Ramat and Paolo Ramat (1997).

Chapter 7: Portuguese

Two useful sources were *A History of Portuguese Overseas Expansion, 1400–1668* by Malyn Newitt (2005) and *Portuguese: A Linguistic Introduction* by Milton Azevedo (2005).

Chapter 6: Bengali

The definitive book about scripts remains *The World's Writing Systems* (1996) by Peter T. Daniels and William Bright (eds). It's a hefty and expensive tome, but what it doesn't tell you about this subject is not worth knowing (or wasn't at the time of publication). Less complete, but a better and more affordable read, is *Writing Systems: A Linguistic Approach* by Henry Rogers (2005).

Chapter 5: Arabic

The 'Concise Dictionary of Our Arabic' owes a lot to my shelf of etymological dictionaries and various websites: in English, *etymonline.com*; in German, Duden; in Spanish, Coromines; in Dutch, *etymologiebank.nl*; in French, Larousse; and in general, *en.wiktionary.org*. I'm also indebted to *Modern Arabic* by Clive Holes (2004) and *The Arabic Language* by Kees Versteegh (2001).

Chapter 4: Hindi-Urdu

As mentioned in the text, my main sources were Alok Rai's *Hindi Nationalism* (2007) and Tariq Rahman's *From Hindi to Urdu* (2011).

Chapter 3: Spanish

I couldn't have written this without a shelf of grammar books and especially the 'English Grammar' series of the Olivia and Hill Press, which explains nine foreign languages on the basis of English grammar. I also used E.O. Ashton's *Swahili Grammar* and Natalia Lusin's *Russian Grammar*.

Chapter 2: Mandarin

Among many sources consulted, I particularly liked the 1992 article 'Why Chinese is so damn hard' by David Moser (*bit.ly/MoserMandarin*) and his book *A Billion Voices: China's Search for a Common Language* (2016). The book by William Hannas that I mention is *Asia's Orthographic Dilemma* (1997); that by Marshall Unger is *Ideogram: Chinese Characters and the Myth of Disembodied Meaning* (2004).

Chapter 2b: Japanese

The crucial source here was *Schrift in Japan* by Steven Hagers (2005), a concise Dutch-language history of the Japanese writing system for those with no interest in actually learning it. I haven't found a similar source in English; the non-Dutch-speaking world deserves a translation. Chapter 4 of Yoko Hasegawa's *Japanese, A Linguistic Introduction* (2014), looks more briefly into the same subject.

Chapter 1: English

Nicholas Ostler's *The Last Lingua Franca* (2010) comprehensively discusses the past, present and future of lingua francas. High-quality books about the English language are too numerous to list – indeed, David Crystal alone writes faster than God can read (to quote poet Adriaan Roland Holst).

Acknowledgements

Without my wife, my friends, a group of enthusiastic volunteers and a large number of professional experts, writing *Babel* would have been more difficult and less fun – not to mention lonelier than writing a book inevitably is.

Most of the chapters were revised by people who are specialised academics, native speakers, or both. I am most grateful to Abhishek Avtans (Hindi-Urdu), Gabrielle van den Berg (Persian), Ateş Dağlı (Turkish), Steven Hagers (Japanese), Lotte Hoek (Bengali), Maarten Mous (Swahili), Phạm Bảo Thanh Huyền (my Vietnamese teacher and friend), Rui Pombal (Portuguese), Joren Pronk (Mandarin), Tijmen Pronk (Russian), George Quinn (Javanese) and Stefan Weninger (Arabic). If you still find any inaccuracies, blame me, not them, especially as I've occasionally ignored their wisdom. I'd also like to thank Indranil Acharya and Ganesh Devy (Bengali), Janine Berns (French), Andrea Bowden and Jasmeen Kanwal (Punjabi), Jo Rees (Japanese), Geeta Tiwari (Hindi-Urdu), and Jenneke van der Wal (Swahili) who provided me with valuable additional information.

Compared to twenty years ago, when I wrote my first book of popular linguistics, it has gradually become more difficult to find academics willing to share their expertise. At many universities, the workload has grown to such an extent that people feel compelled to choose their commitments judiciously. I fully sympathise, but the downside is that more and more knowledge, paid for by society, remains within the walls of academia. This overload is a problem that needs fixing.

Babel wouldn't exist without another group of professionals, namely the book-loving people working at, or commissioned by, Profile Books. I'd like to say thank you to the editors, Jonathan Buckley and Mark Ellingham, for their *meedenken*, a hard-to-translate Dutch word that literally means 'thinking along' but really comes closer to co-creation. My genuine appreciation also extends to Henry Iles (text design and layout), Jamie Keenan (cover design), Dominic Beddow of Draughtsman Ltd (maps), Susanne Hillen (proofreading), Bill Johncocks (indexing), Drew Jerrison (publicity), Penny Daniel and the Nurnberg Agency (language rights) and Andrew Franklin (enthusiasm). Many thanks also to my agent, Caroline Dawnay. I'd buy all of them several rounds of drinks to celebrate many things and to forget one or two others, if only we weren't such a far-flung bunch without a pub we can all reach.

Some of the people who loved my previous book, *Lingo*, and told me so were invited to embark on the *Babel* adventure with me. Many of them became faithful advance readers and commented on chapters, providing advice and encouragement as well as gently correcting my non-native English. They are Anna Rempe, Bernard Danson, Bill DeFelice, Charlotta Erenmalm, Danlias Howe, Edmund Grimley-Evans, Howard Tindall, Ilaria Bailo, Jen Jennings, Kastytis Šmigelskas, Katharine Miles, Michael Clarke, Michael Loughridge, Rae Bathgate, Randi Hacker, Rui Pombal and Sterre Leufkens. Many thanks, dear Babelistas, for keeping me going!

Before turning to my inner circle, allow me to mention my friendly neighbourhood gym. Here I discovered that a good part of the proverbial ninety per cent perspiration involved in writing a book does not follow, but precedes the ten per cent inspiration – indeed, generates it.

And finally, there are my nearest and dearest to be thanked, for sharing with me the good times and the bad, *Babel*-related and otherwise. They know who they are, and first names will do: Maarten, Karin and Bart, Niala, Stan, Ellen, Erik – and, of course, Marleen, the alpha and omega of these acknowledgements and of most of my days.

Photo Credits

Photos in the book are copyright of the following sources. Every effort has been made to contact copyright holders but if any have been missed, please contact the publishers so information can be corrected on future editions.

Vietnamese: pp.18, 29, 32 (author).

Korean: p.40 (korea.net, Republic of Korea, Flickr); p.47 (Hyunwoo Sun, Flickr); p.50 (korea.net, Republic of Korea, Flickr).

Tamil: p.56 (http://tasveerghar.net); p.59 (Sodabottle/Wikimedia); p.60 (Tamil cinema on Pinterest); p.63 (unknown); p.64 (tamilo.com).

Turkish: p.72 (Topkapi/Wikipedia); p.76 (Fotosearch/Getty Images).

Javanese: p.87 (Tropenmuseum/National Museum of World Cultures); p.89 (Nurphoto/Getty Images); p.92 (painting by O'ong Mariyono).

Persian: p.101 (Jean-Michel Coureau/Getty Images); p.104 (Guennol Collection; purchase through the Lila Acheson Wallace Gift; photo by Marie-Lan Nguyen); p.108 (map by Draughtsman Ltd); p.110 (Stan Termeer).

Punjabi: p.116 (Redferns/Getty Images); p.119 (Pinterest); p.121 (Adam Jones/Flickr); p.125 (Júlio Reis/tintazul, Wikimedia).

Japanese: p.130 (YouTube video 'Onna Kotoba' by Wasabi – Learn Japanese Online); p.132 (Komatsuken, Museum of Fine Arts Boston); p.136 (Mike Licht, based on an 1897 print by Toyohara Chikanobu)..

Swahili: p.145: Swahili in German East Africa ('Under Every Leaf' blog); p.149 (Justin Raycraft/Flickr).

German: p.161 (Nina Stoessinger/Flickr); p.166 (wortreich); p.168 (spreadshirt.de).

French: p.177 (Hulton Archive/Getty Images); p.181, p.183 (public domain).

Malay: p.195 (Scubazoo/Alamy Stock Photo); p.199 (NaidNdeso/Wikimedia); p.201(Wanderlust Diaries blog, *ordersabroad.com*).

Russian: p.207 (Barcroft Media/Getty Images); p.211 (Zeljka Burazin/Alamy Stock Photo); p.214 (Mikhail Yakovlev/Wikimedia).

Portuguese: p.221 (Wikimedia); p.227 (Francisco Santos/Wikimedia); p.231 (FIFA/Getty Images).

Bengali: p.236 (indiarailinfo.com); p.241 (ullstein bild/Getty Images); p.247 (Nguyễn Vũ Hưng/Flickr); p.250 (Wikimedia).

Arabic: p.257 (Themeplus/Flickr).

Hindi-Urdu: p.273 (HomoCosmicos/Alamy Stock Photo); p.278 (Wikimedia); p.281 (Imperial War Museum); p.283 (David Boyk).

Spanish: p.289 (Real Academia Española); p.292 (Bob Daemmrich/Alamy Stock Photo); p.297 (mpclemens/Flickr).

Mandarin: p.302 (unknown); p.307 (DLIFLC PAO/Flickr); p.315 (Lego – Empress of Blandings/Flickr; coffee – Mercury Jin, Flickr); p.322 (Tamaki Sono/Flickr).

English: p.329 (alan.98/Flickr); p.330 (Uri Tours/Flickr); p.333 (*https://learnenglishwithdemi.wordpress.com*); p.337 (unknown).

Index

Note: **Bold** entries indicate tables; *italics*, illustration captions; the suffix 'n' indicates a footnote on that page.

The 20 Babel languages: native speakers

Canada

United States

Mexico

Bahamas
Cuba
Belize
Honduras
Guatemala
El Salvador
Costa Rica
Panama
Haiti
Dominican Rep.
Puerto Rico
Jamaica
Nicaragua

Venezuela
Guyana
Suriname
French Guiana
Colombia

Ecuador

Peru

Brazil

Bolivia
Paraguay

Chile
Uruguay
Argentina

Namibia

Ireland
UK
Germany
France
Portugal
Spain
Tunisia
Morocco
Algeria
Mauritania
Mali
Niger
Senegal
Gambia
Guinea-Bissau
Guinea
Sierra Leone
Liberia
Nigeria
Côte
d'Ivoire
Eq.
Guin.
Cameroon
Gabon